ALTERNATIVES UNINCORPORATED

Cross Cultural Theologies

Series Editors: Jione Havea and Clive Pearson, both at United Theological College, Sydney, and Charles Sturt University, Australia, and Anthony G. Reddie, Queen's Foundation for Ecumenical Theological Education, Birmingham

This series focuses on how the "cultural turn" in interdisciplinary studies has informed theology and biblical studies. It takes its leave from the experience of the flow of people from one part of the world to another.

It moves beyond the crossing of cultures in a narrow diasporic sense. It entertains perspectives that arise out of generational criticism, gender, sexual orientation, and the relationship of film to theology. It explores the sometimes competing rhetoric of multiculturalism and cross-culturalism and demonstrates a concern for the intersection of globalization and how those global flows of peoples and ideas are received and interpreted in localized settings. The series seeks to make use of a range of disciplines including the study of cross-cultural liturgy, travel, the practice of ministry and worship in multi-ethnic locations and how theologies that have arisen in one part of the world have migrated to a new location. It looks at the public nature of faith in complex, multicultural, multireligious societies and compares how diverse faiths and their theologies have responded to the same issues.

The series welcomes contributions by scholars from around the world. It includes both single-authored and multi-authored volumes.

Published:

Global Civilization
Leonardo Boff

Dramatizing Theologies: A Participative Approach to Black God-Talk
Anthony G. Reddie

Art as Theology: The Religious Transformation of Art from the Postmodern to the Medieval
Andreas Andreopoulos

Black Theology in Britain: A Reader
Edited by Michael N. Jagessar and Anthony G. Reddie

Bibles and Baedekers: Tourism, Travel, Exile and God
Michael Grimshaw

Home Away from Home: The Caribbean Diasporan Church in the Black Atlantic Tradition
Delroy A. Reid-Salmon

Working against the Grain: Black Theology in the 21ˢᵗ Century
Anthony G. Reddie

The Non-Western Jesus: Jesus as Bodhisattva, Avatara, Guru, Prophet, Ancestor or Healer?
Martien E. Brinkman
Translated by Henry and Lucy Jansen

Another World is Possible: Spiritualities and Religions of Global Darker Peoples
Edited by Dwight N. Hopkins and Marjorie Lewis

Out of Place: Doing Theology on the Crosscultural Brink
Edited by Jione Havea and Clive Pearson

Christian Worship: Postcolonial Perspectives
Stephen Burns and Michael N. Jagessar

Voices from the Borderland: Re-imagining Cross-cultural Urban Theology in the Twenty-first Century
Chris Shannahan

Forthcoming:

Towards a Systematic Spirituality of Black British Women
Marjorie Lewis

ALTERNATIVES UNINCORPORATED

EARTH ETHICS FROM THE GRASSROOTS

George Zachariah

Routledge
Taylor & Francis Group

LONDON AND NEW YORK

First published 2011 by Equinox Publishing Ltd, an imprint of Acumen

Published 2014 by Routledge
2 Park Square, Milton Park, Abingdon, Oxon OX14 4RN
711 Third Avenue, New York, NY 10017, USA

Routledge is an imprint of the Taylor & Francis Group, an informa business

Notices
Practitioners and researchers must always rely on their own experience and
knowledge in evaluating and using any information, methods, compounds, or
experiments described herein. In using such information or methods they should
be mindful of their own safety and the safety of others, including parties for whom
they have a professional responsibility.

To the fullest extent of the law, neither the Publisher nor the authors, contributors,
or editors, assume any liability for any injury and/or damage to persons or
property as a matter of products liability, negligence or otherwise, or from any use
or operation of any methods, products, instructions, or ideas contained
in the material herein.

British Library Cataloguing-in-Publication Data

A catalogue record for this book is available from the British Library.

ISBN-13   978 1 84553 688 6   (hardback)
            978 1 84553 689 3   (paperback)

Library of Congress Cataloging-in-Publication Data

Sakha_riya, Jorj.
    Alternatives unincorporated : earth ethics from the grassroots /George Zachariah.
        p. cm.—(Cross cultural theologies)
    Includes bibliographical references and index.
    ISBN 978-1-84553-688-6 (hb)—ISBN 978-1-84553-689-3 (pb) 1. Human
ecology–Philosophy. 2. Environmentalism--Philosophy. 3.
Environmentalism–Moral and ethical aspects. 4. Environmental ethics.
I. Title. GF21.S335 2010
179'.1–dc22
                                        2010000595

Typeset by S.J.I. Services, New Delhi

Contents

Preface

Academic research is a collective journey, surrounded, challenged, mentored, and nourished by companions and fellow sojourners. This project is the fruit of such a collective journey, where community continued to happen in diverse ways and forms. Recognizing and acknowledging the companions in the journey is more than an inherited practice in the academy. It is a humble attempt to celebrate the midwives of this book.

The theological and ethical reflections narrated in this book are autobiographical and they have evolved from the faith journey of a generation of ecumenical youths in India. Traditionally we consider our homes and churches as the spaces and instruments of our faith formation. Through extensive and exclusive modes of faith formation and indoctrination, our churches mould us into being the faithful followers of their respective faith and practices. It is in this context that I was introduced to the Student Christian Movement of India (SCM). The history of SCM is the story of a different type of faith formation and nurturing which inspired several generations of young people to re-imagine Christian discipleship and to engage in radical forms of public witnessing in Church and society. The last two decades of the previous century witnessed the emergence of several social movements in India that challenged the dominant ways of understanding society, and initiated alternative political practices informed by the lived experiences of the subaltern communities. Participation in the struggles of the subaltern movements such as traditional fisher people, dalits, adivasis, and women was a new baptismal experience for many of us. These movements challenged us to rethink the content and pattern of Christian mission in India. M. J. Joseph, Poulose Mar Poulose, M. M. Thomas, and a host of others instilled in us the passion for doing theology in solidarity with the subalterns and their social movements, and they accompanied us on this journey.

My dream to initiate research towards constructing an earth ethics from the grassroots and affirming the social movements as "text" started as a dissertation project at the Lutheran School of Theology at Chicago. Vítor Westhelle, my academic advisor, enriched this project enormously with his comments and critiques, and encouraged me always by reminding me of the significance of this work. Ron Engel, Larry Rasmussen, and Linda Thomas were more than just readers. They accompanied me on this journey with constant support, and surrounded me with their love. David Rhoads and Barbara Rossing were always there to refresh my spirit.

There are several other mentors and friends who sojourned with me reading and correcting the manuscript, and pushing me further to perceive, think, and write differently. They include K. C. Abraham, Jione Havea, M. P. Joseph, Seth Kasten, Sarosh Koshy, Shiju Sam Varghese, and Rob Worley. The staff at the JKM Library owned this research as their project and extended their wholehearted support. I am grateful to Sarosh Koshy for coining the title "Alternatives Unincorporated."

This research would not have been possible without the support of the friends at the Narmada valley. The activists of the Narmada Bachao Andolan and the people of the valley welcomed me and provided all assistance for my field research. Alok Agarwal, Joe Athialy, Devram Bhai, Shripad Dharmadhikary, Ashish Mandloi, Philip Mathew, Chittaroopa Palit, Medha Patkar, Vinod Patwa, Maju Varghese, Keshav Vasave, Kamala Yadav, and a host of others accompanied me in my immersion in the text called NBA. The documentation centers at the NBA office, Badwani, the Manthan Adhyayan Kendra, Badwani, and the Delhi Forum, Delhi, provided me access to their resources.

Being an international student without institutional and ecclesiastical sponsorship it would have been impossible for me to complete this project without the love and solidarity of friends and communities. The faith communities at the Purna Jiwan South Asian Church, the Mar Thoma churches in Chicago, and the First Presbyterian Church of Homewood welcomed me and my family into their communities, and accompanied us on our journey. It was the friendship and fellowship that we received from Pastor Eardley Mendis and the community of Purna Jiwan that sustained us in this sojourn.

My deep gratitude goes to the editors of the Cross Cultural Theologies series of Equinox Press for selecting my manuscript for publication. I am grateful to Jione Havea for his comments and encouragement. Thanks to Janet James and Valerie Hall for their support. Thanks also to Sarah Norman, the copyeditor, for making this book more readable.

I had the opportunity to present sections of the manuscript to different academic and activist communities in South Asia and to revise it based on the critical observations I received from them. In this regard, I am grateful to the Senate of Serampore College (University), the Christian Institute for the Study of Religion and Society, and the National Council of Churches in India. I am also grateful to the Gurukul Lutheran Theological College and Research Institute, Chennai, India for the support and encouragement that I continue to receive from the community.

Our parents and siblings, though separated by oceans and continents, surrounded us with their love and prayers. I thank God for them. Amritha and Aruna, our daughters, who grew up with this project, bringing laughter and fun to our otherwise stressed-out and busy life, reminded us always that life blossoms in our life together. This journey would have remained a dream without Sheila (Anshi), my love and my soul-mate. Her love and solidarity that hovered over this project made it a reality.

George Zachariah

Introduction

To engage in disengaged academic endeavors, and disembodied career search, when the Other is destined to die before their time, raises problematic questions about the very vocation of doing theology in our times. With the idols of death becoming the presiding deities a hegemonic war against the movement of life has been unleashed. Death by starvation increases in spite of food surpluses. Rain forests are denuded, rivers are dammed, and ocean beds are raped. The commons are being snatched away from the communities, and are now on sale for corporate plunder. For the "common good" and "national interest" millions have been uprooted from their abodes. Suicide seems the only dignified option in life for those who used to live in communion with nature. Preemptive killing has become the doctrine of the day where collateral damage has only statistical relevance. But in the midst of this reign of death, we also see a new celebration of life in the affirmation that another world is possible. Such affirmations continue to arise in the small pockets of resistance in the villages and small towns and the metropolises where people gather together to resist the reign of death. This polyphony of new harmonies is a contemporary experience of epiphany, one which not only invites but inspires us to do theology differently. A view from the grassroots – the standpoints of those who are uprooted from life – is the key to experiencing this epiphany.

One of the major contributions of the theologies that emerged in the twentieth century is the realization that all theologies are products of specific contexts, and the attempt to apply it to different contexts, by claiming universality, is problematic. The issue is larger than the notions of binary opposites like west and east or first world and third world. Rather, in the midst of pluralism and diversity, dominant theologies have a tendency to project what is particular to them as universal to all. This common-denominator approach is also a process of universalization through which particular experiences, values, events, or symbols are being made normative for doing theology and making ethical decisions, which has resulted in the theological colonization of peoples and communities all over the world.[1]

The awareness of the danger of universalization has led to the emergence of social location and lived experience of the community as the loci for doing theology. The objective realities of poverty, racial, caste, gender discrimination and the like thus became important categories in theological and ethical discourses. However, contextual articulations of theology, in general, tend to ignore the methodological significance of the collective politics of the grassroots communities, and lead to an apolitical essentialism in contemporary discourses. In this way a view from the grassroots reiterates the interrelationship between theology and political praxis. Underscoring the importance of the political praxis of social movements for critical theory, Nancy Fraser states that, "first, it valorizes historically specific, conjectural struggles as the agenda setters for critical theory; second, it posits social movements as the subjects of critique; and third, it implies that it is in the crucible of political practice that critical theories meet the ultimate test of viability."[2] The dominant strands of eco-theology and environmental ethics are examples of the common-denominator approach, where dominant readings of the crisis of the earth, viewed from nowhere, are presented as meta-narratives, and panaceas are prescribed, claiming universal validity and applicability. As Fraser rightly puts it, our attempt to go beyond the universal categories needs to be mediated through a view from the grassroots, affirming the agency of the social movements.

This book, therefore, attempts to construct an earth ethics from the grassroots, in the crucible of subaltern political praxis, and proposes that social movements as discursive sites can inform the construction of a subaltern earth ethics that is life affirming, communitarian, and liberating. Drawing from the collective biography of the Narmada Bachao Andolan (the Save Narmada Movement – hereafter NBA), a social movement in India, the book does witness to the creativity and potential of a social movement to become a theological text.

The book is the outcome of research which involved deeper engagement with a combination of primary and secondary sources. During field research in the Narmada valley and other related sites in India, different social movement research methods were used. *Semi-structured interviewing* helped to understand social movement mobilization from the perspective of the movement actors. *Field-driven* and *theory-driven participant observation* enabled one to observe, and also to some degree participate in the action being studied, as the action was happening. *Protest event analysis* and *historical analysis* studied secondary sources such as newspapers, articles, and research on particular protest events that occurred in the history of the movement.[3] The secondary sources mainly included library research of various published books, articles, researches, videos, and newspaper clippings. It is important to acknowledge the significance of non-conventional transcripts of the movement, such as songs, slogans, posters, for this research.

Why an Earth Ethics from the Grassroots?

Recent decades have witnessed the emergence of a new awareness of the need to protect and save the environment from decay and destruction. This awareness has also paved the way to the construction of a variety of theories on environment and nature. Environmental ethics is a new discipline which deals with issues related to the environmental crisis using different moral theories. In Christian theology and ethics we see a similar commitment to respond to the environmental crisis from theological and ethical perspectives.[4] All these theological articulations are attempts to make sense of the distress that we face today and to inspire the faith communities to the care of creation.

However, eco-theology and environmental ethics, in general, construct their analysis and arguments based on the false notion of universality, as they draw from ecological and cosmological metanarratives. Concerns such as wilderness preservation, population explosion, biocentrism, intrinsic worth of non-human beings, sustainable development, and so on, thus become the major themes of mainstream theological and ethical literature on ecology. At the same time, there is a new initiative to affirm the interrelationship between ecological justice and wider social justice in recent times.[5] However, a methodological commitment to recognize the agency of the victims of environmental destruction seems to be missing here.[6] This is the context in which a constructive attempt towards an earth ethics from the grassroots becomes relevant.

The notion of "subaltern" is important in constructing an earth ethics from the grassroots, and hence a clarification of how the term "subaltern" is being used in this book is in order here. Antonio

Gramsci, the Italian Marxist, elaborated the notion of subaltern to explain the inability of the Italian bourgeois liberal state to embody a national popular will. Analyzing the Italian context, he observed that, "The 'national' does not coincide with the 'popular' because in Italy the intellectuals are distant from the people, i.e. from the 'nation.' They are tied instead to a caste tradition that has never been broken by a strong popular or national political movement from below."[7] The Subaltern Studies Collective of South Asian Scholars has popularized this concept over the last few decades. Ranajit Guha defines "subaltern" as a name for the "general attitude of subordination in South Asian society whether this is expressed in terms of class, caste, age, gender and office or in any other way."[8]

Mark Lewis Taylor's analysis of the linguistic construction of the term "subaltern" is important. "Clearly, the term signals an interest in otherness (difference, diversity, deferral in a flux of signification and location) by way of its major linguistic unit, '-altern' (from Latin *alter*, 'other'). Nevertheless, its prefix, 'sub-,' deepens and orients its interests in alterity to experiences of *sub*-ordination."[9] Based on this analysis, Taylor provides a unique perspective for subaltern studies: "To study the subaltern is to study the subordinated others, usually, the others who have been subordinated because of their otherness or because their otherness was a convenient stigmatizing mechanism for organizing their subordination."[10] An earth ethics from the grassroots, hence, is the narrative of the subalterns, the mechanisms that perpetuate their subordination, and their resilient resolve to transform their destiny.

An analysis of the concept of hegemony is also important to understand the rationale for an earth ethics from the grassroots. Antonio Gramsci's interpretation of the concept of hegemony enables us to see the ideological function of hegemony to perpetrate and perpetuate bourgeois values. According to him, capitalism, along with its political and economic coercion using force and violence, functions at the level of culture and values to indoctrinate the community with bourgeois values. Hegemony, for Gramsci, is the cultural process, initiated by institutions in the civil society, through which the dominant persuades the subaltern to internalize the dominant values and worldviews as truth and normative. To put it differently, hegemony is the art of the dominant class to universalize the way it wants to see the world so that the subaltern may receive it as common sense and internalize it losing their distinct moral agency and vantage point to see the world as it is.

The term subaltern, hence, is inherently a social critique. It exposes the deep-rooted sinfulness of our social fabric. The subalterns are the subordinated others. They are the victims of the clandestine violence of hegemony, which strips away their moral agency. At the same time, they are more than victims as they are involved in the resistance against the mechanisms and systems that enslave and subordinate them. They are also engaged in creating a different earth by dismantling the prevailing dominant social and ecological relations. The term subaltern in this book therefore stands for the engaged collectivity of the subalterns – their social movements – that strive for a redeemed earth where life flourishes abundantly. An earth ethics from the grassroots, therefore, affirms the situatedness of earth ethics in the crucible of the political praxis of the subordinated others who are pushed to the peripheries of the dominant construction of knowledge.

The Latin American Subaltern Studies Group helps us to understand further the politics of subaltern studies. "It [subaltern studies] appears and develops as an academic practice in a contemporary setting in which globalization is producing new patterns of domination and exploitation and reinforcing older ones ... Subaltern studies is not only a new form of academic knowledge, then; it must also be a way of intervening politically in that production on the side of the subaltern."[11] Said differently, subaltern studies is primarily a commitment to engage in the political praxis of the subalterns.

An earth ethics from the grassroots, hence, is the vision of an engaged collectivity of the subaltern communities about their lives on earth in communion with all other living beings. A perspective from the grassroots enables earth ethics to understand the very subalternity of earth, and to see how the otherness of nature and the otherness of the subordinated others are correlated. It describes how the subordinated others at the grassroots perceive the realities that continue to make them powerless, and reduce all life forms into commodities to be plundered and exploited. An earth ethics from the grassroots envisions the interconnectedness between social justice, differences and environmental degradation. It unmasks the brutal face of development and globalization. A host of social, environmental, and political theories are being analyzed and used as resources in this constructive endeavor. An earth ethics from the grassroots recognizes and retrieves the liberative strands in the religious traditions, scriptures, rituals, and cosmogonies of the communities, and uses them as resources in their struggles. The awareness of the interconnectedness between the struggles for redistribution, recognition, environmental justice, and human rights enables the earth ethics from the grassroots to initiate solidarity networks between different social movements. It underscores the reclamation of the moral agency of the uprooted at the grassroots as foundational to their political praxis. An earth ethics from the grassroots, therefore, is a vision and praxis *to interpret* the reality and *to change* it radically from the subaltern standpoint so that a different world may become a contemporary reality.

Alternatives Unincorporated irrupts out of an engaged praxis with the NBA, which is engaged in a historic struggle against a massive multipurpose river valley project in the River Narmada in India. This project has led to the colonization of all life forms in the region. The first chapter presents the crisis of the earth as perceived from the grassroots. Using the Habermasian concept of the colonization of the lifeworld, this chapter elucidates how development and neoliberal globalization continue the colonial legacy of colonizing the lifeworld and erasing the moral agency of the subaltern communities. The way God-talk functions as a sacred canopy to legitimize and to perpetuate the conquest of the lifeworld is also presented in this chapter.

The second chapter narrates the story of River Narmada. It is a narrative of the lifeworld of the valley, the history of the river valley project, and the "coming to voice" of peoples' resilience to resist the colonization of their lifeworld. This chapter closely examines how development emerged as a fetish in postcolonial India, exhorting the subalterns to suffer and sacrifice for the "progress" and "economic growth" of the country. It further exposes the color line of the development gaze. The descriptive narrative of the story of the NBA attempts to understand the politics of the movement in depth.

The third chapter presents and reflects upon the methodological proposal that social movements are texts through a deeper engagement and conversation with the epistemologies from the grassroots. It exposes the hegemonic nature of the regime of truth, and underscores the agency of oppositional consciousness and knowledges that stem from the subaltern counterpublic spheres – the social movements. The last chapter is the constructive attempt to map the earth ethics from the grassroots. The book concludes with a manifesto of the earth ethics from the grassroots, reclaiming the moral agency of the subalterns to dream and to midwife alternatives that are "unincorporated."

Can the Subaltern Speak?

This Introduction cannot be concluded without an engagement with Gayatri Chakravorty Spivak's penetrating critique of the dominant project to represent the subalterns, as articulated poignantly in her famous essay "Can the Subaltern Speak?"[12] According to Spivak, both "speaking for" in the sense of political representation and "speaking about" (re-presenting) in the sense of creating a portrait, not only leads to subaltern silencing, but also veils the dominant project of representation. One may wonder about the relevance of Spivak's critique to this work. The radical self-reflexive nature of her critique of representation warrants a critical engagement with it. Ilan Kapoor's exposition of Spivak is instructive here. "Knowledge is always imbricated with power, so that getting to know (or 'discursively framing') the Third World [the subaltern] is about getting to discipline and monitor it, to have a more manageable 'Other'."[13] Arundhati Roy's critique of "fly-by-night PhDs pretending to be on the inside-track of peoples movements,"[14] further contextualizes the need for a radical self-reflexive at the very outset of this journey.

Being a western educated, lower-middle-class, dominant caste, male, heterosexual person, I come from a social location of privilege, supremacy, and dominance in Indian society. My academic engagement to work on this book further puts me in the Spivakian category of "native informant," where I join the *diaspora* third world researchers who speak on behalf of the third world for the benefit of western scholarship. In his critique of the native informant's desire to "don ethnicity as a badge," Kapoor reminds us that "valorizing the 'ethnic' may end up rewarding those who are already privileged and upwardly mobile, at the expense of the subaltern."[15] Whether we agree with it or not, the commodifcation of difference and the Other for professional upward mobility is a common practice in the academy today. It is in this context that Kapoor raises some pertinent questions on the politics of research such as the present one:

> What are the ethico-political implications of our representations for the Third World, and especially for the subaltern groups that preoccupy a good part of our work? To what extent do our depictions and actions marginalize or silence these groups and mask our own complicities? What social and institutional power relationships do these representations, even those aimed at 'empowerment', set up or neglect? And to what extent can we attenuate these pitfalls?[16]

Along with our positioning informed by our social location, our institutional affiliations also influence the way we represent and construct the subaltern which ultimately would lead to the reinforcement of subaltern speechlessness. This realization is articulated well by John Beverley when he observes that "literature and the university are among the practices that create and sustain subalternity."[17] Our representation of the subaltern from our institutional positioning is nothing but a "new Orientalism," where we valorize and romanticize difference and the Other for the dominant political agenda. The third world has been reduced as repositories for mining "different" data for academic theorizing and systematizing in the West, while at the end of the day, the speechlessness and the powerlessness of the subalterns remain unchallenged. Again, as Kapoor reminds us, "when we act in accordance with personal, professional, organizational interests, our representations of the Other say much more about us than about the Other, or at a minimum, they construct the Other *only in as far as* we want to know it and control it."[18]

Where does this radical self-reflexivity lead us? Is it still possible to listen to "the small voice of history" at the grassroots without a colonial and orientalist attitude to control and manage? What are the ethico-political concerns that we need to keep in mind as we engage in conversation with the subalterns? First of all, we must begin with an honest acknowledgement of our own embeddedness in locations of privilege, supremacy and dominance which tint our perception of the reality and influence our inferences. Even while we critique something, we are seduced by it. This acknowledgement is important because, as Spivak rightly puts it, it enables us to negotiate by "persistently transforming conditions of impossibility into possibility."[19] Such an acknowledgment is the first step to begin a "journey of unlearning" our dominant ways of knowing and representing. However, Spivak also reminds us about the need to begin this journey "without guarantees." It is an invitation to be "open to the 'non-speakingness' of the subaltern, its refusal to answer or submit to the gaze and questioning of the ethnographer. Thus, the subaltern's various silences (as distinguished from its silenc*ing*) need to be recognized as forms of resistance and agency."[20]

Second, our commitment to enable the subaltern voice to insurrect demands an equally passionate political praxis in our own respective social locations, engaging in acts of resistance and creating alternatives. Such political actions against the subtle and obvious acts of violence and silencing perpetuated by institutions such as family, religion, academy, ethnicity, and state make our engagement with the grassroots more credible and authentic. This provides a liberatory *a priori* dimension to our social existence, to consistently challenge hegemonic structures of exclusion and silencing so that just and inclusive social relations become a contemporary possibility.

Third, the call for radical self-reflexivity is an invitation for an ethical relationship with the grassroots. The naked face of the subaltern becomes the site of new epiphanies. Our political praxis in solidarity with the subalterns becomes our Damascus experience where we encounter the Divine as the represented One. Our organic fellowship with the subalterns enables us to learn what it means to be human. Jack Hill's engagement with Indian Christian ethicists is instructive here. Hill learned from India a new conception of ethics as "being pulled by others in experiences of *communitas*."[21] This experience of being pulled by encounters of subalternity provides us a new vision of being and becoming ethical. In our times, it is the encounter with the social movements that provides us new ethical groundings. We become ethical as we partake in their project of liberation which mediates our liberation as well.

Our attempt in this book is not to solve or fix Spivak's conundrum. Rather, the autobiographical moorings of this book make it imperative to recognize the challenge of radical self-reflexivity as we continue to engage with the subalterns. In that sense, this work is more than an academic pursuit to construct an earth ethics from the grassroots. As Larry Rasmussen reminded us in the context of "Katrina's epiphany," our engagements with the subalterns are "epiphanies for those of us who buffer ourselves well with privilege and see the world not as it is but as we are."[22] The ethical discernment to view the world from the grassroots marks the beginning of a new discipleship journey – a detour in the way we live out our faith.

1 The Crisis of Earth: A View from the Grassroots

The negation of the fundamental right to live is the everyday life experience that binds land, water, forest, and subsistence communities at the grassroots in the era of globalization. Such negations manifest in diverse ways as a reign of death, leading the movement of life into jeopardy. The reign of death becomes hegemonic when it colonizes the minds of the communities and denudes them of their sense of moral agency. Communities without moral agency are mere "dead men [sic] walking." The ethical imperative in such historical contexts is nothing but to reclaim the moral agency of the victims of the reign of death. A critical analysis of the reign of death is, hence, the starting point in our ethical praxis as it helps us to understand the distress of the earth and its inhabitants. This chapter presents how an earth ethics from the grassroots problematizes the crisis of earth.

The Colonization of the Lifeworld

The Colonization of the Lifeworld: The Problem for an Earth Ethics from the Grassroots

The threat to the movement of life in late-capitalist societies can be narrated, analyzed, and approached in different ways. In this book we use the concept of the "colonization of the lifeworld" developed by Jürgen Habermas, to problematize the crisis of earth. Habermas uses this concept to develop his critique of modernity and advanced capitalism.

According to Habermas, society can be seen as divided into "system" and "lifeworld." System refers to the sphere coordinated by the instrumental rationality of the market economy and the administrative state. Lifeworld, on the other hand, represents the organic sphere of communicative rationality. Cultural reproduction (the interpretation and transmission of cultural traditions from one generation to the other), social integration (the institutionalization and

coordination of patterned practices of everyday life), and socializa-
tion (formation of personal identities) are the processes associated
with the lifeworld.[1] Habermas then presents the colonization of the
lifeworld as the pathology of modernity. The uncoupling of system
and lifeworld, and its colonization, leads to the ascendancy of instrumental rationality of market and state, which then strips away the
moral world and agency of the lifeworld.[2]

The Habermasian concept of the colonization of the lifeworld
has been used by various Christian theologians and ethicists to analyze late-capitalist societies and to develop theological and ethical
critiques of modernity.[3] The crisis of our time is the colonization
of the lifeworld. The morality of the market and the bureaucratic
state has become the norm that guides decisions in the lifeworld in
the contemporary world. Knowledge becomes a commodity with a
price tag, and a means to have dominion and hegemony over others. The hegemony of instrumental rationality and its penetration
and invasion into the lifeworld castrates the community of its moral
agency. The distress of the earth which we mourn today is therefore
the consequence of the colonization of the lifeworld.

David Tracy's observation about Habermas' critical theory of society summarizes the significance of the concept of the colonization
of the lifeworld:

> His critical social theory helps analyze and test the social systems of our
> society: the economy and political administration and their media of
> money and power; and their invasion, if unchecked, of the commu-
> nicative rationality necessary to the social action in the lifeworld of the
> society; especially in the public realm. Indeed, to understand why the
> "public realm" has become impoverished in our society and why the
> lifeworld has been "colonized" by the systems of the economy and po-
> litical administration demands a social analysis that can show how the
> communicative rationality of the "citizen" can gradually be affected by
> the purposive rationality of the client and the consumer in developed
> modern societies.[4]

The systematic societal analysis which Tracy proposes will expose us
to the process of invasion and colonization that is taking place in our
history such as commodification of labor and nature, desertification
of rain forests for development projects, forceful displacement and
subsequent refugization of subsistence communities from their commons and homelands, depletion of the biomass for commercial fishing, bio-imperialism through gene manipulation and agro-business,

and the doctrine of preemptive war. These are the narratives that are silenced by the hegemonic bandwagon of progress, growth, development, and globalization. Re-engaging these narratives is the starting point of an earth ethics from the grassroots.

The Colonization of the Lifeworld: Subaltern Narratives

It was a winter night in December 1984. The city of Bhopal in India froze with the cold wind. Sometime during the night that cold wind became a hurricane of death, containing the poisonous gas leaked from the Union Carbide plant in the city. It was India's Hiroshima. For thousands, it was their last night. Those who survived the gas became the living dead. The environment was yet another casualty. The lifeworld could literally smell the colonization of their being, while the state and the multinational corporation legitimized the genocide as a sacrifice that the subjects of an "underdeveloped" nation are called to bear for progress and growth.

A decade later, on the first day of 1994, as the US initiated the North American Free Trade Agreement (NAFTA), in the jungles of the Mexican state of Chiapas there emerged a movement called the Zapatistas, out of peoples' collective resolve to end the five hundred years of oppression and the five decades of development. They articulated succinctly their perception of the colonization of the lifeworld and declared *basta*:

> [We understood] that our misery meant the wealth of a few; that on the bones and the dust of our ancestors and our children the powerful built their house. [We understood] that our steps could not enter that house, and that the light that brightened it was fed by the darkness [imposed on] our people. [We understood] that the abundance on the table at that house was fed by the emptiness of our stomachs, and that their children were borne by our misery. [That house's] roof and walls were built over the fragility of our bodies; and the health that filled its spaces resulted from our death; and the wisdom lived in that house nourished itself of our ignorance. The peace that sheltered it was war waged on our people.[5]

Lawrence Summers, the former chief economist for the World Bank, issued a memorandum in 1991 encouraging the bank to export toxic waste to the third world because it is "economically efficient." According to him, "a given amount of health-impairing pollution should be done in the country with the lowest cost, which will be the country with the lowest wages." He also warned the Bank of some resistance in the name of "social concerns" and "moral reasons" that "could be turned around and used more or less effectively against every Bank proposal for liberalization."[6]

Summers' memo was not a surprise to the third world as their history is a history of pillage in the name of progress and development. The following testimony from Guatemala is a witness to this. "I saw them bury a dead child in a cardboard box. (This is true, and I don't forget it.) On this box there was a stamp: 'General Electric Company – Progress is our Most Important Product'."[7]

Bhopal and Chiapas are living examples of subaltern lifeworlds being colonized and massacred. As Summers' memo categorically reveals, these are not accidents. These events also expose the nexus between global capital, indigenous elites, and the postcolonial state. The co-existence of massacre and accumulation is the hallmark of our times. These narratives interpret the colonization of the lifeworld as a process of disempowering a people by stripping them of their moral agency, and unleashing on them a regime of social engineering to accumulate more wealth.

The Colonization of the Lifeworld: A Theological Project

An analysis of the history of the colonization of the lifeworld will also expose us to the God-talk that has been used to legitimize the process of invasion. Differently said, the colonization of the lifeworld has always been a theological project, and God-talk has always functioned as a "sacred canopy" to face the legitimation crisis of the system. Enrique Dussel, in his exposition of modernity, conquest, and globalization, categorically presents this use of theological claims. For Dussel, the Europeans (the conquistadors) portrayed themselves as "the missionaries of civilization to all the world, especially to the barbarian people."[8]

Dussel further traces this same God-talk in the conquest of the Spaniards, calling it the "spiritual conquest." The conquistador invasion, like all other expressions of the colonization of the lifeworld, required divine legitimization. The following excerpt from the requirement (*requerimiento*) that the conquistadors read to the Indians before the battle reveals the violence of their God-talk. "If you refuse to try to protract this process by malicious delay, I certify that with the aid of God I will wage mighty war upon you in every place and in every way… I will seize your women and sons and sell them into slavery. I will rob you of all your goods and do to you every evil and injury in my power."[9]

The insights from the Latin American narratives help us to analyze more deeply the God-talk of the colonizers. The God-talk of the colonization of the lifeworld involves three categories: the affirmation of the divinely destined agency of the colonizer to invade and conquer the Other; the teleological vision of an ideal state of maturity, progress, and growth which they want to impose upon the colonized with missionary zeal; and finally the strong sense of a deontological call to be the missionaries of this new religion. As Larry Rasmussen rightly puts it, "when Columbus sailed from Cadiz, theft was his religious right and conquest his Christian duty, necessary for the safe deliverance of the colonized themselves."[10] The following excerpt from a French document published in 1897 supporting colonialism categorically explains the deontological foundation of colonialism:

> Colonization is not a question of interest but a question of duty. It is necessary to colonize because there is a moral obligation, for both nations and individuals, to employ the strengths and advantages they have received from Providence for the general good of humanity. It is necessary to colonize because colonization is one of the duties incumbent upon great nations, which they cannot evade without failing in their mission and falling into moral dereliction.[11]

The colonization of the lifeworld has always been a project filled with violence. And more than anything else, it has been God-talk that has helped the colonizers to legitimize violence thanks to the theological concept of "sacrifice." As Dussel rightly states, "the Indians were victimized in the name of an innocent victim and for the sake of universal rights."[12]

The violence of colonization seeks theological legitimization in two ways: firstly, by invoking a particular interpretation of the doctrine of atonement to glorify victimization – imposed sacrifice as redemptive (civilizing); and secondly, by focusing on a utopian *telos* which promises progress, growth, and human rights. In this way the God-talk of colonization is a doctrine combining a masochistic soteriology with an eschatological vision of progress and development mediated by a chosen race. The "realized eschatology" of the "developed" nations is being invoked in this doctrine to invite the "underdeveloped" to convert to this religion. This spiritual conquest is fought masked in messianic claims of missionary agency and zeal to civilize and emancipate the Other, and the casualty of this subtle proselytization is the moral agency of the communities. The spirit of this spiritual conquest is well articulated in the following observation by Dussel: "Modernity elaborated a myth of its own goodness, rationalized its violence as civilizing, and finally declared itself innocent of the assassination of the Other."[13]

Such discernment of the violence of colonization is apolitical if we fail to understand modernity as capitalist modernity. Christian social ethicists like Larry Rasmussen and Elizabeth Bounds, along with Enrique Dussel, enable us to see this perspective. For Rasmussen, capitalist modernity is "killing us. It slowly devours its own children as well as the children of others"[14] whereas for Bounds, "capitalism is able to organize the most intimate areas of lives and shape profoundly our consciousness."[15] This violence and sacrifice is divinely sanctioned for the realization of the *telos* of the messianic project of modernity.

> The sacrificial capitalist economy commenced its five hundred year history by worshipping money as its fetish and by celebrating its earthly (unheavenly) religion during the week, instead of on the Sabbath… The year 1492 ushered in a new era which has been immolating the colonized peoples of the periphery, or the so-called Third World, on a new god's altar.[16]

To sum up, the colonizers have always been successful in constructing and effectively using God-talk that legitimizes different manifestations of colonization. It continues as new colonies and erasures of landscapes and livelihood emerge at the peripheries and grassroots. Such God-talk is not only hegemonic but toxic with the potential to colonize the minds of the communities.

Contemporary Manifestations of the Colonization of the Lifeworld

The historical analysis of the colonization of the lifeworld does not mean that the invasion of the lifeworld came to an end with the demise of colonialism. Clarification of certain important terms is in order here. Even though the terms colonialism and imperialism are often used interchangeably, we need to be aware of their distinctiveness. According to Mark Lewis Taylor, colonialism is "the organized deployment of racialized and gendered constructs for practices of acquiring and maintaining political control over other social groups, settling their lands with new residents, and/or exploring that land and its people through military and administrative occupiers."[17] Imperialism, on the other hand, refers to the organized and specific actions of the colonizers which make them "a political machine that rules from the center, and extends its control to the farthest reaches of the peripheries."[18] So colonialism can be considered as the consequence of imperialism.

The erstwhile colonized nations began to gain independence and to become sovereign nations in the last century through a process known as decolonization. However, decolonization does not mean the collapse of the reign of subjugation. Rather, subjugation – which is known as recolonization in today's world – continues in new forms and ways. Neocolonialism is the term that is used to represent the contemporary process of recolonization, where the subjugation of the lifeworld of the communities at the peripheries through the economic and military hegemony of the Empire and the transnational corporations continue with the support of theological legitimization. This process of colonization happens not only in the southern hemisphere, but also at the margins of the affluent societies where the "social junk" – the poor, the colored, the homeless, the jobless, and the elderly, the disposable – reside.

Development and globalization are two contemporary manifestations of the process of the colonization of the lifeworld. The Indian physicist and environmentalist Vandana Shiva, in her critical analysis of globalization, identifies three waves of globalization by tracing the interconnection between the European colonization of the rest of the world, the imposition of "development" in the post-World War II period, and contemporary neo-liberal globalization.[19] This discernment is foundational for theological and ethical reflections on earth ethics, as it clarifies contemporary manifestations of the colonization of the lifeworld. Hence we devote the remaining part of this chapter to examining the way development and globalization continue to invade and commodify the lifeworld in our times, leading to the distress of the earth and its children.

Development as the Colonization of the Lifeworld

The invention of development

"Like a towering lighthouse guiding sailors towards the coast, 'development' stood as *the* idea which oriented emerging nations in their journey."[20] This introductory statement by Wolfgang Sachs in his celebrated work *Development Dictionary* summarizes the history, politics, and theology of development. Following the breakdown of the European colonial powers, Sachs further observes, "the US found an opportunity to give worldwide dimensions to the mission their founding fathers had bequeathed to them: to be the 'beacon on the hill.' They launched the idea of development with a call to every nation to follow their footsteps."[21] The rest is history.

Development is a contested concept. The foundational question here is rather a straight and direct one: Is development yet another (neo)colonial mechanism to invade, control, and plunder the world, or is it capable of enabling the flourishing of life in community? Let us begin with a historical sketch of the evolution of the concept of development in the twentieth century.

The meaning of the term development in its contemporary sense is derived from the modern development thinking and project inaugurated after World War II. So we are limiting our analysis to the twentieth-century phenomenon of modern development. Up until the last two decades of the twentieth century the teleology of modern development was uncontested though the means to reach that *telos* was subject to a variety of criticisms. "In development, all the modern advances in science, technology, democracy, values, ethics, and social organization fuse into the single humanitarian project of producing a far better world."[22] Here one can identify the rootedness of development in the dominant Enlightenment principles of belief in progress, reason, science, and modernity. Modern development in common parlance is understood as humanitarian technical assistance, wherein northern "experts" help southern governments to reach the standards attained by the North through the mediation of western technology, institutions, and practices. Ivan Illich summarizes the notion of development in the following words:

Development can be imagined as a blast of wind that blows people off their feet, out of their familiar space, and places them on an artificial platform, a new structure of living. In order to survive on this exposed and raised foundation, people are compelled to achieve new minimum levels of consumption, for example, in formal education, public health measures, frequency in the use of transportation and rental housing. The overall process is usually couched in the language of engineering – the creation of infrastructures, the building and co-ordination of systems, various growth stages, social escalators.[23]

Being a humanitarian project with a teleological vision of a better world, and a deontological commitment to bring in civilizational transformation at the peripheries, development has been considered as the panacea for the accumulated ills of societies and nations at the margins. Initially, objections to this project only concerned the paths to development. However, there has been an eruption of voices from all over the world raising fundamental questions about the very paradigm of modern development, which in recent times has become a monolithic hegemonic doctrine called "developmentalism." Developmentalism is primarily a belief in the economic growth model of development as the only viable paradigm of development in the contemporary world.

Jan Nederveen Pieterse's analysis of developmentalism, based on tracing the interconnection between power and truth, is instructive for our attempt to understand development critically:

> The central thesis of developmentalism is that social change occurs according to a pre-established pattern, the logic and direction of which is known. Those who declare themselves furthest advanced along its course claim privileged knowledge of the direction of change. Developmentalism is the truth from the point of view of the center of power; it is the theorization (or rather, ideologization) of its own path of development, and the comparative method elaborates this perspective.[24]

This interplay of power, knowledge, and truth, and its manifestations in coercive interventions all over the world for social engineering, are a contemporary reality. The truth from the center of power does claim universal validity, and hence it is imperative for the rest of the world to welcome this truth into their lifeworld. The heretics of this gospel are destined to remain in their primitive state of affairs. For developmentalism, they are "development's Others" – communities diagnosed as pathological and to be cured by development interventions. The best example to explain developmentalism is the modernization paradigm elaborated by Walt W. Rostow in his celebrated work, *The Stages of Economic Growth: A Non-Communist Manifesto*.[25] As Rostow categorically explains, the challenge of the time is that of "creating, in association with the non-Communist politicians and peoples of the preconditions and early take-off areas, a partnership which will see them through into sustained growth on a political and social basis which keeps open the possibilities of progressive, democratic development."[26] The *a priori* ideological position of developmentalism as explained in this statement endorses Pieterse's definition of developmentalism, identifying the interconnection between the center of power and center of knowledge. The very title of Rostow's book exposes its political agenda – to develop a growth-oriented development model and to create an international coalition to prevent radical social transformation (communism) which is detrimental to the interests of the western centers of power.

Rostow's theory identifies five economic stages to describe the path of growth that the countries undergo in their journey towards development. These stages are the traditional society, the preconditions for take-off, the take-off, the drive to maturity, and the age of high mass-consumption. The uniqueness of Rostow's model is the use of the metaphor of an airplane to describe the project of development, where, like an airplane that generates its speed on the runway and climbs upward consistently overcoming all obstacles on its way, development also, ignited by the engine of growth, can take the countries in the world to the ultimate destiny of the age of high mass-consumption.[27]

A closer look at the five stages of economic growth of Rostow's theory further explains the ideological and of course the theological foundations of developmentalism. The first stage is the traditional society which in Rostow's project is a stage of low productivity due to the ignorance of modern science and technology. The second stage that initiates the transition from tradition to modernity is christened as the "preconditions of take-off." To put it in Rostow's words, in this stage "the idea spreads not merely that economic progress is possible, but that economic progress is a necessary condition for some other purpose, judged to be good: be it national dignity, private profit, the general welfare, or a better life for the children."[28] This stage also witnesses the emergence of a new indigenous elite class. Take-off, the third stage, is the stage in which growth overcomes the legitimation crisis and becomes natural. When growth becomes natural, and compound interest becomes habit, a new social ethos of accumulation becomes the dominant worldview of the society. In economic terms, the take-off stage visualizes a substantial increase in the Gross National Product (GNP), commercialization of agriculture, and industrialization with accelerated use of modern science and technology. The "drive to maturity," the fourth stage, is the liminal stage between take-off and maturity. The final stage is the "age of high mass-consumption" where profit is shared with the workers to promote more consumption.

The following observation by Ivan Illich succinctly summarizes the contemporary state of development of which we have become prisoners.

> We have embodied our world-view in our institutions and are now their prisoners. Factories, news media, hospitals, governments and schools produce goods and services packaged to contain our view of the world. We – the rich – conceive of progress as the expansion of these establishments. We conceive of heightened mobility as luxury and safety packaged by General Motors or Boeing. We conceive of improving the general well-being as increasing the supply of doctors and hospitals, which package health along with protracted suffering. We have come to identify our need for further learning with the demand for ever longer confinement to classrooms. In other words, we have packaged education with custodial care, certification for jobs, and the right to vote, and wrapped them all together with indoctrination in the Christian, liberal or communist virtues… Rich nations now benevolently impose a straightjacket of traffic jams, hospital confinements and classrooms in the poor nations, and by international agreement call this 'development'.[29]

Development as discourse

Development as the colonization of the lifeworld is best articulated in the poststructuralist and postcolonial critique of development popularly known as post-development theory. In this section we analyze post-development theory to examine how development is a neo-colonial discourse and project. The poststructural turn in development studies, thanks to the engagement with the critical theory of Michael Foucault and postcolonialism, has radically transformed the development debate in recent times. Popularly known as post-development,[30] this shift is more than an academic exercise. It is rather a subversive political engagement affirming the subjectivity and agency of the new social movements. Gustavo Esteva echoes the same in his observations on the Chiapas movement. "The revolt was not a response to a lack of development – a call for cheaper food, more jobs, more health care and more education – or to poverty or misery. It was a dignified reaction to too much development. It arose because people opted for a more dignified form of dying."[31] Morgan Brigg summarizes post-development as follows.

By drawing inspiration from the discursive turn in the social sciences and local and indigenous knowledges, post-development effects a move away from the centering of economic relations which characterize neoliberal, political economy, regulation school and other variants of development studies. In doing so, it initiates a wider critique of development than has hitherto been possible. This indicates the possibility of criticisms and analyses that promote more ethical and nourishing engagements across cultures and lifestyles that coalesce at the site of development efforts.[32]

Unlike other theories of development, post-development is unique as it rejects the very concept and practice of development. This rejection does not arise out of the failure of development; rather, it is the success of development as a neocolonial discourse and project that leads to its outright rejection. James Ferguson's findings from his research on development interventions in Lesotho give us a foretaste of the post-development perspective:

It may be that what is most important about a "development" project is not so much what it fails to do but what it does do... The "instrumental-effect," then, is two-fold: alongside the institutional effect of expanding bureaucratic state power is the conceptual or ideological effect of depoliticizing both poverty and the state... If the "instrumental-effects" of a "development" project end up forming any kind of strategically coherent or intelligible whole, this is it: the anti-politics machine.[33]

Post-development perspective, therefore, is an approach that critically looks at the aforementioned instrumental effects of development on communities. The instrumental effects of development can be translated as the colonization of the lifeworld because the success of the "anti-politics machine" of development is based on its ability to disempower the moral agency of the communities. The problematization of poverty in development discourse apoliticizes the lifeworld by presenting it as a problem that can be technically fixed

through social engineering by development interventions. Such realization leads us to a closer look at "development as discourse" which
unleashes a hegemonic regime of truth that constructs "underdevelopment" as the "Other," and perpetuates and legitimizes the domination of the centers of power and their violent interventions at the
peripheries.

The post-World War II period witnessed a new realization in
several countries, as they began to perceive themselves as "underdeveloped," subsequently leading them to begin a new journey
of "un-underdeveloping" by "subjecting their societies to increas-
ingly systematic, detailed, and comprehensive interventions."[34]
Development as discourse is a theoretical and political engagement
to deconstruct this ideological construction of "underdevelopment,"
to expose its continuity with the politics of colonialism. Edward Said's
critical study of Orientalism provides us insights to understand development as discourse. "Orientalism can be discussed and analyzed as
the corporate institution for dealing with the Orient – dealing with it
by making statements about it, authorizing views on it, describing it,
by teaching it, settling it, ruling over it; in short, Orientalism as a western style for dominating, restructuring, and having authority over the
Orient."[35] In the Saidian sense, development as discourse enables
us to understand how "underdevelopment" and "third world" were
produced discursively by the West to continue their imperial project,
disguised as humanitarian and philanthropic interventions.

Homi Bhabha, in his analysis of the colonial discourse apparatus,
helps us to understand how the discursive construction of the Other
perpetuates and legitimizes the domination over it. "The objective
of colonial discourse is to construe the colonized as a population of
degenerate types on the basis of racial origin, in order to justify conquest and to establish systems of administration and instruction."[36]
Following this imperial legacy, development has succeeded in creating an apparatus for producing the regime of truth and knowledge about the third world to colonize it through "developmental"
interventions.

Development as discourse, according to post-development
scholars, begins with "discovering" poverty in the post-World War II
period as a social problem requiring systemic, economic, and technological interventions by the first world. The problematization of
poverty sanctified a new discourse with its universal prescription of

economic growth. This monotheistic religion of progress professes economic growth as the only way to attain salvation.

Post-development scholars in their critical analysis consider Harry Truman's second inaugural address as the president of the United States on January 20, 1949 as "the invention of underdevelopment." President Truman declared on that day that,

> [W]e must embark on a bold new program for making the benefits of our scientific advances and industrial progress available for the improvement and growth of underdeveloped areas. The old imperialism – exploitation for foreign profit – has no place in our plans. What we envisage is a program of development based on the concepts of democratic fair dealing.[37]

Reflecting on the inaugural address from a post-development perspective, Gustavo Esteva makes the following observation:

> Underdevelopment began, then, on January 20, 1949. On that day, two billion people became underdeveloped. In a real sense, from that time on, they ceased being what they were, in all their diversity, and were transmogrified into an inverted mirror of others' reality: a mirror that belittles them and sends them off to the end of the queue, a mirror that defines their identity, which is really that of a heterogeneous and diverse majority, simply in the terms of a homogenizing and narrow minority.[38]

The problematization of underdevelopment thus became an epistemological and political construction of the third world as the "Other" waiting to be invaded by the salvific bandwagon of development and progress. The six decades of development with new adjectives and sub-categories added to it such as "Women in Development," "Participatory Development," and "Sustainable Development" have categorically demonstrated the process of creating "development's Other" all over the world by reducing them to objects to be acted upon.

Having said this it is important here to look at how the post-development school defines and conceptually explains development. According to Escobar, "Development was – and continues to be for the most part – a top-down, ethnocentric, and technocratic approach, which treated people and cultures as abstract concepts, statistical figures to be moved up and down in the charts of 'progress.'"[39] The institutional and professional mechanisms of modern development are the missionaries who continue this evangelization and proselytization of the world. When social reality is reduced to a technical problem, there emerges a new priesthood – the development professionals – who have the know-how to fix and manage the problem through the apparatus of planning, and development projects.

Escobar succinctly summarizes this predicament in which the countries at the periphery have ended up after six decades of development:

> At times, development grew to be so important for Third World countries that it became acceptable for their rulers to subject their populations to an infinite variety of interventions, to more encompassing forms of power and systems of control; so important that First and Third World elites accepted the price of massive impoverishment, of selling Third World resources to the most convenient bidder, of degrading their physical and human ecologies, of killing and torturing, of condemning their indigenous populations to near extinction; so important that many in the Third World began to think of themselves as inferior, underdeveloped, and ignorant and to doubt the value of their own culture, deciding instead to pledge allegiance to the banners of reason and progress; so important, finally, that the achievement of development clouded the awareness of the impossibility of fulfilling the promises that development seemed to be making.[40]

More than the failures of development, post-development is concerned with the success of development in being an "anti-politics machine." The imperial politics of messianic and hegemonic propagation of this monotheistic religion, with a universally applicable salvation package, transformed communities with moral agency into a faceless crowd in the statistical records of the state waiting to be represented by and intervened upon to become developed. In this sense, modern development is the colonization of the lifeworld.

Development as redemption: the God-talk of development
Developmentalism is a secularized version of the Christian understanding of history as salvific process. The very title of Gilbert Rist's book reinforces this perspective: *The History of Development: From Western Origins to Global Faith*. Rist further explains this doctrine of redemption: "An American evangelist would have said much the same thing. Jesus Christ offers salvation to those abandoned to sin and death, provided that they fall in with what the faith demands of them; for that is how they will attain eternal life, and enjoy the bliss promised to the elect."[41]

Jan Nederveen Pieterse helps us to critique the God-talk of developmentalism. "Providence recast as Progress. Predestination reformulated as determinism. The basic scenario of the scripture, Paradise – Fall – Redemption, comes replicated in evolutionary schemes. Primeval simplicity and innocence, followed by the fall from grace, which is in turn to be followed by a redeeming change."[42] When it comes to practice, we see the same spirit of missionary zeal to civilize and convert the world into the new faith. "Developmentalism and its master plan is not merely a matter of reason and logic, it [is] also, at heart, the performance of a religious duty, the quest of a utopian rendezvous, the pursuit of a messianic course."[43] This sounds similar to the God-talk of colonialism. Agency, duty, and eschatology are the basic categories in the God-talk of development too. The God-talk of development is an anti-politics discourse which has the potential to colonize the minds of the community. Stated differently, the God-talk of development corrodes moral agency. The following observation by Jose Maria Sbert articulates how progress, the engine of developmentalism, colonizes the lifeworld and erodes moral agency.

> Faith in progress is entrusted with stripping the common man [sic] – who as yet has not progressed, but has already been cut off from his common land and deprived of his traditional means for autonomous subsistence – of all the cultural footholds that could give him spiritual autonomy and personal confidence as he face the market, industry and the nation-state. Disembedded from his community and caring only for himself, free from his elders' beliefs and fears, having learned to look down on his parents and knowing he will find no respect in what they could teach him, he and his fellows can only become *workers* for industry, *consumers* for the market, *citizens* for the nation and *humans* for mankind [sic].[44]

Globalization as the Colonization of the Lifeworld

The last two decades of the twentieth century witnessed the resilience of neo-liberalism. Globalization thus became the mantra of our times. Let us now explore how globalization continues the legacy of colonialism and development in colonizing the lifeworld. Globalization is an ambiguous concept with multiple meanings such that it takes diametrically opposite meanings depending on the social location of the subjects. Hence it is wrong to develop a universal definition of globalization. However, from the vantage point of this book, which affirms the situatedness of knowledge, particularly in the victims of the system, we will analyze globalization as the colonization of the lifeworld. Recognizing this ambiguity, North American ecofeminist theologians Heather Eaton and Lois Ann Lorentzen explain globalization in the following way.

Globalization can mean: (1) An *economic agenda* that traverses the world, promoting market economies and enhancing trade in the service of capital growth; (2) An *ideology* representing values, cultural norms, and practices, seen by some as a superior worldview and by others as cultural hegemony; (3) A *corporate structure and mechanism* that may supersede the rule of nation-states and challenge or even threaten democracy; (4) A *global village*, the consequence of vast cultural exchanges, communication technologies, transportation, migrations, and a wide array of global interconnections, including the globalization of ideas such as ecofeminism; or (5) A *grassroots globalization* or *globalization from below* as witnessed in anti-globalization or pre-democracy movements emerging in resistance to economic and cultural globalization.[45]

This perspective of globalization highlights certain fundamental characteristics of the phenomenon. It is a hegemonic ideology of homogenization with an economic agenda to protect the flow and plunder of transnational capital by corporations, disempowering the sovereignty of democratic bodies such as nation-states. At the same time, ironically, globalization enables the consolidation of resistance to global capital as well. Having identified these fundamental characteristics of globalization, let us look at the historical development of neo-liberal globalization.

Globalization: a neo-liberal project
Globalization needs to be understood as part of the ideology and socio-economic and political project of neo-liberalism. How did neo-liberalism emerge as the overarching economic truth of our times? Within the neo-liberal project, one can identify two distinct models of political economy – *laissez-faire* and social equity or welfare liberalism. Social equity liberalism is in general associated with the theories of John Keynes. Developing his theories in the context of the Great Depression, Keynes proposed governmental initiative to invest in public work projects when private entrepreneurs refused to invest in employment generating sectors. According to him, "unemployment, resource misuse and increasing monopolization ran

contrary to the credo of the *laissez-faire* equilibrium theorists."[46] Hence he opposed self-regulating markets.

The Keynesian economic model, according to feminist ethicist Rebecca Todd Peters, "has been labeled 'social equity' liberalism because it exhibits concern for the devastating human effects that accompany unemployment and inflation, particularly among the poorer classes in society."[47] However, for Keynes, concern for the poor was part of the neo-liberal economic agenda of growth because the availability of more money in the hands of the poor and the working class would eventually stimulate the economy. In short, the main characteristics of the Keynesian model are the affirmation of the economic agency of the government in stabilizing the market, and a concern for the poor and their welfare.

The contemporary expression of globalization begins with an ideological ascendancy of the *laissez-faire* model over the social equity liberalism model of Keynes. This has been achieved by a combination of economic and moral arguments. The Lutheran feminist ethicist Cynthia Moe-Lobeda identifies two basic premises for the dominant version of neo-liberalism: "First, the freedom of markets from state intervention contributes to wealth-creation and social well-being. Second, the freedom of individuals to act in perceived self-interest in economic life is a moral right and contributes to wealth-creation and social well-being."[48] This rhetoric, based on individual freedom and moral right to self-interest to enhance wealth, and the potential of an unregulated market to create wealth and thereby social welfare, remains the legitimizing argument of the system. Let us now explore how the unregulated free-market model of neo-liberalism became the ruling economic model.

The post-World War II era of developmentalism can also be understood as an era of experimenting with different approaches of neo-liberalism worldwide. It has almost become a ritual in globalization studies to trace back the history of neo-liberalism to the emergence of the Bretton Woods institutions in 1944. It was in Bretton Woods that the World Bank and the International Monetary Fund (IMF) were established to regulate countries facing fiscal deficit, and to promote development in the "underdeveloped" regions through financial aid. Their objective at the time of inception did not include intervention and control of the economies of sovereign nations.

In 1948, the US government introduced the Marshall Plan, a massive economic program to help European economies devastated by war. This plan was inspired by the Keynesian model as "for the first time in the history of capitalism, the general interest of society seemed to have taken primacy over the interest of particular investors or nations."[49] Over the next two decades we see various neo-liberal economic projects – both the *laissez-faire* model and the welfare liberalism model – being imposed on "underdeveloped" nations by the Bretton Woods institutions.

By the time the *laissez-fair* model gained ascendancy, thanks to the "development" lending of the Bank, most of the countries in the South fell into the debt trap. Servicing of debt became the major economic activity of those countries. In 1982, Mexico became the first country to become bankrupt. Neo-liberal globalization thus became the universal economic model. It became the common belief that free trade and linking of national economy with global capital will lead to the "trickling down" of wealth to the poorer sections of the society. Voices of dissent to this hegemonic bandwagon were dismissed by labeling them as "anti-development," "left-wing folly," "economic suicide," "going back to the dark ages," and so on. The failure of the East European and the USSR model of state socialism was an additional blessing to the process of globalization. As Susan George observes, "so, from a small, unpopular sect with virtually no influence, neo-liberalism has become the major world religion with its dogmatic doctrine, its priesthood, its lawgiving institutions and perhaps most important of all, its hell for heathen and sinners who dare to contest the revealed truth."[50]

The 1980s witnessed an increased intervention of the Bretton Woods institutions in the economic affairs of the countries in the South to redesign their budgets and economies in accordance with the principles of *laissez-faire* capitalism. The redesigning in 1986 took the form of a new form of lending known as Structural Adjustment Loans. With the emergence of structural adjustment lending, the welfare state, which is sarcastically called the "nanny state" by pro-globalization propagandists, became extinct and instead the state became the policeman of global capital. The conditions or the reforms that the structural adjustment lending imposed on nations in the debt trap can be summarized as follows.

(1) To allow markets to work by allowing the free market to determine prices. (2) To reduce the state control on prices, such that prices may be set by scarcity values. (3) The divestiture of resources held by the state, into the private sector. (4) The reduction of the state budget as far as is possible. (5) A reform of state institutions to reorient the role of the bureaucracy towards the facilitation of the private sector.[51]

Liberalization, deregulation and privatization thus became the catch-phrases of the time, while globalization hit the marginalized sections violently thanks to the total withdrawal of the state from social welfare programs. Addressing the South Summit in April 2000, President Fidel Castro of Cuba represented the anguish and indignation of the South. "For two decades, the Third World has been repeatedly listening to only one simplistic discourse while one single policy has prevailed. We have been told that deregulated markets, maximum privatization and the state's withdrawal from the economic activity were the infallible principles conducive to economic and social development."[52] It is in this context that we try to grapple with questions such as what has globalization to do with the colonization of the lifeworld, and why do we consider globalization as an issue in subaltern earth ethics?

Globalization and the colonization of the lifeworld

Neo-liberal globalization, with its inherent logic of commodification and marketization, is in practice a social fascism that excludes, displaces and annihilates communities and nature through the colonization of the lifeworld. It was prophesied five decades ago by Karl Polanyi in his critique of the marketization of society: "To allow the market mechanism to be sole director of the fate of human beings and their natural environment…would result in the demolition of society."[53] In Polanyi's analysis this is a shift from a "society with market" to a "market society." Put differently, it is a shift from a society where economic relations and practices were "embedded" in the social relations to a society colonized by the hegemonic logic and practice of the market.

The suppressed voices and narratives of our times, which we heard at the very beginning of this chapter, speak out from the peripheries of our "market societies" – stories of "tortured bodies" and "altered earth." There are other stories too. From 1986–1991 Zimbabwe had to remit $2.6 million in debt service alone. How did it affect the community? Susan George narrates this story: "Sex can become the only commodity left to sell, not only for girls but for their mothers as well. In the town of __ in the __ district, I have spoken to women working as prostitutes and they have cited their children's school fees as a primary reason for selling sex."[54]

From India, Vandana Shiva shares with us the story of "the suicide economy of corporate globalization."[55] Shiva, in her article, exposes how the earth, the most generous employer in a country of a billion people, becomes colonized by the "market society," and thereby is reduced to being a helpless witness to the suicide of more than 25,000 peasants between 1997 and 2004. The Structural Adjustment Program (SAP) insisted that India open its economy, including the seed sector, to transnational corporations. As a result, corporations such as Cargill, Monsanto, and Syngenta invaded the country and replaced the indigenous "farm saved seeds" with "corporate terminator seeds" which requires pesticides and fertilizers to grow. The terminator logic of Monsanto is antithetical to nature's organic ability to regenerate, and hence becomes an imperial invasion whose aim is the unrestricted growth of capital. This shift has pauperized the peasants, and suicide became the only option for them to have human dignity rather than living in perpetual debt.[56]

The stories of the prostituted women in Zimbabwe and the peasants in India show the violent face of the colonization of the lifeworld. Communities which used to be the subjects of their destiny in their subsistence economies have been sacrificed on the altar of neo-liberal globalization. The farmers' charter announced by the peasants' movements in India on March 7, 1996 articulates their moral indignation over the colonization of the lifeworld: "We are original breeders of seed and our resource and intellectual rights are prior to, and set the limits for, corporate monopolies from any intellectual property rights regimes. This further includes our fundamental rights to exclude patents on plants and life forms because they violate our ethical values and cultural traditions."[57]

M. P. Joseph, reflecting on the philosophy of the exclusion of contemporary globalization, identifies three fundamental changes that the transnational invasion brings into social relations in India: (1) A radical shift in the ownership pattern – from small land-owning farmers providing jobs to other marginal farmers to industrial houses and transnational corporations with large land holdings; (2) A shift from labor-intensive appropriate technologies, to capital-intensive and penetrating technologies; and (3) A change in the pattern of production – from subsistence farming to export-oriented agribusiness. The casualty of this shift is the land, and the communities living in communion with the land. Joseph concludes with the observation that "globalization has reduced land to a commodity and communities as economic territories to be exploited by transnational capital."[58]

A closer look at two of the conditionalities attached to the Structural Adjustment Program as representatives reveals the agenda for the colonization of the lifeworld inherent in globalization. Under the demand conditionality, countries in the South were asked to reduce the spending power of their people via a devaluation of local currency and wage reduction. This has affected the livelihood of the common people and particularly the marginalized sections of society. In the case of Brazil, after the devaluation of the currency in 1983, the price of beans increased by 769 percent and rice by 188 percent. The working hours needed to procure food for a month rose from 127 in 1982 to 242 in 1984.[59]

Supply conditionality is the means to discipline government spending on welfare programs. The government of India, as a faithful servant of global capital, even established a ministry for divestment to systematically monitor the privatization of public-sector undertakings. Government subsidies on agriculture, education, health, electricity, and the like were taken away as part of fiscal disciplining. In her article "Free Trade is War," Naomi Klein narrates the impact of the demise of the welfare state in the following way: "On Monday, seven anti-privatization activists were arrested in Soweto for blocking the installation of prepaid water meters. The meters are a privatized answer to the fact that millions of poor South Africans cannot pay their water bills. The new gadgets work like pay-as-you-go cell phones, only instead of having a dead phone when you run out of money; you have dead people, sickened by drinking cholera-infested water."[60]

The reality of hunger created by SAP conditionalities has provided the environment for the development of a new type of slavery all over the world. The colonization of the lifeworld hits the majority in the form of a crisis of livelihood. In the struggle for survival, they fall into the trap of slavery. According to a major investigative study by the International Labor Organization (ILO), 12.3 million people live in a condition of "modern slavery."[61] Are the poor who work for Wal-Mart in a Chinese sweatshop for 13 to 23 cents an hour and forced to work for 60–70 hours a week under conditions of a prison anything more than slaves? How do we classify the 12 to 13 year old girls in many of the Asian countries who are forced to work for Nike for 15 cents an hour for more than 50 hours a week? According to ILO statistics reproduced by David Baake, "three out of four forced laborers [are] usually enslaved by private agents, with 11% forced into prostitution or another form of commercial sexual activity and 64% working as bonded laborers in traditional sectors of the economy… Slavery is an extremely lucrative industry, generating 31.6 billion dollars in profit each year."[62] A closer look at modern slave farms, known as Export Processing Zones (EPZ), further exposes the color line of the slaves. To conclude, contrary to what the proponents of globalization would like us to believe, inequality and exclusion are not just problems of wrong implementation; rather, they are part of the package.

One of the contemporary manifestations of the colonization of the lifeworld is the rise of religious fanaticism and violence. Religious fundamentalism is a complex reality with socio-economic cultural and political roots. In spite of the danger of over-simplification and reductionism, new studies are coming out that expose the correlation between communalization of the lifeworld and neo-liberal globalization.[63] Riaz Ahmad, in his study of the communal riots in Gujarat, India, opines that "the current Gujarat violence is a glimpse of the ugly face of the convergence of the processes of globalization, authoritarianism and communalism."[64] He substantiates his observation with the data that in the city of Ahmedabad alone, 50 textile mills were closed down in the 1990s as part of the globalization process, robbing 100,000 people of their livelihoods. Gujarat has been a laboratory for Hindutva[65] forces, and globalization provided them a lumpen crowd to unleash a reign of terror in the name of religion.

Rachel Corrie, the American peace activist who was brutally killed by the military bulldozers while participating in the resistance against Israeli aggression, could identify the economic interests behind Israel's religious claims over the "Holy" land. For Corrie, participation in the anti-globalization march in Seattle and her presence in the Gaza strip were closely interrelated. During her stay in Gaza, she saw water being diverted from Gaza to Israeli agricultural lands. To put it in her words: "so much of what happens in Rafah is related

to this slow elimination of people's ability to survive...
particular, seems critical and invisible."[66] Unlike the domina .. narrative of the crisis in the Middle East depicting a religious war between the Zionists and the Jihadis, Corrie's personal testimony exposes the rootedness of the crisis in the colonization of the lifeworld. Vandana Shiva, in her reflections on 9/11, observed that globalization is contributing to the Talibanization of the world.[67] Her analogy of terrorism as cannibalism is a powerful exposition of the colonization of the lifeworld by market forces. In the factory farms where freedom is limited to the walls of cages, even the peaceful animals and birds show tendencies of "cannibalism." The pigs and the chickens "attack" each other. The factory administration is not concerned about the question of why those non-cannibal creatures become violent. Instead they solve the violence by debeaking and sterilization. The problem, Shiva concludes, is "the factory cage – not the teeth and tails of pigs, the beaks of chicken, the horns of cattle. It is the cage that needs removing, not the tail, or beak or horn. When animals are denied their basic freedoms to function as a species, when they are held captive and confined, they turn to cannibalism."[68] Shiva then raises the pertinent question:

> Could the 'war against terrorism' be equivalent to the detoothing, debeaking, dehorning of pigs, chickens and cattle by the agribusiness industry because they are turning violent when kept under violent conditions? ... The cages that humans are feeling trapped in are the new enclosures which are robbing communities of their cultural spaces and identities, and their ecological and economic spaces for survival. Globalization is the overarching name for this enclosure.[69]

Shiva's invoking of the memory of enclosures reiterates the continuity between colonialism and globalization.[70]

Globalization is now searching to "discover" new places to invade and plunder. In her article "The Rise of Disaster Capitalism," Naomi Klein helps us to see the new discoveries of capitalism. The article exposes the vulturous spirit of capitalism to convert the humanitarian response to one of the most tragic disasters that recent history has witnessed – the tsunami that hit South and South East Asia on December 26, 2004 – into a systematic attempt of radical social and economic engineering to maximize corporate interests. To put it in her words, "There is, however, plenty of destruction – countries smashed to rubble, whether by so-called Acts of God or by

Acts of Bush (on orders from God). And where there is destruction there is reconstruction, a chance to grab hold of 'the terrible barrenness'...and fill it with the most perfect, beautiful plans."[71] According to Herman Kumara of the National Fisheries Solidarity Movement in Sri Lanka, her country is facing "a second tsunami of corporate globalization and militarization, potentially even more devastating than the first. We see this as a plan of action amidst the tsunami crisis to hand over the sea and the coast to foreign corporations and tourism, with military assistance from the US marines." The vulturous face of globalization as the colonization of the lifeworld stands naked here.

"The realized eschatology": the God-talk of globalization
As in the case of previous versions of conquest and invasion, God-talk has been playing an undisputed role in the propagation of the new religion of "*money*theism" of globalization. Globalization, similar to its precursors – colonialism and developmentalism – is in itself a God-talk with the vision and promise of a teleology, and a missionary zeal motivated by a sense of deontology. The teleology of globalization, unlike that of developmentalism, is much more persuasive and convincing now that the gospel choir of globalization has succeeded in popularizing a chorus of "There is No Alternative." But the uniqueness of globalization is its emergence as a new religion with the market as the presiding deity. In the place of the old dictum of "no salvation outside the church" there emerged the new dictum: "no salvation outside the market."

Dwight Hopkins, in his study of the religion of globalization, in a convincing manner articulates globalization as a religious system. He defines religion as:

> a system of beliefs and practices comprising a god (which is the object of one's faith), a faith (which is a belief in a desired power greater than oneself), a religious leadership (which determines the path of belief), a theological anthropology (which defines what it means to be human), values (which set the standards to which the religion subscribes), a theology (which is the theoretical justification of the faith), and revelation (which is the diverse ways that the god manifests itself in and to the world).[72]

This descriptive definition provides us with a methodology to understand critically the religion of globalization. The god of globalization, according to Hopkins, is the monopoly of capitalist wealth. This god is Mammon whose *telos* is to maximize wealth by commodifying and marketizing living beings. The Indian Jesuit theologian Sebastian

Kappen in his compelling analysis of the religion of globalization exposes the spiritual legitimization that the "Christian Ungod" provides to neo-liberal globalization. According to him, the omnipresence of this ungod in our times is a historical continuation of the spiritual legitimization that the Christian Ungod has been doing. Explaining the "Christian Ungod" Kappen writes:

> It is the God whom Christians fashioned to legitimize their lust for wealth and power. It is this Ungod who inspired Kings, and Popes to embark on the Crusades and massacre of millions of Jews and Turks, who in the person of the Grand Inquisitor indulged in the brutalities of witch-hunting and the burning of heretics, who authorized the Christian Kings of the West to colonize and enslave all 'pagan' nations, who gave the green signal to slave trade involving the transportation across the Atlantic of 30 million Africans, who connived at the brutal extermination of the indigenous tribes of the Americas and Australias, who steadied the hands of those who dropped atom bombs over Hiroshima and Nagasaki, who in his new incarnation as an illustrious preacher stood by the side of president Bush in 1991 as the latter knelt down to invoke divine blessing on his projected war on Iraq, that was to kill thousands of Iraqis, men, women, and children. He is a god who will not hesitate to avenge the death of one North American marine with the death of ten times the number of Somalis. In short, he is a god who takes the side of the affluent against the poor, of the powerful against the weak, a god with hands dripping with the blood of the innocent.[73]

The analysis of the religion of globalization further enables us to critically evaluate the theological anthropology of globalization. We encounter here a new anthropology, according to which human beings are primarily motivated by self-interest. Adam Smith himself laid the foundation for this anthropology. "It is not from the benevolence of the butcher, the brewer, or the banker, that we expect our dinner, but from their regard to their own interest. We address ourselves, not to their humanity but to their self-love."[74] The theological anthropology of globalization in short presents a vision of being human which will further widen prevailing asymmetrical social relations. As Hopkins rightly puts it, "people are baptized into a lifestyle to fulfill the desire for commodities and to follow further the commodification of desires."[75]

Globalization as a religious system has succeeded in facing the legitimation crisis of the system. This success story of the missionaries of the new religion converts the existential crisis that humans and the wider community of life face today into a crisis of faith. M. P. Joseph, in his analysis of this crisis of faith, identifies the primacy of market as the mediating agent, a theological and ethical issue deserving serious engagement.[76] With the exclusive power of mediating agency, market becomes the true "ecclesia" of our times, according to Joseph. The concept of Divine is the major casualty in this new ecclesia of market because "unless the divine appears in the form of a colorful thing, with a decent price tag, and musters the ability to compete with other divine images in the market place, it deprives its charm. Ability to turn as an idol thus is an existential need for the concept of divine."[77] Idolization of the Divine is certainly a crisis of faith because "the ungod of death is worshipped as the real god when the God of life is alienated and peripheralized as a heresy."[78] Doesn't such idolization make globalization a fundamental theological problem of idolatry?

To Interpret and to Change: *Reclaiming Moral Agency*

Globalization as the colonization of the lifeworld is a fundamental ethical issue because it not only robs the moral agency of the community, but it also assumes moral agency through its claims of universality and the propaganda slogan of "There is No Alternative" (TINA). Thus the ethical imperative in the contemporary world is to reclaim the moral agency of the dispossessed. Moral agency empowers the community with the discernment of its historical responsibility to be sensitive, critical, morally indignant, compassionate and creative to understand what the reality *is*, and to strive collectively to transform it radically to what it *ought to be*. Put differently, moral agency is the political and spiritual power *to interpret* and *to change* the world. A people with moral agency are, therefore, the architects of a different world because they believe that "another world is possible."

When the people are empowered to reclaim their moral agency, they are able to see and analyze politically the reality from their own vantage point. This knowledge has the potential to unleash a revolutionary journey towards freedom and dignity. Cynthia Moe-Lobeda's interpretation of moral agency is instructive here. Moral agency, according to Moe-Lobeda, "is the power to subvert, that is, to resist and to live toward alternatives. That subversive and multifaceted activity is political...that is, it constitutes participation in the shaping of public life. The moral norm of active, embodied love is a call to political participation on behalf of life and against what destroys it."[79] The priests of neo-liberal globalization know it very well, so they systematically corrode the moral agency and the political will of the community through colonizing their lifeworld.

Conclusion

The threat to the movement of life that we face in the contemporary world under the hegemonic domination of neo-liberal globalization and development is a crisis of faith and ethics. The colonization of the lifeworld is systematic political, social, and economic engineering to apoliticize the discourses of our times, and thereby to create a public sphere filled with chanting and worshipping of the ungod of capitalism. Such a religiosity is the new opium that tranquilizes the communities of their historical subjectivity, and robs them of their moral agency. The discernment of this predicament of the disempowerment of moral agency, as articulated in the various theoretical discussions above, affirms the agency of the new social movements in reclaiming the moral agency of the community *to interpret* and *to change* the reality from their vantage point.

2 The Narmada Saga: A Valley that Refuses to Die

Introduction

When the colonizing gaze of development and globalization conquers the lifeworld, the lifeworld feels the smell and touch of death in its very body. Like the plagues of the ancient times, death then visits all living beings. Whether it is physical death due to impoverishment, or cultural and spiritual death due to uprooting and displacement, or political death due to disempowerment through taking away the moral agency of the communities, the movement of life is in jeopardy. Eulogies become celebrations and proclamations of "mission accomplished," inviting the "yet to be dead" to choose the only truth that is available for them to avoid "dying before their times." However, in spite of this culture of death, subaltern communities at the grassroots are engaged in struggles to resist the colonization of their lifeworld. The Narmada saga is the story of such a struggle – the struggle of a river valley that refuses to die.

The Narmada Valley: The Story of a Subaltern Lifeworld

The Narmada valley is inherently diverse in its landscape, demography, culture, worldview, and religiosity. It is the River Narmada that transforms these diversities into communities, primarily in their commitment to respect and venerate the river as mother. The veneration of the river as mother or Goddess is based on the cosmogonies and legends of various religious traditions in the valley. The religio-cultural ethos of this understanding of Narmada as a sacred river is foundational to the community's perception of their lifeworld. Whether it is the followers of the classical Hindu tradition or the indigenous communities living in the valley, the fact that they all share a pantheistic attitude towards their lifeworld makes it imperative that we be familiar with the cosmogonies and the legends of the valley. Before we begin our expedition into the world of their ancestors and gods, it is important to have some basic information about the river and the valley.

The River, the Valley and the Communities

River Narmada is considered the lifeline of Central India as it flourishes and nourishes life in diverse ways in three central and western Indian states, namely: Madhya Pradesh, Maharashtra, and Gujarat. The *Jivan Shala* campuses (Schools for Life) in the Narmada Valley vibrate with the song *Ma Reva*, a tribute to Mother Narmada which describes the river's voyage, giving life in abundance to the valley. This song narrates the story of the river. Narmada begins its journey from the Maikal ranges at Amarkantak in Madhya Pradesh, which is situated about 1057 meters above sea level. Along its voyage, Narmada flows through a diverse terrain which includes dense forests, mountain ranges, and plains before it reaches its final destination in the Arabian Sea. The Narmada travels 1312 kilometers and its basin covers 98,796 square kilometers, populated by an estimated population of 25 million people.

The Narmada valley is of great archaeological importance with the discovery of an almost complete skull of *Homo erectus* in the valley which may date back 150,000 years. It is considered the most ancient human remains recovered on the Indian subcontinent.[1] The Narmada is also known to have one of the richest deposits of mammalian fossils. The diverse and rich terrain, consisting of a vast savannah along with swamps and lakes, fertile agricultural land, rock shelters and hundreds of tributaries, has made the Narmada valley the perfect habitat for living beings from time immemorial.

The Narmada valley is blessed with rich and diverse flora and fauna. The valley is famous for its biodiversity. Kipling's *Jungle Book* was conceived and written with the forests of Seoni and Betul in the valley as the background. Sal (*Shorea robusta*), anjan (*Hardwickia binata*), kanji (*Pongamia glabra*), teak, bamboo, saj (*Terminalia tomentosa*), bija (*Pterocarpus marsupium*), and hirda (*Terminalia chebula*) constitute a green canopy providing shade and shelter to numerous living beings. The valley – especially the Nimad region – is known for its fertile land. The main agricultural products are wheat, millet, lentils and rice. With the dawn of globalization, market forces have caused farmers to shift from traditional food crops to cash crops such as cotton, sugar cane, and linseed. It is common in the region today for farmers to use terminator seeds and pesticides extensively. The faunal remains found in archaeological research substantiate the argument that the valley was the abode of wild animals such as rhinoceroses, elephants, boars, tigers, and buffalos.

The demographic diversity is yet another important characteristic of the Narmada valley. Archaeological and anthropological studies observe different stages in the evolution of human civilization in the valley based on rock paintings dating between 1400 and 1500 BCE. Demographically, the valley can broadly be classified into adivasi[2] and non-adivasi areas. The Nimad region in the central Narmada basin is the plain fertile land of migrants from Gujarat and other Northern states belonging to caste communities such as Jats, Patidars, Yadavs, Gujjars, Bharuds and others who settled in the plains after the sixteenth century. The early settlers in the Nimad region are called Nimadis. The Urdu-speaking Muslim community traces their history back to the Pindari marauders who settled in the seventeenth and eighteenth centuries. Most of the people in the Nimad region are land-owning farmers and agricultural workers. Along with innumerable adivasi and other dialects, Hindi, Marathi, Gujarathi, and Urdu are the major languages spoken in the valley.

Among the adivasis, Bhils, Bhilalas, Korku, Gonds, Pardhans, Bharia-Bhumia, and Kol are the main sub groups. These communities have been living in the valley from time immemorial, and they are mostly concentrated in the hilly regions. Among them Bhils and Gonds are the main groups. The adivasis in general are a subsistence community. They depend on the forest for their subsistence, such as food, fodder, fuel, fruits, and building materials. Their relationship with "market" is minimal. The adivasis who live on the plains, according to Amita Baviskar, are under the influence of "sanskritization."[3] "Living within a system of occupational specialization closely related to caste divisions, Bhils and Bhilalas have become more and more assimilated into the caste system, so that, in the plains, they are even considered as a caste."[4] So they remain in the plains as marginal landless agricultural laborers struggling to harmonize their adivasi heritage with the worldview of the plains.

The Narmada *Mata*

This section will now explore the cosmogonies and creation myths of different communities in the valley in order to understand how the Narmada influences their perceptions of the lifeworld. I have no intention of romanticizing the religio-cultural ethos of the communities or of claiming that popular piety and devotion towards Narmada is the only decisive influence that constructs the lifeworld in the valley. We will discuss in detail these issues later on and also address the danger of accepting lifeworld as given without bringing critical questions to it. The attempt here is to understand the religious and cultural significance of River Narmada for the communities in the valley, and how it enables them to construct their perception of the lifeworld.

The Gayana: the song of creation of the Bhilalas

The *Gayana* is an epic poem of the Bhilalas, celebrating fertility and bounty of earth, and sung during the *Indal pooja*, an annual festival.[5] The *gayana* helps the community to situate itself and the ancestors who live there in relation to a specific locality or site. For example, the *gayana* of Anjanvara (cited in the endnote) has the flow of Narmada as the locality to which it situates the community. Baviskar observes that "by establishing a religious connection with their environment and acknowledging its power to affect their fortunes, people also 'naturalize' their own existence, explaining and, at the same time, claiming for themselves their physical world. Appropriation, explanation and legitimation occur simultaneously."[6]

As mentioned above, *gayana* is sung during the *Indal pooja*, the communal celebration when a family shares its bounty with the community while invoking and celebrating the gods. So in *gayana* we see a celebration of the interdependence of a community with their natural world and gods. It is a ritual enactment of their social relationship, reminding and celebrating the embeddedness of their relationality in the world of their gods, ancestors, and nature. In that sense, a sacralization of the lifeworld and social relationship takes place in this ritual.

The song of *gayana* is the creation story of the Bhilalas. In this song they articulate the origin of their universe which includes the natural world, the world of the beasts and human beings, and social differentiation. The *gayana* has four episodes. The second episode narrates the journey of Narmada to the sea, her fiancé. On the way, because of her kindness and love for the living beings on the banks, she stops everywhere to bless the shores with life and fertility. However, these stops delay her journey and cost her dearly. Her lover changes his mind and chooses Tapti, her sister. Narmada remains forever unwed nurturing life on her shores.

"Throughout the *gayana* flows the Narmada, bestowing life-giving gifts to all whom she meets, naming and making sacred the geography along her banks."[7] We cannot write off this observation of Baviskar as the romantic poetic outburst of a researcher. According to Bava Mahalia, an adivasi leader from the valley, "we [tribal peoples] worship our gods by singing the *gayana* – the song of the river… The Narmada gives joy to those who live in her belly."[8] During my own interactions with the adivasis in the valley, I have come across similar retellings of the *gayana* where Narmada was affirmed as the life-giving source of the community. I heard new layers to the story, as people explained the curves in the route of the river as due to Narmada's attempt to stretch out to bless communities in different hamlets in the region.

Coming back to Baviskar's observation, the *gayana* is a powerful and inspiring myth that enables the community to consider nature as sacred. To ascribe the title of "natural environmentalists" or "ecological ethnicities" to adivasis, or to essentialize them as by nature protectors of environment is debatable.[9] However, the pantheistic ethos of their religiosity creates in them a worldview which holds the earth as sacred. The controversy over essentialism simply misses the point. The perception of the lifeworld of the adivasis is influenced by a variety of factors. Among them myths such as *gayana* have a significant impact on their everyday life in making social, political, and economic decisions in the community.

The Narmada Parikarma

The River Narmada is considered one of the holiest rivers in Hinduism. Unlike other holy rivers, such as the Ganges where one has to dip for the cleansing of sins, the simple seeing of the Narmada is sufficient for absolution. Legends in circulation in the valley claim that even the Ganges has to bathe in Narmada once a year to purify herself. Chris Deegan summarizes the diverse ways in which the Narmada becomes a sacred space for the community. "As a river, it is also an idol (*murti*). As a deity, it is subject to and giver of *darsan* (auspicious sight). As a temple, it is circumambulated. As a *tirtha*, it is a sacred crossing."[10] The Narmada *Parikarma* is the pilgrimage of circumambulation of the river. Several texts in the Hindu sacred literature praise Narmada as a deity, and describe the benevolence of the river to the community and to nature.

There are diverse descriptions of the origin of Narmada in different *Puranas*.[11] The legends associated with Lord Shiva are also diverse – Narmada being originated from the sweat of the dancing Shiva, from the sweat of the meditating Shiva, and from the *somakala* on the head of Shiva.[12] A commonality here is that all these legends ascribe the origin of Narmada to Shiva. The story of the nativity of Narmada, as narrated by Govind Prasad Dvivedi, the chief priest of the Narmada temple at Amarkantak, is as follows: "There was drought on earth and famine... The *devas* (gods) appealed to Shiva to relieve the dreadful thirst of the land. Shiva meditated for many days. So powerful was his *tapasya* (meditation) that a drop of sweat formed on his forehead and fell on the ground. From it arose a maiden."[13] These legends, in spite of their diversity, affirm Shiva as the source of Narmada, and present Narmada as a benevolent mother who cleanses the sins of the people.[14]

The name *Nar-mada* means endower of bliss. The opening verses of the *Narmada Purana* describe the features of the river through different names such as *Surasa* (flavorful or sweet), *Kripa* (of graceful attitude), *Karabha* (one who radiates happiness), *Vipapa* (without sin), and *Maharnava* (survivor of world destruction).[15]

The Narmada *Parikarma* is a sacred ritual practiced from ancient times in which pilgrims circumambulate the river barefoot. Traditionally, the *parikarma* takes three years, three months and three days to complete. The pilgrims on *parikarma* are required to follow certain ascetic practices which include going barefoot, not cutting any hair, collecting food through alms, eating only once a day, bathing in the Narmada once a day, abstaining from sexual activity, suppressing desire, and refraining from speaking lies, malice and hostility. The pilgrims will visit all sacred places and sites such as temples on their way. The pilgrims, in their prayers, uphold others in their family and community. Vijay Paranjype describes succinctly the cosmic vision that the pilgrimage provides to the pilgrims:

> Through this assemblage of cultures the pilgrim must pick his [sic] lonely and difficult path, past the humblest of ritual stones, beyond the gloriously carved soaring temples, through the lush, dense forests with their

incredible variety of vegetation and teeming wild creatures, keeping pace with the most sacred of rivers in all her moods until he [sic] reaches the final glimmer of understanding, of the oneness of all creation and his [sic] own place in it. The *parikarma*, in other words, enables the pilgrim to perceive the universe in its physical as well as mystical form.[16]

The exposition of the *gayana* and the Narmada *parikarma* serves as a window into the religious ethos of the communities in the valley.[17] Despite the demographic differences, and the differences in their religious doctrines and practices, they do share in common a notion of nature as sacred space. The Narmada as mother and endower of bliss is a tangible sacred presence which nourishes their worldview with a culture of reverence for life. The cosmogonies and the legends around River Narmada enable them to situate themselves in communion with the natural world and the world of the gods and the ancestors. This culture of life is the spirit of the lifeworld in the valley.

The Narmada Valley Development Project: The Development Gaze

India's "tryst with destiny" on the midnight of August 14, 1947 was not just the inauguration of an independent nation, but also the beginning of a regime of development. Freedom from the shackles of British imperialism was perceived by Jawaharlal Nehru, the first prime minister of the nation, as the historic opportunity for development through modernization and industrialization. The development gaze which came out of that nationalist mold perceived the commons such as land, forests, and waters as untapped resources to be plundered for the "common good" and "national interest." The lifeworld could feel the penetration of the invasion of a different logic in its body. The Narmada Valley Development Project came into being from this logic and gaze of development.

Independent India: The Fetishism of Development

The development paradigm popularly known as the Nehruvian model can be analyzed using the method of development as discourse.[18] Even though the Nehruvian model emerged during the anti-colonial struggle as the panacea for India's "underdevelopment," within the logic of modernity. The National Planning Committee under the leadership of Nehru, which was formed almost a decade before Indian independence, prepared a set of development goals for independent India. With the objective of creating a self-sufficient India, the committee included goals such as improvements in nutrition, clothing, and housing standards, a boost in agricultural and industrial production, generating more employment, a rise in per capita income, spread of literacy, enhancing public utility services, better health care, and an increase in life expectancy. Independent India continued this pattern of centralized planning and development through a series of Five Year Plans.

Partha Chatterjee provides a new perspective to nationalist historiography through presenting three "moments of maneuver" in the nationalist movement associated with three important leaders: Bankimchandra, Gandhi and Nehru.[19] For Chatterjee, with the sole exception of Gandhi, the colonial Indian middle-class thought as reflected in the nationalist movement was a "derivative discourse" of "post-Enlightenment rationality."[20] Bankimchandra's effort to combine the superiority of western material culture with the spiritual richness of the East is a classic example of this. For him, "the day the European industries and sciences are united with Indian dharma, man [sic] will be God."[21]

For Nehru the "derivative discourse" of the "post-Enlightenment rationality" became transparent with his "fetishization of the modern nation-state." According to Gabriele Dietrich and Bas Wielenga, "[T]his state embodies for him the spirit of modern progress which is needed to reorganize and increase economic production with the help of the latest science and technology so that enough wealth is created to ensure social justice for all."[22] We can derive three fundamental principles of the Nehruvian model from this analysis. (1) The centralized state as the legitimate agency to intervene and initiate development projects of modernization and industrialization to enhance economic growth. (2) A strong faith in science and technology as the vehicle to propel India to the category of developed nations. (3) A genuine commitment to eradicate the contradictions in the social fabric of the nation such as poverty, illiteracy, and the like which is generically named as "underdevelopment."

Nationalism emerged from the Nehruvian "moment of maneuver," which, in the words of Gyan Prakash, "hijacked even Gandhi's anti-modern ideology in its drive to create a nation-state devoted to modernization, and turned him into a figure revered for his ability to appeal to the 'irrational' peasants and for the mystical bond that he was seen to have with the masses."[23] With Gandhi reduced to marble statues that overlook the city squares, and to a face that adorns postal stamps, scientific temper, economic growth, modernization and industrialization became the national ideology. The liberal commitment to social equity and the perception of modernization as liberative in the context of social injustices elevated the Nehruvian development model to the pedestal of a national religion.[24]

It is in this context that the identification of river valley projects as an important means for nation building and economic growth by the postcolonial state in India becomes important. The multipurpose nature of the river valley projects such as generation of power, water to agriculture and industries, controlling of floods, and reducing droughts legitimized the government's commitment to build more large dams. The following oft-quoted statement by Nehru on the occasion of the inauguration of the Nangal canal in Punjab in 1954 is the best illustration of the emergence of big dams as a symbol of patriotic pride, and of course as a fetish.

> What a stupendous, magnificent work – a work which only that nation can take up which as faith and boldness! ... it has become the symbol of a nation's will to march forward with strength, determination and courage… As I walked around the (dam) site I thought that these days the biggest temple and mosque and *gurdwara* is the place where man [sic] works for the good of mankind [sic]. Which place can be greater that this, this Bhakra-Nangal, where thousands and lakhs [hundreds of thousands] of men [sic] have worked, have shed their blood and sweat and laid down their lives as well? Where can be a greater and holier place than this, which can regard as higher?[25]

According to the official records of the Central Water Commission of the government of India, out of 4,291 large dams that India had in 1994, 3,998 were constructed after independence. Out of these more than half were undertaken during the 1970s and 1980s. Half of the large dams in India are situated in Maharashtra and Gujarat, and three-fourths lie within Maharashtra, Madhya Pradesh and Gujarat.[26] These statistics prove the government of India's loyalty and commitment to continuing the dream of Nehru.[27]

The Narmada Dammed

"Harnessing the untapped waters of Narmada for the survival of millions of people and environmentally sound sustainable development of western India by providing the essence of life-water and energy"[28] is the mission for the damming of Narmada, according to Sardar Sarovar Narmada Nigam, Ltd. (SSNNL). The mission to harness Narmada has been on the rulers' agenda for at least a century. Studies were commissioned in 1946 to look into the possibility of developing the entire Narmada basin. In 1948 the Khosla committee recommended the Tawa, Bargi, Punasa, and Bharuch projects. A parallel study shortly after identified 16 sites with the hydro-electric potential of 1300 MW.

The reorganization of states in the 1950s, and the tension between the riparian states in sharing the benefits of the proposed project, led to the formation of several committees, and finally to the enactment of the Inter-state Water Disputes Act 1956. According to this Act, the Union government was entrusted with the responsibility to form a tribunal whose decisions would be final and binding on all the states involved in the project. After a decade of deliberations, in 1979 the Narmada Water Disputes Tribunal (NWDT) announced its final award. The Narmada Valley Development Project (NVDP) in a nutshell is an inter-state multipurpose river valley project consisting of 30 major dams, 135 medium dams, and 3000 small dams on the River Narmada and its 41 tributaries. The Sardar Sarovar Project (SSP) and the Narmada Sagar Project (NSP) are mega dams and centers of international attention. Because of the enormity of this project, we will limit our analysis to the SSP. At the same time, we will keep the integrity of the whole project by including stories and analysis from different projects within the NVDP.

"Say yes to Narmada," says one of the most televised commercials of the SSP in India. This is a clarion call to affirm and support the most ambitious river valley project ever conceived and initiated in human history. Though some critics call it "India's greatest planned environmental disaster," the ruling class and the elites have succeeded in gathering the support of all pillars of the democratic system in the country, international monetary agencies, and transnational capital to damn the lifeworld with the damming of the river.

The Sardar Sarovar dam is situated in Navagam, Gujarat. Prime Minister Nehru laid the foundation stone of the dam on April 5,

1961, but the work commenced only in 1987. According to the Gujarat government, the SSP would provide irrigation to 1.8 million ha (445 million acres) in Gujarat and 75,000 ha (185 thousand acres) in Rajasthan, the neighboring drought-prone state. It would provide drinking water to 8,215 villages and 136 towns in Saurashtra, North Gujarat and Kutch along with 131 villages in Rajasthan. The Narmada River water estimated at 28 MAFT (Million Acre Feet – 1200 billion liters) annually, is to be shared with Madhya Pradesh (18.25 MAFT), Gujarat (9 MAFT), Rajasthan (0.5 MAFT) and Maharashtra (0.25 MAFT). It is estimated that the dam would generate 1450 MW of power, and would be shared in the ratio of 57%: 27%: 16% among Madhya Pradesh, Maharashtra and Gujarat respectively.[29] This is the rationale for the government to call the SSP the lifeline of Gujarat.

Given the multipurpose nature of a project like SSP, it provides other benefits as well. Flood protection is estimated at 30,000 ha, in 210 villages including Bharuch city. The environmental benefit that the dam provides is to be shared by Dumkhal Sloth Bear Sanctuary; Wild Ass Sanctuary Kutch; Black Buck Sanctuary, Velavader; Indian Bustard Sanctuary and Nal Sarovar Sanctuary. Other benefits include fisheries development, tourist and recreational facilities, agro-industrial development, and employment generation at the construction sites.

Apart from the debate on the very development model of big dams, the controversy over the NVDP has focused mainly on issues such as displacement, rehabilitation, and environmental impacts. The SSNNL and the government of Gujarat refuted these criticisms, and instead presented the SSP as the most environmentally friendly dam. They also challenged the allegations regarding resettlement and rehabilitation (R&R). Patrick McCully helps us to understand the subtle ways in which a project like SSP creates livelihood problems to communities.

Eight hundred families lost their land to the new town built for the SSP construction workers. Although land acquisition began in 1961, the families were still fighting for adequate compensation 35 years later. Tens of thousands of adivasis could be thrown off their traditional land to make way for a wildlife sanctuary supposed to 'mitigate' the loss of wildlife to the SSP reservoir. Thousands are being deprived of access to cropland which the government is turning into tree plantations to 'mitigate' submerged forests. Tens of thousands who grow crops, gather fuelwood and fodder, or are employed on the forest and farm land being taken over to resettle the reservoir oustees are suffering what is known as 'secondary displacement'. An estimated 140,000 landholders would lose at least some of their land to SSP's network of irrigation canals, with 25,000 ending up with less than two hectares, regarded as the minimum viable holding. A large area of farmland, many villages and even whole towns could eventually be flooded by the so-called 'backwater' effect, used by the gradual rise in water levels due to sedimentation in the upper reaches of the reservoir. Downstream, SSP is planned to eradicate the flow of the Narmada between the dam and the sea for most of the year, destroying the livelihood of thousands of fishing families and affecting the water supply of up to a million people.[30]

This long quotation is important as it provides a new meaning to displacement and rehabilitation. The official meaning of displacement and the official category of Project Affected Peoples (PAPs) do not recognize the enormous impact of this project in creating livelihood and survival problems for communities. Informed by McCully's narration, let us examine the official claims of R&R.

The official claims of the SSNNL as posted on its website regarding R&R portray a different picture of the reality. The three states have "liberalized" the R&R regulations proposed by the NWDT Award, and the primary objective of the policy, according to SSNNL, is that the economic condition of the PAPs must improve significantly after resettlement. A short visit to the valley is more than sufficient to see the gap between claims and reality. A simple issue is the definition of PAPs. In the narrative of McCully we see a host of instances of livelihood attrition due to the dam. However, most of these "refugees" such as people affected by the canals, communities living in downstream who lost their traditional livelihoods such as fishing and related occupations, and landless artisans who survived on the economy of the submerged villages are not eligible to be considered as PAPs. This list goes on and on.

The SSNNL claims that a minimum 2 hectares of land for agricultural purposes of the size equal to the area of land acquired shall be given to all PAPs. We need to juxtapose this claim with the categorical statement from the government of Madhya Pradesh that it is impossible for the government to provide cultivable land for acquired land.[31] I saw PAPs in Madhya Pradesh confronting the moral dilemma of whether to accept cash compensation for their land. The NWDT Award foresaw this possibility and addressed this issue drawing from past experiences.

Cash compensation (under the provisions of the Land Acquisitions Act, 1894) was the practice, which resulted in the resettlement of displaced families becoming unsustainable due to squandering away of the compensation money. This type of rehabilitation programme deprived the poor and illiterate tribals from their land, houses, wages, natural environment and their socio-economic and cultural milieu.[32]

The Award failed to limit the impact of cash compensation to adivasis. The two major thriving businesses in the Nimad region (the non-adivasi area) when the cash compensation was distributed were gold and motorbikes!

The construction of the SSP was stopped by the Supreme Court of India based on the comprehensive writ petition filed against the project. After a long litigation, on October 18, 2000 the court's final verdict rejected the petition, and ordered the work to resume. While the majority judgment of Justices Kripal and Anand rejected the petition, the minority judgment of Justice Bharucha stopped the dam construction until environmental clearance was accorded.[33] The fundamental propositions of the majority judgment as summarized by L. C. Jain reflect the very logic of the NVDP:

Large dams have improved the living standards of the displaced persons – predominantly tribals. Large dams are cost effective. The phenomenal increase in food production is due to large dams. Large dams have improved the environment. Hydro power is ecologically friendly. Higher electric consumption is an indicator of progress in living standards.[34]

The displacement of adivasis is a major issue in all development projects in India, and in particular in the case of the NVDP. In the case of the SSP 57.6 percent of the displaced are adivasis.[35] This statistic makes sense only when we juxtapose it with the statistical record that adivasis constitute only 8 percent of the Indian population. We must consider the response of the dam lobby, including the majority judgment regarding the issue of adivasi displacement. B. G. Verghese, a pro-dam journalist, justified the displacement of adivasis as a means for their development. "All development entails some initial disturbance and if this is not allowed then all progress must come to a standstill; the right to life must include the right to development, the right to prosperity and the right to a better standard of life."[36] Put differently, it is the powerful – the state and the upper class – who decides what is best for the adivasis. The majority judgment went further, to give legal legitimation to adivasi displacement. "The displacement of the tribals and other persons would not per se result in the violation of their fundamental or other rights... The gradual assimilation in the mainstream of the society will lead to betterment and progress."[37]

The NWDT final Award in 1979 gave the green light to the governments to go ahead with the project. Even before that, from 1978 onwards, the World Bank had been showing interest in associating with this project by extending a loan. However, the NWDT Award created spontaneous protests all over the valley. Almost all political parties in Madhya Pradesh opposed the Award because of its impact on communities. In the 1980s, the government of India formed the Ministry of Environment and Forests (MoEF), and it produced guidelines for river valley projects. The MoEF did not approve the project because several important studies had not been completed. Meanwhile, in 1985, the World Bank sanctioned a loan of US$ 450 million on the basis of its own staff appraisal reports. The dam lobbies used the World Bank loan to pressure the MoEF to issue clearance. Finally in 1987, the MoEF gave conditional clearance to SSP.

The presence of the World Bank in the valley in fact internationalized the struggle. Ever since, the international fraternity of nongovernment organizations (NGOs) and social movements lobbied for a review of the project and for the withdrawal of the World Bank from the NVDP. They succeeded in convincing the World Bank of its failure to comply with its own policies regarding issues such as R&R and environmental and social impacts before sanctioning the loan. The World Bank appointed an independent Review of the Project under the chairmanship of Bradford Morse, the former chairman of the United Nations Development Project (UNDP). It was a comprehensive study involving all parties concerned. In my visit to different villages in the valley I was able to see how people still respect the visit of Morse and his team, as the committee took pains to visit even unreachable hamlets in the valley, and to see and hear their stories. Finally they presented their report:

> We think the Sardar Sarovar Projects as they stand are flawed, that resettlement and rehabilitation of all those displaced by the Projects is not possible under prevailing circumstances, and that environmental impacts of the Projects have not been properly considered or adequately addressed. Moreover we believe that the Bank shares responsibility with the borrower for the situation that has developed...it seems clear that engineering and economic imperatives have driven the Projects to the

exclusion of human and environmental concerns... As a result, we think that the wisest course would be for the Bank to step back from the Projects and consider them afresh.[38]

The Morse report exposed the inherent contradictions in the NVDP. Finally, in March 1993, the World Bank decided to withdraw from the project. The Morse report was a great blow to the dam lobby as it exposed the nexus between the Indian government and the World Bank. The withdrawal of the Bank was also a vindication of the global struggles against the invasion of international monetary agencies to promote the capitalist agenda.

However, by 1991 India opened up the energy sector for privatization. Within a year, the Maheshwar dam in the Narmada valley became the first Indian hydro-electric project to be privatized. This added a new dimension to the struggle in the valley. The people of the valley could feel globalization as a concrete reality of displacement, deforestation, and police brutality. S. Kumars, the Indian textile giant, took over the project. The historic struggle of the people in the valley with the support of solidarity groups in Europe and the North America succeeded in the withdrawal of corporations such as Bayernwerk, Siemens, and Ogden Energy from the project.

Right from the beginning, the NVDP has been presented as a symbol of nation-building. One can identify a combination of religious and patriotic motifs in the propaganda campaigns. These motifs provided the NVDP a sacred status as they symbolize nationalism and faith. The same logic has been used to brand and condemn the communities and movements that resist the NVDP, as anti-development and unpatriotic. On October 31, 2000, when the BJP government in Gujarat resumed the work of the SSP, based on the final verdict of the Supreme Court of India, the whole ceremony was orchestrated as a ritual exorcising of the resistance by calling it anti-progress and unpatriotic. The guests of the day were all *Hindutva* leaders such as L. K. Advani, the Union Home minister, and Keshubhai Patel, the chief minister of Gujarat. Advani in his address accused those who oppose the dam as doing so at the behest of some foreign nations. He then went on to compare the SSP with the successful nuclear test that India conducted at Pokhran in 1998.[39]

Development as the Colonization of the Lifeworld

We began this section with an analysis of the dominant development model. The damming of Narmada is yet another manifestation of the colonization of lifeworld. William Fisher[40] helps us to understand it clearly.

The Sardar Sarovar Dam is a vivid example of modernist convictions that one can obtain mastery over nature, and that the failure to do so will mean ruin. It derives from the conviction that as humans we can and must make our own destiny, that human history has been a history of progress, and that we can find technological solutions to all the problems we encounter. It reflects Descartes' conviction that the general good of all humankind could be pursued by the attainment of knowledge that is useful in life so as to make ourselves 'the masters and possessors of nature.'[41]

The logic of this development model reduces nature to violence, which needs to be contained. At the same time, it views nature as a "stockroom of resources" which has to be plundered using our scientific and technological knowledge. A metamorphosis of the river takes place under the gaze of development. In that process the river becomes reservoirs and canals, with private companies having exclusive rights for fishing and transportation in the reservoirs. The theological significance of this development-induced metamorphosis is the denuding of the river's sacredness through human technological intervention to commoditize the waters, and the elevation of the dam as sacred. "The emergence of the dam as a sacred icon of modernization has the unfortunate consequence of presenting the dam as an end rather than a means of development."[42] The legends and oral histories of the valley describe River Narmada as the lifeline of Central India. But today we are informed by the propaganda machine of the state that the dam and the canal system are the lifeline!

Fisher summarizes the consequences of the colonization of the lifeworld in the Narmada valley as follows.

One is the transfer of redistribution of resources from low-resource-use populations to high-resource-use populations – a transfer that is done without the consent of the low-use group and justified in terms of both human need and progress. Resources perceived as unused or wasted are taken as part of the manifest destiny of high-use portions of the population. Second, this diversion of natural resources is done in such a way that it entails further alteration and domination of nature. Third, the process allows and even requires that governments consolidate their control over both resources and people.[43]

With the final verdict of the Supreme Court the SSP is nearing completion. The Narmada valley is about to be declared as developed. What did development bring to the communities in the valley? Arundhati Roy helps us to answer this question:

> The 'fruits of modern development,' when they finally came, brought only horror. Roads brought surveyors. Surveyors brought trucks. Trucks brought policemen. Policemen brought bullets and beatings and rape and arrest and in one case, murder. The only genuine 'fruit' of modern development that reached them, reached them inadvertently – the right to raise their voices, the right to be heard.[44]

The story of the Narmada Bachao Andolan (NBA) narrates a community's determination to affirm their right to raise their voices, to say no to the colonization of their lifeworld.

Resistance in the Valley: Reclamation of the Lifeworld

The damming of the river is a process of colonization as it operates within the logic of imperialism. The erasure of the landscape and the destruction of the livelihoods of the subaltern communities in the name of "common good" and "national interest" is the logical end of the development gaze. One of the inner contradictions of the dominant system is the possibility for the emergence of collective voices of protest and resistance – an alternative discourse and politics – from within. This happens when the communities reclaim their moral agency. Jürgen Habermas, in his analysis of the colonization of the lifeworld, underscores the emergence of what he calls "the new social movements" as a response to the colonization of lifeworld.[45] In that sense, the Narmada Bachao Andolam (NBA) is a new social movement emerging out of a community's collective experience of colonial invasion of their lifeworld, and their collective determination to be the subjects of their life story.[46]

Narmada Bachao, Manav Bachao (Save Narmada, Save Humanity)

The Narmada valley has a long history of subaltern resistance against the invading spirit of colonial rulers.[47] There are also stories of popular resistance against big dams and other development projects elsewhere in the country. The *Chipko Andolan* (Hugging the Trees Movement) in the Himalayas, the *Tehri Bandh Virodhi Sangharshan Samiti* (Stop the Tehri Dam Project Movement), and the National Fishworkers' Federation are the most popular ones in this tradition. Way back in 1921 the peasants in Mulshi valley near Pune waged a struggle against a hydro-electric power dam initiated by the Tata Company. Their resistance exposed the capitalist invasion of the life-world, and they questioned the logic of public good and the method of cost–benefit analysis. Instead, they affirmed their sovereignty and opposed the dam, despite Gandhi's position.[48] There are also a host of people's movements or social movements in different parts of the country, articulating the collective resistance of communities to diverse manifestations of colonization, marginalization, and pauperization. Most of them fall into the category of subaltern politics with diverse ideological moorings such as socialist, Gandhian, Marxist, feminist, and dalit. So the NBA is not an isolated example, and it therefore has to be understood and analyzed in this great tradition of counter-discourses and resistance.

The post-independent initiative of the NVDP revived the legacy of subaltern politics in the valley. As we have seen earlier, the genesis of the current project to harness the river started in 1946. But the people destined to sacrifice for the project came to know about it only when the officials came to the villages to place the stone markers that would indicate the water level of the reservoir. The state has never recognized nor respected peoples' right to information about policies that affect their landscape and livelihoods. As the valley became crowded with surveyors, construction workers and law enforcement officials, people began to talk about the deluge. As early as in 1972–75, under the banner of the *Narmada Bachao-Nimad Bachao Samiti,* people in the valley raised critical questions about the SSP. In 1978, after the NWDT award was announced, the Congress party organized a protest against the SSP in the Nirmad region, and formed an organization called Nimar Bachao Andolan.

The people in the valley soon realized the motives of the Congress-led movement, and it just withered away.

ARCH-Vahini was a Gujarat-based NGO which started to work in the 1980s among the SSP-displaced tribal peoples in Gujarat. From the very beginning their focus was on rehabilitation and resettlement. Even though in the beginning ARCH-Vahini opposed big dams, by the late 1980s and early 1990s it became the propaganda machine for the state and the SSNNL. The staff of the NGO used to plead and convince the adivasis in the affected villages to move out of their hamlets and resettle in better facilities. ARCH-Vahini also supported the World Bank intervention in the project, thinking that it would enhance a humane R&R policy. In short, eventually the NGO became the mouthpiece for the dam lobby to condemn the NBA.

The activist-researchers associated with *Kalpavriksha*, a Delhi-based organization, exposed the inherent problems of the NVDP and its impact on the tribal peoples and the environment through their research in the valley in 1983. They succeeded in generating an awareness of the tragedy of the valley among concerned people all over the country. Organizations such as *Khedut Mazdoor Chetna Sangath* (The Peasants' and Workers' Consciousness Union) working among the adivasis in the Alirajpur region in Madhya Pradesh also played a significant role in enabling the community to reclaim their moral agency. The Union helped them to assert their communal rights over the forest, and to resist the attempt of the state to colonize their landscape and livelihoods. *Jangal jamin kunin se? Amri se! Amri se!* (Whose is the forest land? It is ours! It is ours!) is one of their slogans which categorically articulates the politics of the Union.

Medha Patkar, a social scientist from the Tata Institute of Social Sciences in Bombay, came to the valley in 1986 to study displacement and rehabilitation. She decided to work in the submerging villages in Maharashtra. The *Narmada Dharangrasta Samiti* (NDS) was formed in 1986. For the next two years the *Samiti* questioned the rationale behind the SSP, and organized the villagers to resist the dam. Similar work was done by the *Khedut Mazdoor Chetna Sangath* among the tribal peoples in Alirajpur, Madhya Pradesh. In the Nimad region there also emerged an organization in 1986, called *Narmada Ghati Navrirman Samiti* (NGNS). The people who were ousted from their villages in 1961 for the construction of the SSP staff colony in Gujarat got organized in 1988 under the banner the *Narmada Asargrasta Sangharsha Samiti* (NASS).

Meanwhile, the Ministry of Environment and Forest (MoEF) objected giving clearance to the SSP. The government of Gujarat tried to pressurize the prime minister into bypassing the directive of the MoEF. This political drama in Delhi led to the first nationwide response to the Narmada struggle. A group of three hundred people from all walks of life, from different regions, religions, and political backgrounds submitted a memorandum to the prime minister to stop further work on the Narmada Valley Project until a thorough review was completed. It was also the beginning of Narmada becoming a major issue for national and international media. The emergence of different organizations of the project affected people in all the three states, and the materialization of support groups all over the country revived the dream for a joint front to continue the struggle in the valley. That dream came into being in the form of the *Narmada Bachao Andolan* in the late 1980s.

The Narmada Bachao Andolan

The NBA stands in the great tradition of the subaltern movements in India and elsewhere, continuing the subaltern discourse and politics by creating a subaltern counter public sphere. It has been possible because of the *Andolan* (movement) characteristic of the NBA. Unlike a traditional NGO with a hierarchical organizational structure, centralization of policy decisions, funding from transnational agencies/foundations, and well salaried professional staff, the NBA has succeeded in keeping its organic movement nature providing a unique model of peoples' resistance and alternatives. In this section we explore how NBA becomes an alternative expression of subaltern politics by analyzing its movement dynamics, means of struggle, and alternative politics.

The NBA as a grassroots subaltern movement

Ramachandra Guha, the environmental historian, named the environmentalism of the southern movements like the NBA the "environmentalism of the poor."[49] However, there has been a host of critical observations over the years questioning the class nature of the NBA.[50] As we have already seen, the Narmada valley consists of communities of diverse ethnic, caste and class background. Moreover, the NBA is also blessed with a large number of activists from outside the valley, and a host of support groups both within the country and outside the country. The question of whether the subaltern can speak has always been an issue in the debate on the NBA.[51] So an analysis of the structure and the *modus operandi* of the NBA, with a focus on its hybrid nature, is in order, to understand better its subaltern politics.

According to Subodh Wagle, the NBA exhibits three "salient features of a true grassroots initiative":

> First, the primary commitment of the NBA has always been the livelihood concerns of the threatened communities. Second, the NBA has always insisted on participation of members of local communities, especially women and youth, in every activity and program in the decade-long struggle, be it *jal-samadhi dal* (self-drowning team) or receiving prestigious international awards. Third, despite a vast network of outside supporters, the local communities have always remained the main sources of strength for the initiative.[52]

The local people and their leaders, continues Wagle, "have played a prime role in shaping both the agenda and the action of the grassroots struggle."[53] Ranjit Dwivedi, on the other hand, has a different perception of the composition of the NBA.

> Notwithstanding, the leadership's claims of being a locally embedded representative voice of the affected people in the valley, organizationally, the NBA comprises of (a) a close-knit core group of activists from outside the valley – comprising educated professionals, (b) a charismatic leader at the helm of affairs, and (c) a network of support groups – activist and advocacy groups, NGOs, academic and research institutions, media organizations – in addition to drawing support from a section of the affected people in the Narmada valley.[54]

Dwivedi is not raising questions about the popular base of the movement; rather he wants to underscore the need for multi-level mobilization of resources and discourses to build an effective and strategic resistance to the dam lobby. The hybrid nature of the NBA therefore permits different people to contribute different approaches based on their political interests.

Sripad Dharmadhikari, a long-time activist of the NBA, endorses Dwivedi's position when he discusses the advocacy skills and systems developed by the NBA. For Dharmadhikari, mobilization and empowerment are the essential prerequisites for any movement. However, a movement also needs support systems in areas such as information systems, peoples' science and scientific research, media management and innovative use of media, networking, interaction with existing institutions, judiciary and the like. However, for him, the most important issue in developing support systems is the litmus test of "people centricity."[55]

The hybrid composition of the NBA is well articulated by Baviskar:

> For some hill adivasis the Narmada movement is a fight to hold onto their precious land; for the engineering student it may encapsulate [sic] the hope of a technologically-appropriate utopia; for the leftist radical from Kerala the dam represents the evils of global capital; for the veteran Gandhain the movement promises to breathe life into a vision of village-centered development.[56]

This hybridity in ideological moorings and ethnicity becomes reconciled in the politics of the *Andolan* by affirming the primary agency of the communities in the valley.

The process of decision making in the NBA is yet another important factor to understanding its subaltern politics. Chittaroopa Palit, who currently leads the struggle against the Maheswar Dam, narrates the decision-making process in the *Andolan*.

> The rhythm of activism is also dictated by the pattern of the seasons. Every monsoon as the people of the Valley face the rising waters, we hold a mass meeting. People from the various villages affected will come together for a whole day, sometimes two, to discuss the situation. How much submergence will take place, and how might it best be confronted? If the dam wall has increased over the last year, what are the implications? What forms of resistance are most appropriate for each *satyagraha*? How should the logistics of wood, water, grain and transport be managed? … After each set of meetings we hold a collective consultation, in which representatives from the different regions come together to work out broader strategies for calling attention to the distress and struggle of the Valley people. Further discussion takes place on the Coordination Committee, …comprised of intellectuals and activists from outside the movement who contribute to forging wider links. Ground level resistance needs to be supported by legal initiatives and media campaigns, and by alliances at national and international levels.[57]

Palit's narrative represents the pattern in which the NBA plans its strategies and makes decisions. As Dharmadhikari and Dwivedi explained, the complexity of the struggle demands multi-level actions, lobbying and mobilizations, which inadvertently requires the involvement of "outsiders" in the decision-making process and in the implementation of the decisions. However, the NBA has always insisted on the epistemological privilege and agency of the communities in the valley when making decisions.

The NBA and grassroots subaltern praxis

The method of struggle in the valley also needs our attention. Though the NBA is not a Gandhian movement per se, it has adopted non-violence as a philosophy in its non-party politics. The NBA is one of the isolated examples of the enlivening of the Gandhian resistance called *Satyagraha*. Satyagraha, in the Gandhian sense, is a moral political action where we bear witness to truth using non-violent means. The various forms of *Satyagraha* that have evolved in the NBA's struggles include protest marches both in the valley and at the centers of power – state capitals, national capital, and the capitals of transnational capital, hunger strikes, road blockades and civil disobedience. In the case of Maheswar Dam, the people have occupied the dam site repeatedly and blocked the construction work despite police atrocities. The monsoon *Satyagrahas* were organized around the slogan *Dubenge par hatenge nahin* (we will drown but not move). *Jal Samarpan* (facing the waters) was a tool of protest that emerged during the monsoon *Satyagrahas*. Let us now analyze one particular struggle in the history of the NBA to understand the use of diverse tools of protest in the struggle.

On Christmas day in 1990, the *Jan Vikas Sangharsh Yatra* (the March of Struggle for Peoples' Development) started from the Nimad region when 6000 people consisting of adivasis, peasants, and comrades from other movements began their long walk towards the dam site in Gujarat. It was the march of a ragged army celebrating unity in their determination to resist the SSP. The dam lobby in Gujarat made all arrangements to prevent the march from entering Gujarat. Ironically, they received the support of some NGOs including those who belong to the Gandhian clan. The rally was stopped at Ferkuwa, the border village, and it became the *Sangharsh Gaon* (Village of Struggle). The ragged army decided to camp there. Six activists, consisting of adivasis, peasants, activists, and comrades from other movements, immediately began a fast unto death. While the government of Gujarat continued to use state tyranny to face the moral power of the people, the victory came in the form of a historical announcement from the World Bank of the Independent Review of the project. This is the first time in the history of the Bank to agree on a review of an ongoing Bank-funded project. On January 22, 1991, after 22 days, the activists called off their fast.

Jan Vikas Sangharsh Yatra did not end there. A new slogan for the movement emerged – *Hamara gaon mein hamara raj* (our rule in our villages). Again drawing from the Gandhian tools of protest it was a praxis of civil disobedience and non-cooperation with a deaf state, insensitive to the plight of its subjects. They boycotted government officials and prevented dam-related activities in their villages. It was an affirmation of their sovereignty and self-determination. Meanwhile, they focused their attention on alternative activities, such as adult education, health training, soil conservation, and irrigation works.

To resist and to re-create: the subaltern politics of the NBA

One of the hard lessons that the NBA and its predecessors learned in the course of struggle was the futility of fighting the battle by focusing on resettlement and rehabilitation. There are several reasons that prompted them to make this shift in focus to a total rejection of big dams. When the peoples' right to information is not recognized and honored, the state can make decisions to the extent of selling their traditional habitats and livelihoods to foster development and capitalist growth. The project was approved by the government and the court, and the construction continued before the resettlement and rehabilitation were completed. The government legitimized this action by citing the legal concept of *pari passu*.[58] From this experience, the NBA learned that a grassroots subaltern politics should go beyond bargaining and negotiating with a state that is reduced to be the watchdog of capital.

The grassroots subaltern politics articulates its perspective through non-conventional transcripts such as slogans, posters, and songs. The shift towards a "no to big dams" was articulated well in the slogans of the NBA. *Koi nahin hatega, bandh nahin banega* (Nobody will move, the dam will not be built) remains the collective resolve of the valley, as it proclaims the determination of the people. The NBA's rationale to stop bargaining for better rehabilitation can be summarized in a set of basic questions: Whose development are we talking about? What is the cost? Are there any quantifiable and non-quantifiable costs, and do they outweigh the benefits? Is this development sustainable and just? How is this project going to serve the national interest? Who are the communities (class, caste, ethnicity) being asked to make sacrifices in the national interest? How are they going to be compensated for their loss of community life and livelihood? Why did the project start before the completion of a comprehensive study of its impact on communities, and the environment?

The story of the *Andolan* is the story of a consistent, creative, and alternative politics resisting the colonization of the valley and their livelihoods. The questions posed above witness to the complexity and the comprehensiveness of the struggle. For NBA the politics against the colonization of the lifeworld consists of a consistent resistance against the development gaze and apparatus, and an imaginative determination to re-create alternatives. To understand more deeply the politics of the NBA, let us now analyze these two focuses of the *Andolan*.

Resistance to development

The development discourse in the struggle against big dams in the Narmada valley is rooted in the assertion of the moral agency of the people. The uniqueness of the NBA is its ability to extend its language of protest and discourse on big dams beyond the impacts of the NVDP and the mechanisms of rehabilitation and compensation. It was not that the NBA got co-opted by the anti-globalization networks. Rather, an affirmation of the subjecthood and self-determination of the community enabled the NBA to develop an alternative politics which strives for alternatives to development. As Claude Alvares rightly puts it, this comes out of an assertion of peoples' right to "pursue one's way of life, irrespective of nuclear plants, dams, thermal plants, or big industries; the right to refuse to be developed according to the whims and fancies of outsiders who think they know best."[59] We need to look at the development discourse of the NBA from this perspective.

Vinash nahin Vikas chahiye (We want development not destruction) has been one of the slogans right from the beginning of the struggle. The adivasis in the valley are denied the fruits of development even after six decades of independence. Electricity, drinking water, hospitals, schools, roads – all visible expressions of development – are still a distant dream for the majority of the people affected by the project in the Narmada valley. But they were content with their subsistence living. Development incarnated in their lifeworld as an elitist vision of gigantism with a clarion call to "sacrifice" for the "common good" and "national interest." They experienced the inherent *himsa* (violence) of development in their bodies.

The people in the Narmada valley know how the state treated those who sacrificed for other gigantic projects. The story of the evacuees of the Bhakra dam, as told by K. L. Rao, the Union Irrigation minister, is just one example. When the dam was built (commissioned in 1963), the village Bhakra was submerged, and the people moved to neighboring hills. "The project resulted in great suffering to the people of the village, but nobody took note of the peoples' representation. It was many years later, during one of my visits to the dam site, that I found that the new village of Bhakra had neither drinking water nor electricity, though surrounded by blazing brilliant lights."[60]

Ram Bai hails from a village submerged in the Bargi dam in the Narmada valley. Now she, along with thousands of other displaced people from the region, lives in a slum in Jabalpur. Once they were self-sufficient subsistent farmers and artisans living on the banks of the river. Now they find habitats in the slums of the cities with the eschatological hope of the trickled-down benefits of development, pulling cycle rickshaws and working as contract laborers for global and indigenous capital. She asks, "Why didn't they just poison us? Then we wouldn't have to live in this shit-hole and the Government could have survived alone with its precious dam all to itself."[61]

Let us now try to understand the NBA's development discourse in perspective. Right from the beginning the NBA articulated its language of protest in the form of a critique of the dominant development model. They exposed the violation of human rights in the compulsory displacement, social and environmental impacts, lack of accountability, violation of the right to information, absence of peoples' participation, and neo-liberal agenda of the transnational agencies. *Jan Vikas Andolan*, an alliance of similar social movements including the NBA, in a statement in the late 1980s, observed that "what today goes on in the name of development is not genuine development but it is in fact socially disruptive, biologically and genetically homogenizing and environmentally destructive."[62]

The National Alliance of Peoples' Movements (NAPM) was formed in 1992 as a nationwide alliance of various social movements in India. The NBA has been part of this alliance right from its inception. Dwivedi summarizes one of the NAPM's statements as follows: "For the NAPM, local communities are losing control over land, forests and water, at the same time as globalized control over technology, fertilizers, seeds and water is rapidly destroying the self-sufficiency of agricultural communities and alienating them from their natural habitat and resource base."[63] The shift that the state has undergone from a welfare state that initiates projects for poverty eradication, rural employment generation, drinking water and sanitation, public distribution system, and elementary education, to an overseer of global capital with new projects such as big dams, express ways, airports, techno-parks, and the like intensifies the *himsa* of development.

The assertion of the subjecthood of the people is also an assertion of their traditional knowledge systems. The dominant development model as a product of modernity represented by technology, scientific rationality, and an apparatus of planning and implementation is in fact a valorization and undemocratic imposition of a knowledge system reducing the traditional knowledge systems of the communities into superstitions. Stated differently, it is a process of converting communities into objects for intervention. The assertion of the selfhood, therefore, is the reclamation of the moral agency.

What is their alternative vision to development? The Jan Vikas Andolan statement tries to answer this question. "The Andolan's demand is for real development, in which the over-riding objective is not just a higher growth rate regardless of its human and environmental cost, but the fulfillment of basic human needs and the creation of just and humane conditions of life for all our people."[64] The NBA's alternative politics seeks to create a new world which goes beyond development. Esteva and Prakash articulate this politics succinctly:

> The struggle surrounding the Narmada reminds us of the way in which people's imagination was captured by developers' promises; how they suffered the destruction of their cultures and environments as a result of chasing the illusions of developers; how their resistance was coopted or refunctionalized by developers; and how people at the grassroots are now continuing their search for new directions – where developers and development cannot pursue them any more.[65]

To sum up, the perception of the Narmada valley as a stockpile of untapped resources is yet another example of development gaze. When development becomes a fetish, development gaze assumes the authority of "normative gaze."[66] The Narmada saga is the story of conquest and colonization of land, water, and forest. In the name of development, growth, progress, and national interest a whole valley has been desecrated. The people of the valley became refugees in their own country, and as the logical end of the process, ended up in the slums of the cities as providers of cheap labor to indigenous and global capital. Affirming the right to determine their lives, asserting their right over land, water, and forests, insisting on their right not to be incorporated into the "realized eschatology" of development, and striving to renew their lifeworld by creating a just, equitable, participatory and non-discriminatory social relations the communities in the valley are in the process of creating alternatives to development. Resistance and reconstruction (*sangharsh aur nirman*) are the two-fold foci of the movement. Re-creation is the self-assertion that there are alternatives to development.

Re-creating alternatives

The development discourse of the NBA, as we have seen in the previous section, is founded on the assertion of the subjecthood of the people. The assertion of subjecthood empowers them and provides them moral agency. When they become subjects of their lives, they create new discourses informed by their knowledge, with the potential to create alternatives. As Smitu Kothari rightly puts it, the NBA is questioning the development truth claims of the experts – the economists, the surveyors, the engineers, the consultants, the bureaucrats and the like, by underscoring the agency of the communities to create viable alternatives:

> They are demonstrating how this arrogance has reduced complex natural and social systems into commodities, into fragments whose monetary value supersedes all other values. They are showing how such an approach has also erased all sensitivity to the historically evolved systems of land and water management, how those who are marginal to the dominant model are capable of identifying more sustainable alternatives, and why, even if this knowledge has been eroded, a dialogue between traditions (the modern with the traditional, for example) needs to be promoted as a principle.[67]

This reconstruction in the valley is not a monolithic process. Rather, it is a comprehensive attempt to create peoples' alternatives to transform their lifeworld into sustainable communities. They articulated their determination and dedication to strive for alternatives in the slogan *Nahin hatenge, nahin doobenge, hum karenge navnirman*

(We will not move out, nor be drowned, we will recreate our lives). *Jeevan Shalas*, as the name itself indicates, are schools for life, where adivasi children share knowledge, power, and grain. Started in 1991, these schools are situated in remote adivasi villages where the state is yet to fulfill its constitutional obligation to provide compulsory and free primary education to all citizens. There are now 13 *Jeevan Shalas* with 1500 pupils and 36 teachers. These are residential schools, and the medium of instruction is Pawri or Bhili, the adivasi languages of the region. They have even developed a set of text books in Pawri.

The idea behind the *Jeevan Shalas* is not to replace the responsibility of the state in the field of education. When the state failed in fulfilling its constitutional responsibility to provide free and compulsory education for all children the NBA took up the challenge to educate them along with creating in them respect for their cultures and knowledge systems. The syllabus combines the state syllabus and peoples' traditional knowledge systems such as land and water management, farming, animal welfare, herbal medicine, music and culture. The motto of the schools for life – *Ladai aur padai saath saath* (struggle and study together) – articulates the philosophy of this alternative experiment. The children learned not only their history, geography and environment, but also how to face police atrocities and submergence. When the school of Chimalkhedi was submerged, the children witnessed it by sitting on its roof. The NBA has received the support of activist-educators who are involved in the alternative education movement elsewhere in the country in developing the curriculum and structure of these schools.

The monsoon *Satyagrahas* are like an annual gathering of the valley in the adivasi villages facing submergence, where along with confronting waters, they discuss reconstruction. The comrades from outside who are involved in alternative movements such as peoples' science movements, organic farming, and the like, enable the NBA to experiment with alternatives in areas such as forestry, health, agriculture, irrigation, and hydro-electric power.

The adivasi hamlets in the valley are dark at night because they don't exist in the maps of the state electricity department. However, the people of Bilgaon, with the technical support of People's School of Energy (PSE), Kerala, recreated their village through "peoples' energy." Today, the Bilgaon micro-hydro project radiates in the valley as yet another example of the peoples' resolve to recreate their life

without following the route of "development." The power generated by tapping a natural waterfall is sufficient to light all the twelve
hamlets in Bilgaon. The turbine also drives a flour mill. The electricity is used during the day to pump drinking water. The peoples'
energy also helps the farmers to raise a second crop with access
to water. The *Bilgaon Navnirman Samiti* (the Bilgaon Reconstruction
Committee), consisting of all families in the village, ensures responsible and equitable use of electricity by prioritizing energy use in the
order of the lighting of homes, the pumping of drinking water, community agriculture, livelihood creation, and entertainment.[68]

Under the logic of gigantism, it is wrong to compare the Bilgaon
project with the SSP. However, Ravi Kuchimanchi, an NBA activist,
helps us to understand things in perspective by juxtaposing the two
projects:

> While the Bilgaon project lights up 12 unelectrified hamlets of Bilgaon
> village, the SSP dam produces very little electricity and none of the
> Adivasi villages will be electrified by it. The installation cost of the Bilgaon
> project is Rs. 40,000 a KW while the SSP is wasteful for Maharashtra at
> Rs. 56,000 a KW. Thirty three tribal villages in Maharashtra and tens of
> thousands of hectares of forest land are being submerged by the Sardar
> Sarovar dam. The Bilgaon project has not caused any damage and all the
> work was *shrmadan* (voluntary) saving Rs. 2.5 lakhs in the eight months
> of work.[69]

Anil of PSE, who came from the state of Kerala to help the community with this project, articulates the politics of alternatives. "It is the
politics of water, of use and control of resources, of the overall development paradigm of the country. That is what the NBA is fighting for
and that is why we came here – to strengthen the NBA's struggle."[70]

Conclusion

The Narmada saga, as we have seen in this chapter, is a concrete example of the colonization of the lifeworld. The logic of the Narmada
Valley Development Project is the same logic of modernity – to reduce everything to commodities in service to the flourishing of global
capital. In the Narmada valley we also see the use of God-talk and
patriotism to buy legitimacy for conquest. The Narmada saga unveils the nakedness of the inherent *himsa* (violence) of development.

It exposes the undemocratic nature of the pillars of democracy. It reveals the neo-liberal agenda behind the erasure of peoples' control over their lives. Borrowing James Ferguson, development intervention in the Narmada valley is an "anti-politics machine," which disempowers the community by taking their moral agency away.[71] The significance of the NBA is its alternative politics, which have empowered and politicized the community to reclaim their moral agency through resistance and by recreating their lifeworld through creating viable alternatives. The Narmada saga is more than a story of colonization. It is the story of a valley that refuses to die.

3   Social Movements as Text: Subaltern Reflections on Epistemology

Introduction

The history of the colonization of the lifeworld is the history of the "regime of truth," and the politics of knowledge of the colonization process manifests itself in a variety of ways. Monopolization of the access and right to knowledge by the dominant class, caste, race, and gender; scriptural and theological legitimization of the epistemic agency of the dominant; universalization of the knowledge systems of the dominant as "the Truth"; and the contempt of the knowledge systems of the subalterns are some of the basic characteristics of this regime of truth. The regime of truth is a reign of hegemony. Hegemony, as Antonio Gramsci analyzes, is an exercise of power without overt use of force, but creating consent through the institutions in civil society. The regime of truth in this sense is hegemonic as it covertly anoints the dominant knowledge systems as "the Truth."

From a feminist perspective, Simone de Beauvoir articulated this succinctly a long time ago. "Representation of the world, like the world itself, is the work of men; they describe it from their own point of view, which they confuse with absolute truth."[1] A critical engagement with the theories of knowledge, hence, is imperative in our search to resist, and to develop alternatives to the colonization of the lifeworld. Such an engagement, I believe, is nothing but an alternative politics of knowledge which affirms the epistemic agency of the collectivity of the politically conscious subalterns. This chapter delineates the rationale for the method of this book: social movements are texts.

The Hegemony of the Regime of Truth

The Regime of Truth as Subaltern Exclusion

The history of the construction of knowledge and epistemic agency under systems of asymmetrical social relations can be traced back to the moment when knowledge became a source of power. Erasure of the subalterns from the epistemic terrain is foundational to the regime of truth. The following excerpt from Aristotle is an example of the systematic negation of the cognitive authority of the subaltern: "The freeman rules over the slave after another manner from that in which the male rules over the female, or the man over the child; although the parts of the soul are present in all of them, they are present in different degrees. For the slave has no deliberative faculty at all; the woman has, but it is without authority, and the child has, but it is immature."[2] It is interesting to note here the hierarchical gradation in this doctrine of exclusion. The subordinated are further divided and categorized as without cognitive ability, with cognitive ability but without authority, and with cognitive ability but immature.

The Aristotelian articulation of the regime of truth is representational to a host of other constructions of knowledge and truth in history. A casual reading of this canon of knowledge may veil the regime of terror and erasure inherent in this politics of knowledge. The dalit eruption against brahmanical Hinduism, informed by a critical engagement with its regime of truth, reveals the inherent *himsa* (violence) of the dominant politics of knowledge. According to the cosmology of classical Hinduism, as recorded by the Vedas, the four castes were created by God from his own body. The *Brahmins* (the priestly class) were God's mouth, the *Ksatriyas* (the warriors) his arms, the *Vaishyas* (the traders) his thighs, and the *Sudras* (the serving caste) were created from his feet.[3] The dalits, who are not part of this fourfold structure, are ontologically devoid of participation in the Divine being.

This Vedic creation story is the scriptural legitimization of the caste-ridden regime of truth still prevalent in India. A closer look at this text reveals the canonization of the exclusion of the outcastes from the knowledge field. At least two issues demand our closer attention. First, the very exclusion of the dalits from the fourfold system not only underscores the ontological separation between the *savarnas* (the dominant castes) and the dalits, but also asserts the inherent absence of the Divine *ousia* in the dalits. That means dalits are essentially devoid of authoritative cognitive capacity which provides them the right and authority to construct knowledge and truth claims. Hence their discursive practices and knowledge systems lack validity and authority. Second, this cosmology bestows authority on the dominant caste production of knowledge because *Brahmins* are created from the head/mouth of the God. So the knowledge and truth claims of the dominant castes are essentially authoritative, and hence have universal validity. This analysis of the Vedic creation story also points to the commonality in the politics of knowledge in the dominant epistemological projects.

There are several other examples of the scriptural legitimization for the erasure of the cognitive authority of the dalits. The story of Ekalavya is from *Mahabharaa*. Ekalavya was an outcaste boy who had to cut off his right thumb for learning archery. *Manusmriti* instructed to pour melted lead into the ears of the dalits who crossed the epistemic terrain by attempting to hear or read the Vedas. The *Ramayana* narrates the story of Samvuka, a *Sudra*, who violated the epistemic rules of the Vedas by undertaking *taps* (penance and meditation) to attain divinity. Because of the *taps,* a Brahmin boy died. Lord Rama came to know about it, and he killed Samvuka and restored the life of the Brahmin boy. The dalit movements have rightly identified that the canonized regime of truth, as articulated in the scriptures, is the base on which the superstructure of the caste system was built and has been perpetuated. This is evident in their outright rejection of the scriptures that legitimize the universality of the dominant caste knowledge system. Dalit leaders such as Jotirao Phule, Babasahab Ambedkar and E. V. Ramaswami Naicker in their respective movements rejected *Manusmriti* and the Vedas, and some of them even went to the extent of burning these scriptures in public.

The Enlightenment Project as a Regime of Truth

With the Enlightenment, the regime of truth became a systematic science of knowledge, thanks to the epistemological theories of Descartes. The perception of reality as "out there" led to the development of the notion of knower as a detached observer. The disengaged and passive subject of knowledge can observe reality "objectively," so that s/he can make truth claims with universal validity. The knowledge thus created is value-free and neutral because it is untainted by the subjectivity of the autonomous knower who is a featureless abstraction. "Reason alone" thus became the catch word for the new epistemology.[4]

Lorraine Code summarizes the basic features of the Cartesian theory of knowledge as follows:

> Its [knowledge's] alleged derivation from detached, pure thought permits it to claim superiority over modes of thought infected with emotional involvement and feeling. Out of this conception of the autonomy of scientific knowledge the conviction emerges that 'real' knowledge must be autonomous, detached from the subjective idiosyncrasies and circumstances of both "observer" and "observed"; abstract, independent, and depersonalized.[5]

The claim of objectivity is based on the assumption that in the process of observation and construction of knowledge, the observer can remain neutral and passive so that the truth can be discovered objectively. The Cartesian system does not recognize the social embeddedness of both the observer and the observed. The Cartesian subject is a disembodied self.

The politics of knowledge inherent in this system is not much different from its predecessors, which we examined earlier. The primary function of any regime of truth is the systematic exclusion of certain sections of the population from the epistemic terrain, and to legitimize it with the mediation of theory. For example, in the Cartesian project, all acts of knowing do not qualify to be considered as "knowledge." The feminist critique of this model rejects the epistemological privilege of reason as a sexist construction to erase women's knowledge. Sandra Harding, in a compelling way, exposes this by raising foundational questions about mainstream epistemology:

> Who can be subjects, agents, of socially legitimate knowledge? What kinds of things can be known? ... Can ... socially situated truths count as knowledge? ... What is the nature of objectivity? Does it require point-of-viewlessness? ... What should be the purpose of the pursuit of knowledge? Can there be "disinterested knowledge" in a society that is deeply stratified by gender, race and class?[6]

"To Add and to Stir": The Liberal Project of Exclusion

The classical liberal strategy of taming dissent succeeded in dealing with the suspicion created by feminist and other subaltern criticisms of the universal validity of the truth claims, and the neutrality and disembodiedness of the knower. This approach reduces the critique to the level of individual representation without challenging the politics and mechanics of knowledge production. Liberalism, as Mary McClintock Fulkerson explains, "is a politics that solves gender, race, class, and sex oppressions by adding the pertinent 'other' to institutions."[7] This "add and stir" method in reality is a strategy of the dominant to perpetuate its epistemic interests by co-opting individuals from the margin. It is important here to recall the Latin American saying that "liberals are fascists on vacation."[8] The following poem illustrates how liberal strategy continues to perpetuate the fascism of the regime of truth by "adding and stirring" differences into the monolithic truth.

"My name is *Ubuntu*" is a poem written by an anonymous author articulating the anger of the African people against the co-opting of the concept of *Ubuntu* in dominant discourse.

> I am the Goddess of Africa. I am bringing my tears before you Yahweh, the God of Israel and Christ. You are the only one who understands my pain. During the years of suffering I was the fountain of life for my people. I was the strength that sustained them. I remained hidden carefully from the eyes of your people. Your people did not know me. I was the secret of my people... But NOW your people have found out about me. They try to drag me away from my people. They try to rape me, cheapen me, turning me into a whore... Making me into an object of their commercial interests. They use my name as if I was a sales slogan: Ubuntu bus tours, Ubuntu game park, Ubuntu service station, Ubuntu shopping centre...[9]

It has become a ritual to invoke concepts such as "Other," "boundary crossing," and the like in hegemonic epistemic terrains of asymmetrical power relations in order to acquire legitimization in the name of diversity and multiculturality and without political commitment to recognize the epistemic agency of the silenced voices. To put it differently, stirring some disengaged individuals from marginalized locations into institutions, which claim that their foundational doctrines developed in particular locations of supremacy and privilege are disembodied and hence universal, is traitorous to the struggles of the marginalized. The recommendations for the African Descent Ministry Strategy of the Evangelical Lutheran Church in America reflect this anguish: "In many ways, people of African descent continue to suffer from internalized oppression... We have internalized the insidious nature of racism and now contribute to our own oppression. We have believed the distortion of God's image in us; namely, that we are to become European in our expression of Lutheran theology and ethics."[10]

A conscious attempt to confront the regime of truth, therefore, demands a collective politics and commitment to understand and affirm the epistemic agency of the collectivity of the subalterns. This political commitment is crucial as more and more concepts and reflections of the marginalized are being grafted into the dominant institutions and markets of knowledge. R. S. Sugirtharajah's observation about the danger of commodification that happens to liberation theologies in dominant societies is important here.

> Liberation theologies are not just a collection of neutral texts. Their intention is to subvert the system that marginalizes people. When such theologies are introduced neglecting the historical and political circumstances of their production and contextuality of their development, then liberation becomes a commodity which can be theorized, talked about, traded and exchanged among many other interesting theological commodities that are on offer... When liberation becomes a commodity, involvement is kept at a minimum and a cloak of neutrality is maintained without the need to take sides. In other words, the vocabulary of liberation is appropriated devoid of its liberative content, treated as an object to be studied and categorized.[11]

The narratives of the regime of truth illustrated above, including the liberal inclusionary project, enable us to understand the politics of the dominant mainstream epistemology which controls the discourses of our times. The hegemony of this regime of truth has been contested by subalterns such as feminists, black feminists/womanists, chicana feminists, *Mujeristas*, dalits, Latinas by initiating counter discourses and creating alternative epistemic principles and terrains. In this search for a new epistemology, Vítor Westhelle's observations are insightful. "It [justification] authorizes the emergence of other voices dissonant from the prevailing regimes of truth and power. Justice begins here; it begins not by fulfilling the requirements of the prevailing regimes, but by setting other conditions, other parameters, which indeed sound foolish or inane."[12] Let us listen to the subaltern articulations of epistemic agency and politics of knowledge.

Epistemologies from the Grassroots

Sati, the Hindu practice of widow sacrifice in the funeral pyre of the deceased husband, has always been a site for the contest of different epistemologies. The interlocutors varied from the "oriental despotic Hindu fanatics" and "the white men who wanted to save the brown women" in the colonial period to the "right-wing Hindu male chauvinists" and feminists and human rights activists in the postcolonial period. The contest has always been filled with arguments based on authoritative sources such as scriptures, jurisprudence, and traditions. In their arguments and counter arguments *representing* the widow, her voice always goes unnoticed. Instead, the body of the widow became the site for elaborating and contesting theories on *Sati*. Put differently, she became a subject of discourse devoid of subjectivity. This is the context in which Gayatri Chakravorty Spivak's penetrating question "Can the subaltern speak?" emerged.[13]

The subaltern discourse on the dominant debate over *Sati* raises fundamental questions about the politics of social theories. Unlike the Cartesian project of disinterested and disembodied production of knowledge and truth, the social theories developed and used by the subalterns are inherently political. As the black feminist scholar Patricia Hill Collins rightly affirms, "Social theories emerging from and/or on behalf of historically oppressed groups investigate ways to escape from, survive in, and/or oppose prevailing social and economic injustice… Social theories from these groups typically do not arise from the rarefied atmosphere of the imagination; instead, they often emerge in conjunction with freedom struggles."[14]

Collins' notion of social theories from the grassroots has an *a priori* dimension. Struggles for survival and the annihilation of the prevailing social order are the wombs from which subaltern social theories emerge. Stated differently, the papyrus on which the subaltern social theory takes the form of alphabets is the collectivity of the subalterns known as social movements. It is from this perspective that we can explore more deeply epistemologies from the grassroots.

Subaltern Knowledge as Collective Ethical and Political Praxis

As we have seen in the previous section, the regime of truth is founded on the myth of the disembodied and neutral Cartesian subject. Our analysis of this myth further clarified that there is a "non-innocent" relationship between the subject, the knowledge or truth that is produced, and the location of the subject in the power structure of social relations. In other words, "knowledge is not *tainted* by interest; it *is* interest."[15]

This realization is foundational to North American feminist standpoint epistemologies. A standpoint is neither an engaged observation of an individual activist nor the detached observation of a disembodied observer. "A standpoint is a 'vantage point' formed by the efforts of a mass movement; it is the result of praxis, combining both political action on the part of an oppressed group… and critical reflection on that action."[16] This definition further clarifies the inseparability between epistemological standpoint and ethical standpoint. All constructions of knowledge and truth are political acts with values inherent to them. The feminist standpoint epistemologies, hence, begin their discourse on knowledge with an *a priori* ethical judgment. As Donna Haraway puts it, "politics and ethics ground struggles for and contests over what may count as rational knowledge."[17] Knowledge is always constructed and contested based on ethics and politics. This truth has been veiled in the myth of the disembodied observer of the Enlightenment project.

The recognition and affirmation of the inherent politics and ethics of knowledge are central to the project of feminist standpoint epistemologies, and they construct this counter-hegemonic epistemology as an oppositional political and ethical praxis. For example, according to Nancy Hartsock, knowledge "exposes the real relations among human beings as inhumane, points beyond the present, and carries a liberatory role."[18] Donna Haraway shares a similar position when she claims that her search for knowledge is "potent for constructing worlds less organized by axes of domination."[19] For the grassroots communities, to summarize the positions of Hartsock and Haraway, knowledge is a political and ethical praxis which enables them to understand critically asymmetrical social relations, to make ethical judgment on the dominant social structures that push them to the peripheries and erase their cognitive agency and to dream and design new worlds together.

I would like to juxtapose here the dalit understanding of epistemology. Commenting on the language of dalit–bajujan political discourse, Gopal Guru states that, "Yet, in the domain of politics, these categories do not acquire an arbitrary character; they are not an aimless or passive representation of the world out there but are conscious constructions with either a positive or negative agenda as chalked out by their users."[20] Guru does not stop with an analysis of knowledge; rather he unveils his perspective about the dalit epistemology too. The dalit category "is not a metaphysical construction. It derives its epistemological and political strength from the material social experience of its subjects. The dalit category, in fact, promotes both the cognitive and emotional response of the collective subjects to the immediate world and its reconstruction."[21]

The dalit feminist standpoint is even more fluid in its construction, as it articulates the identity of standpoint epistemologies as conscious collective political activity. The dalit feminist standpoint, according to Sharmila Rege, "therefore, is not to be seen in terms of aggregates of individuals, it is a collective subject position that requires an always contingent transformation of complex subject positions."[22]

To summarize the feminist standpoint and the dalit positions, there is an interrelationship between the ethical standpoint and the epistemological standpoint of a community as they are informed by the understanding of the prevailing social relations and the vision of the future mediated through their political struggles. It is important here to return to Patricia Hill Collins, who raises three basic questions in her search to define the epistemological criteria for critical social theory. Does the social theory enable people to see the truth about their lived reality? Does the social theory equip and empower people to resist their oppression? And does the social theory inspire people to struggle? "When informed by truths, armed with tools of resistance, and moved by faith in justice, proclaimed love that struggles without end can make a profound difference."[23] An epistemological standpoint, born out of the collective praxis of a grassroots subaltern movement with the political commitment to strive for the realization of a different world devoid of the axis of domination, is an ethical standpoint. In other words, a standpoint epistemology emerges at the interface of ethics, politics, and knowledge.

The Situatedness of Knowledges: The Subaltern Objectivity

The epistemological discourses to emerge from the grassroots as standpoint epistemologies introduce the lived experiences of the community as the loci for constructing knowledge and truth. This radical shift from the objectivity of the dominant epistemologies to subjective experiences of the community has led to new debates over objectivity and subjectivity. These debates have given birth to new interpretations of objectivity from subaltern standpoints. Donna Haraway's engagement with this debate led to the birth of the concept of "situated knowledges."

The interface of ethics, politics, and knowledge has been central to the epistemological reflections of Haraway. For her, a separation of ethics, politics, and knowledge is detrimental to the interests of the powerless as knowledge and truth claims constructed under unjust power relations have the potential to become both hegemonic and lethal. Of course, the dominant epistemologies claim such knowledge as "objective," and the knowers as disembodied and value-free observers. This is the context in which Haraway reinterprets objectivity, by incorporating responsibility and locatedness, and proclaims that "feminist objectivity means quite simply situated knowledges."[24]

Situated knowledges affirm the partiality and bias of what we perceive from our particular locations. In that sense, it is the situated knowledges that provide objectivity. Haraway does not stop there. In her project, the world is an active entity with agency because "situated knowledges require that the object of knowledge be pictured as an actor and agent, not as a screen or a ground or a resource, never finally as slave to the master that closes off the dialectic in his unique agency and his authorship of 'objective' knowledge."[25] When the knower and the known become situated epistemic agents, the logic of "discovery" will be replaced by a culture of "conversation." The alternative for Haraway is "partial, locatable, critical knowledges sustaining the possibility of webs of conversations called solidarity in politics and shared conversations in epistemology."[26]

The feminist recognition of the situatedness of knowledges reflects its politics of knowledge. It is the realization of the fascist tendencies in the totalizing epistemic projects of the dominant that enabled the feminists not to construct their liberatory epistemic project within the logic of the dominant paradigm. To put it differently, the affirmation of the situatedness and partiality of all knowledge claims is a political rejection of the logic of all totalizing hegemonic knowledges. Even more constructively the feminist politics of knowledge underscores the place of solidarity in politics informed and nurtured by mutual conversations in epistemology.

The epistemologies from the grassroots, as we have seen above, peel away the very edifice of the regime of truth and while negating the logic of the dominant epistemology, they also necessarily revisit some of the basic concepts in epistemology, bringing new meanings to those concepts mediated by their politics. Let us now see how the epistemologies from the grassroots enable us to develop the methodology of social movements as text.

Subaltern Lived Experience as Sites of Knowledge

The affirmation of lived experience as the primary source of knowledge is essentially a revolt against the dominant "reason alone" epistemology. It proclaims the embodiment of knowing in the everyday lived experiences of the communities. The recognition of the cognitive authority of experience is nothing new. The heterodox strand in the Indian philosophical system called *Lokayata* considered experience as a source of knowledge centuries if not millennia ago. However, it is the women's movements across the world that have provided this category a political meaning and content. In the epistemological discourses of these women, lived experience becomes the loci of knowledge.

"All our knowledge," as feminist liberation ethicist Beverly Wildung Harrison asserts, "including our moral knowledge, is body mediated."[27] Over the last few decades, this understanding of experience as the primary source of knowledge became nuanced, thanks to the intense theoretical conversations among women and other subaltern communities. One of the issues that they realized in claiming epistemological privilege to experience is the danger of homogenization, considering women as a homogenous entity. The initial attempt to "fix" this danger was to invoke the plural form of "women's experiences." However, that too failed to address the issue of multiple identities and subjectivities.

"Essentialism" is yet another issue that initiated intense conversations on the epistemological claim of experience. There are a host of issues related to essentialism. According to Uma Narayan, "The feminist critique of gender essentialism does not merely charge that essentialist claims about 'women' are overgeneralizations, but points out that these generalizations are hegemonic in that they represent the problems of privileged women ... as paradigmatic 'women's issues.'"[28] The erasure of differences and the universalization of the dominant experience as the source for knowledge perpetuate asymmetrical power relations. On the other hand, critics would argue that an apolitical emphasis on differences can lead to a reversal of hierarchies with new masters and lords of knowledge who would continue the same logic of the regime of truth. The problem here is the biological reduction of the identity politics which ahistoricizes and thereby apoliticizes the collective experiences of the marginalized communities. Having identified this danger of essentialism, let us continue to explore how the epistemologies from the margins address this danger and re-articulate the centrality of lived experience as the primary source of knowledge.

Ada Maria Isasi-Diaz in her reflections on *Mujerista* theology presents *lo cotidiano* (everyday) as the lived experience for Latinas. Her interpretation of the concept of *lo cotidiano* is instructive for our reflections on the epistemological significance of experience. For her it is not a generic term that describes everyday life. Rather, the epistemological function of *lo cotidiano* is to indicate that "the struggles of the poor and the oppressed taking place in the underside of history constitutes the place, the moment – the horizon – of grassroots people's knowledge of reality. There is a triple dimension to knowing reality: becoming aware/getting to know reality, taking responsibility for reality, and transforming reality."[29]

We see a similar approach in black feminist thought also. While affirming that "the primary responsibility for defining one's own reality lies with the people who live that reality, who actually have those experiences,"[30] Patricia Hill Collins underscores the importance of the politically conscious collectivity of the community to have the cognitive ability to "create the conditions of a shared standpoint that in turn can stimulate collective political action."[31] For Collins the purpose of the mediation of lived experience is "not simply to insert the missing experiences into prevailing wisdom. Instead, when effectively done, claiming the authority of concrete experiences use(d) wisdom to challenge legitimated knowledge."[32]

Through her concept of "oppositional gaze" bell hooks also defines black feminist thought in a similar way. When the oppositional gaze is absent in black women's perception, they do not see the reality differently, thanks to the colonization of their perception by dominant ways of knowing. So an active collective resistance to dominant ways of knowing is a pre-requisite for black women's oppositional gaze. To put it in bell hooks' words, with oppositional gaze "we do more than resist. We create *alternative texts* that are not solely reactions. As critical spectators, black women participate in a broad range of looking relations, contest, resist, revision, interrogate, and invent on multiple levels."[33]

Lived experience, as the survey of feminist literature informs us, is primarily a political category, not a biological or cultural one. It calls for a shift from apolitical essentialist notions to political commitment. The ground for the emerging politics of knowledge is not color or gender per se; rather, "it is the way we think about race, class, and gender – the political links we choose to make among and between struggles."[34] Lived experience becomes epistemological when communities transform this experience into oppositional knowledge. It involves a critical understanding of the reality of subordination, and a vision and the political strategy to replace that reality with just and participatory social relations.

Epistemological Communities as Alternative Texts

Oppositional knowledge, informed by the lived experience of the subaltern communities at the grassroots, legitimizes the "authorization" of their knowledge. Through oppositional knowledge, they affirm their cognitive authority and reclaim their moral agency. In fact, it is the negation of the negation – the rejection of the regime of truth which reduces them to be objects without agency to be represented and colonized. Oppositional knowledge is, therefore, the "coming to voice" and "coming to power" of the politically conscious collectivity of the subaltern communities.

The affirmation of the epistemological authority of lived experience is questioned by the proponents of the dominant politics of knowledge in the name of objectivity. Objectivity in the post-

Enlightenment epistemological project refers to an objectivist view – a dispassionate view from nowhere for everyone. In the dominant discourses, the absence of objectivity is condemned as relativism, which in common parlance means "everything goes." The epistemologies from the grassroots cannot avoid the issue of objectivity vs. relativism as it questions their very epistemic agency. So it is important to understand their approach towards objectivity.

The epistemologies from the grassroots understand objectivity as an ethical category of accountability and responsibility. These ethical categories are absent in the dominant understanding of dispassionate and detached objectivity because there is no relationship between the knower and the object of knowledge. Stated differently, it is the distance from the Other that makes observations and representations made without accountability and responsibility objective knowledge. This realization led feminists to reject the dominant understanding of objectivity: "Feminists don't need a doctrine of objectivity that promises transcendence, a story that loses track of its mediations just where someone might be held responsible for something... Immortality and omnipotence are not our goals."[35]

The feminist affirmation of the situatedness of knowledge gives a new meaning to objectivity. The bottom line in feminist objectivity is accountability and responsibility arising from the relationship between the knower and the object of knowledge. It is no more a "god's eye view from nowhere," but a particular and specific embodiment and relationship. For Haraway, the moral is simple: "Only partial perspective promises objective vision."[36]

The communities at the grassroots share in their bodies the scars of being objectified and represented in the history of knowledge. In this way the reinterpretation of objectivity is autobiographical, as they struggle to expose the claims of objectivity of the dominant epistemology. Haraway succinctly articulates the politics of this new understanding of objectivity. "[C]oming to terms with the agency of the 'objects' studied is the only way to avoid gross error and false knowledge of many kinds."[37] In other words, authorizing epistemological agency of the 'objects' guarantees objectivity.

Having said this, how do we substantiate the claim that epistemological communities are alternative texts? The term "epistemological communities" also has its origin in the feminist epistemological discourses. It comes out of two basic affirmations: First, the agents of knowledge production are politically conscious communities at the margins, not disembodied or engaged activist individuals. Second, not all communities are epistemological communities; communities that are consciously involved in the process of "coming to voice" and "coming to power" have the epistemic authority and cognitive agency to construct knowledge that is counter hegemonic.

The above mentioned foundational characteristics of epistemological communities revive the debate on essentialism. How is this understanding of epistemological communities different from an apolitical and ahistorical identity politics? Isn't it relativism in different attire? Feminist standpoint epistemology does not subscribe to the essentialist position of subalterns as ontologically "natural" knowers. A standpoint, as we have seen earlier, is more than assigning an individual or a group epistemological authority based on the fact that he/she or they belong to an oppressed group. As Shari Stone-Mediatore's commentary on Chandra Mohanty's interpretation of experience rightly suggests, "critical knowledge and political consciousness do not follow automatically from living in a marginalized social location; they develop only with the struggle against oppression, when this struggle includes the work of remembering and renarrating obscured experiences of resistance to, or tension with, social and cultural norms."[38]

The concept of epistemological communities becomes an alternative here. A collectivity that proclaims its testimonies informed by their experience of subjugation and mediated by social theories to challenge the dominant hegemonic discourses has the authority to be considered an epistemological community. The very presence of the epistemological communities is a threat to the regime of truth, as they contest, challenge, and disrupt the hegemonic knowledge and truth claims by being an alternative text.

To exegete further the claim of epistemological communities as alternative text, let us return to the women of color. As we have seen in the *Mujerista theology*, analysis of everyday lived experience, the activity of knowing, involves three things: becoming aware/getting to know reality, taking responsibility for reality, and transforming reality. In black feminist thought, developed particularly by Patricia Hill Collins, the praxis of knowing involves three interrelated components – breaking silence about oppression, developing a self-defined standpoint, and finally talking back.[39] In this process of knowing, along with the epistemological communities, the lifeworld also becomes an active agent. To put it differently, when the epistemological relationship between the epistemological communities and the lifeworld becomes one of "conversation," rather than the dominant models of "colonization" and "discovery" and "representation," the collectivity becomes an authoritative alternative text.

The understanding of epistemological communities further underscores hybridity as it challenges the framework of binary opposites. Coming back to the discourse on *Sati*, Ania Loomba's challenge to move towards a "collective subjectivity of agents" is instructive here. According to Loomba, the collective subjectivity of agents in the case of *Sati* would not be a collectivity of satis or even of widows but rather of huge, if not all, sections of Indian women who suffer form the consequences of the ideology of sati. I would like to suggest that "the subaltern" "in the text of sati," if we must locate one, cannot be understood simply as the immolated widow. The sati is produced by and functions to recirculate ideologies which target and seek to position a large body of women, whose experiences, articulations, and silences are crucial to understanding the relations of power and insubordination which are central to any analysis of "the subaltern."[40] This challenge not only provides room for people from outside of a particular epistemological community to enter into solidarity with the political praxis of that community, but also underscores the importance of networking with other similar epistemological communities.

Social Movements as Epistemological Communities

What is the relevance of the discourse on subaltern epistemologies for this book? To answer that question, we need to place our learnings in this chapter – the realization and affirmation of the epistemological and moral agency of the politically conscious collectivity of the subalterns – in the wider context of this book. To recapitulate our discussion in the first two chapters, let me quote Karl Polanyi again:

> To allow the market mechanism to be the sole director of the fate of human beings and their natural environment ... would result in the demolition of society ... Robbed of the protective covering of cultural institutions, human beings would perish from the effects of social exposure; they would die as victims of acute social dislocation ... Nature would be reduced to its elements, neighborhoods and landscapes defiled, rivers

polluted ... the power to produce food and raw materials destroyed ... Undoubtedly, labor, land, and money are essential to a market economy. But no society could stand the effects of such a system of crude fictions even for the shortest stretch of time unless its human and natural substance ... was protected against the satanic mill.[41]

The prophecy of Polanyi is the best description of the colonization of the lifeworld that communities in the Narmada valley and other parts of the world are facing today. In the Narmada valley, the "satanic mill" of development and globalization has the face of mega dams. Polanyi does not stop with a pessimistic note. In fact, he shares equally the vision of a counter movement. "This was more than the usual defensive behavior of a society faced with change; it was a reaction against a dislocation which attacked the fabric of society, and which would have destroyed the very organization of production that the market had called into being."[42] We have seen this counter movement in the Narmada saga. Our discussions about the interface of the colonization of the lifeworld, social movements, and the epistemologies from the grassroots led us to the constructive proposal that social movements such as the Narmada Bachao Andolan (NBA) are epistemological communities.

To substantiate this proposal, our discussion in the previous section provides us three pertinent insights: First of all, the very premise of our epistemological discourse in the interface of ethics, politics, and knowledge underscores the agency of social movements in the construction of a counter-hegemonic discourse of truth. Second, the affirmation of the situatedness of knowledge and the agency of the politically conscious oppositional gaze or praxis of the collectivity of the subalterns further privileges the epistemological agency and authority of the social movements. Finally, the potential of an epistemological community to become an alternative text by not only contesting and disrupting the dominant discourse, but also by creating viable alternatives that affirm and enhance the movement of life is nothing but the authorization of the alternative text called "social movements."

The New Social Movements

Before we proceed, it is important here to clarify how we use the concept of social movements in this book. Social movement research is an emerging interdisciplinary academic area with new studies and theories surfacing every day. Given the diversity in the theoretical articulations of the phenomenon of social movements, it is not helpful to premise this work on one definition of social movements. Since a comprehensive study of the theories of social movements is beyond the scope of this book, our attempt is confined to the theories of New Social Movements (NSMs), and the way selected feminist social scientists and activists from India and elsewhere appropriate those theories.[43]

The European social theorist Alberto Melucci calls social movements "disenchanted prophets."

> Contemporary movements are prophets of the present. What they possess is not the force of the apparatus but the power of the word. They announce the commencement of change; not, however, a change in the distant future but one that is already a presence. They force the power out into open and give it a shape and a face. They speak a language that seems to be entirely their own, but they say something that transcends their particularity and speaks to us all.[44]

Even though the above mentioned statement is not a definition, it describes the characteristics of contemporary social movements. Through the method of describing the contemporary movements *via negativa,* Melucci clarifies the discontinuity between "old" social movements and the "new" social movements. The term New Social Movements refers to those movements which emerged following the pattern of the student movement of the 1960s as an alternative to the trade unions and the workers' movements, the old social movements. They include second-wave feminism, the animal rights movement, the environmental movement, and the anti-war movement.

One of the oft-repeated questions in the study of the NSMs is what is "new" about the NSMs. Alain Touraine, Jürgen Habermas, and Alberto Melucci, the three main proponents of the NSM theories have attempted to address this question.[45] They premised their argument on the shift that western societies have undergone in terms of mode of organization. This shift, they argued, had resulted in a corresponding shift in the central conflict and struggle in those societies. To explain further, for the trade unions and working-class movements inspired by Marxism, the fundamental conflict was between two classes – the bourgeoisie and the proletariat, and being the agents of history, it was the historical role of the proletariat to overthrow the order and capture power. That does not mean that

Marxism is blind to other social conflicts and struggles. But Marxism in its classical and dominant political articulations tends to reduce all conflicts to a class issue based on the base superstructure analysis.

The theorists of NSMs rejected this reductionist Marxist analysis, and recognized the presence of plurality of conflicts which leads to the affirmation of diverse agents and their social movements. As Nick Crossley opines, "The Marxist discourse on social movement was traditionally focused upon issues of state and revolution," whereas, "NSM theory in contrast, generally focuses upon the ways in which social movements seek to achieve change in cultural, symbolic, and sub-political domains."[46] This position is well articulated by Habermas:

> In the past decade or two, conflicts have developed in advanced Western societies that deviate in various ways from the Welfare State pattern of institutionalized conflict over distribution... The issue is not primarily one of compensations that the welfare state can provide, but of defending and restoring endangered ways of life. In short, the new conflicts are not ignited by distribution problems but by questions having to do with the grammar of forms of life.[47]

Habermas' theory of social movement emerges in the context of his analysis of the colonization of the lifeworld. For him, the "new" in the NSMs is the conflict shift from the capital-labor to the "seam between the system-lifeworld." A commonality in various articulations of the NSMs is the theoretical attempt to present contemporary social movements as over against the working-class movements. In other words, according to the NSM theorists, the struggles for distribution and struggles for recognition are mutually exclusive. In this project, "the grammar of forms of life" is reduced to an apolitical category.

Independent India has produced a host of social movements which can be considered "new" because of the diversity in their ideological moorings and in the perception of the social conflicts. Gail Omvedt, an Indian feminist social scientist, shares the critique of the class-based grand narrative of the Marxist social movements, exposing their "monocolor" character, and their tendency to ignore "nonclass" issues. However, unlike the European theorists of the NSMs, Omvedt brings a nuanced position on Marxism. "They are 'new' in that they themselves, through the ideologies they generate, define their exploitation and oppression, the system that generates these, and the way to end this exploitation and oppression, in 'new' terms – related to traditional Marxism but having clear differences with it."[48] The main difference that Omvedt brings to the discourse on NSMs is the assertion that struggles for recognition and struggles for distribution are mutually inclusive.

The dalit feminist standpoint also addresses the danger of uncoupling the struggles for recognition and the struggles for distribution.

> A dichotomization of injustices into socio-economic and cultural, which had been radically challenged both by Dalit Panthers and the women's movement assumes thus a divide as if between a politics of redistribution and recognition. Such an opposition overlooks the fact that caste is cultural without ceasing to be material and a Brahmanism in its production distribution and effect is economic.[49]

This corrective to the European versions of NSM theories is the strength of New Social Movements in India and elsewhere. Even while raising criticisms of the neo-liberal globalization, the European theorists tend to keep the dichotomization between movements for cultural rights and movements against neo-liberalism.[50] A re-engagement with socialism becomes important in this context, and Gail Omvedt has articulated emphatically the latent socialist commitment of the New Social Movements in India:

> They have been explicitly antisystemic in their ideologies, looking towards a casteless, nonpatriarchal, nonlooting, sustainable society; they are involved, in their own view, in inherent conflict with the current social order. They are analyzing the current situation and causes of exploitation and oppression in new ways (rethinking Marxism), constituting a new interpretation of Indian society and history (reimagining the community), and seeking new modes of action to effect change. In the process of organizing, their songs still echo the aspirations for the creation of a new society of equality and freedom, traditionally known as "socialism."[51]

The corrective to the dominant NSM theories proposed by the communities at the grassroots in India and other countries, through their New Social Movements, is politically significant in the context of the colonization of the lifeworld. Nancy Fraser's analysis of "postsocialist" condition is enlightening here. Fraser identifies three constitutive features of the "postsocialist" condition. First of all, the postsocialist condition represents the absence of a credible alternative vision due to the "exhaustion of utopian energies." Secondly, there is a shift in the grammar of political claims which led to the decoupling of cultural politics from social politics, with the relative ascendance of the former. Thirdly, this shift occurs in a historical context of resurgent economic liberalism through globalization,[52] and it calls for a coalition of theories of recognition and distribution with a common commitment to cultural rights and social justice.

Social Movements as a Subaltern Counterpublic Sphere

The concept of public sphere as a discursive model is an important contribution of Jürgen Habermas.[53] Public sphere is the domain in which public opinion can be formed. This domain is conceptually distinct from the state and the market. It is primarily a discursive site and theater for constructing and circulating discourses that are critical of the state and the market. It is important to note here that Habermas developed the notion of public sphere as part of his theory of New Social Movements.

For Habermas, the New Social Movements of the late 60s (the women's movement, the environmental movement, the anti-war movement etc.) are the source for the public sphere. As we have seen in the first chapter, in his theory of communicative action, Habermas makes a distinction between system and lifeworld, and diagnoses the colonization of the lifeworld by the system as the root cause for the contemporary crisis. System in this model is understood as those administrative areas of modern society coordinated by money and power, and represented by the market and the state. Lifeworld, for Habermas, is the everyday world, the site of symbolic interaction, where we live together and communicate with each other. As we have seen in the previous section, his theory of the NSMs is based on the conflict shift from what was capital-labor to the "seam between the system-lifeworld." This bias against the "old" politics of the labor movements is evident in his rejection of the struggles for distribution. The Habermasian concept of public sphere therefore needs to be understood in the context of his wider project of the colonization of the lifeworld and the New Social Movements.

Habermas presents the public sphere as a discursive site which is conceptually distinct from the state and the market. The public sphere is an arena where the citizens engage in discursive interactions in order to produce and circulate new discourses to bring about political changes. The Habermasian concept of public sphere is problematic from the perspective of the epistemologies from the grassroots. Three things require our attention here. First of all, Habermas' public sphere tends to be a "bourgeois public sphere" which legitimizes the political domination of the state by creating an arena in which citizens can share their opinions about issues of common interest. As we learn from Antonio Gramsci, we witness a shift from a repressive mode of domination to a hegemonic mode of domination, where institutions in the civil society and the public sphere legitimize the domination through non-repressive means. In such a context, the official (bourgeois) public sphere is the institutional domain that constructs the legitimization of the hegemonic mode of domination of the state.

Secondly, the bourgeois public sphere idealizes a universal and normative way of reasoning, and as a result, it excludes the majority of the people – women, indigenous communities, dalits, children – from its discursive arena. As Benjamin Valentine states, such theorizations "seem hostile to cultural difference, and ... do not sufficiently scrutinize the discursive and practical implications of social inequality."[54] Stated differently, the concept of public sphere in this sense is an ideology that erases differences and the discursive authority of the subalterns. Thirdly, the Habermasian concept of public sphere is so monolithic that it does not recognize the presence of counterpublic spheres that exist along with the bourgeois public sphere. Patricia Hill Collins' recollection of the political significance of the black public sphere or black civil society – families, churches, fraternal organizations, and other institutions – is just one example of the host of counterpublics that are erased from discursive authority by the bourgeois public sphere.[55]

This is the context in which the concept of subaltern counterpublic spheres developed by Nancy Fraser becomes paradigmatic for us. Nancy Fraser defines subaltern counterpublics as "parallel discursive arenas where members of subordinated social groups invent and circulate counter discourses, which in turn permit them to formulate oppositional interpretations of their identities, interests, and needs."[56] It is important to note here that in Fraser's project, subaltern counterpublic spheres are not proposed as over against the bourgeois public spheres. Rather, they engage and dialogue continuously with the public spheres. The subaltern counterpublic spheres, therefore, are alternative discursive arenas for the construction and circulation of oppositional knowledge.

To conclude, the subaltern counterpublic sphere enables the communities at the grassroots to articulate the oppositional knowledge and to develop it as a political force to contest dominant knowledge claims. The recognition of the multiplicity of counterpublics further underscores the reality of the multiplicity of oppression that the communities face in their lifeworld, and strengthens the attempts for coalitions of solidarity. In the words of Benjamin Valentine, "the idea of subaltern counterpublics elucidates the possibility of a more comprehensive arena of discourse and association in which more limited, yet significant and contextually specific, public spheres infused with diverse values, identities, cultural styles, and context-specific needs can coexist and, when necessary, unite for a common good."[57]

All these arguments underscore our proposal that social movements are texts. Rajendra Singh helps us to clarify this proposal further:

> [M]ovements are not *made*, much less are they *launched* or led by leaders. Whenever opportunities permit or human disenchantments exhaust the limits of human perseverance, movements decoil (unfold) automatically and reveal themselves in the actions of the awakened conflictual consciousness of the collectivity.[58]

Social movements are communicative media that encode information containing reflections on the context and the vision of an alternative reality. They are signifying systems through which a social system is communicated, critiqued, and explored. As forms of cultural, political, and spiritual expressions, social movements are alternative social texts.

This argument is further elaborated by Alberto Melucci in the following observation about NSMs.

> The very existence and structure of collective action (NSMs) provides the rest of society with a different way of interpreting individual and collective experiences. Linking personal changes with external action, collective action functions as a new media which illuminates the silent and arbitrary elements of the dominant codes as well as publicizes new alternatives.[59]

In other words, the text called social movements provides not only the relevant information, but also the perspective to engage in radical politics. "It [collective action] is no longer considered as a means to an end, and it therefore cannot be assessed only in terms of its instrumental rationality. The organization has a self-reflexive character and its form expresses the meaning (or goals) of action itself."[60]

A deeper analysis of the social movements enables us to see how the dominant codes are being symbolically challenged by the movements. These symbolic expressions of unmasking the dominant codes are in fact a different way of articulating and celebrating a new world. T. V. Reed, in his study of the poetics of social movements based on women's street theatre and novels, makes the following observation. "The totalizing tendencies of (all) theory can be resisted best not by the production of written textual heterogeneity (as some radical formalisms might have it) but by exposure to the actual diversity ('heteroglossia') of living political subjects."[61]

The emergence of a social movement involves a process of creating consensus on diverse views, dialogue, integration, and reflexive articulations of internal differences. So social movement as text may not be a coherent text; but it is an intrinsically heterogeneous text, with subtexts and cotexts and intertextuality. The social movements are, therefore, sites and texts that contain and encourage the multiple voices of the living political subjects in our times. They are counter discourses contesting the dominant discourse, rebellion against the dominant episteme. These texts can inform us in constructing a grassroots earth ethics that can challenge the perpetuation of the colonization of the lifeworld.

Social movements, as intentional political organizations of communities at the grassroots, attempt to understand social reality with a political and ethical motif in order to transform it radically. It is an engaged and collective construction of knowledge mediated by their particular experience of marginality and counter-hegemonic discourses being generated in their struggles. For these reasons, social movements are the sites of an alternative narrative and therefore they have the epistemological agency to construct liberating knowledge.

Social Movements as Theological Texts

This chapter, as we mentioned at the outset, is an attempt to validate the methodological proposal of this book, that social movements are texts. As we have seen so far, this proposal affirms that to reclaim the moral agency of the communities at the grassroots is the initial stage in their exodus from the colonization of their lifeworld. To reclaim moral agency requires mediation through epistemological communities who contest dominant hegemonic knowledge and their interventions of conquest and social engineering, with alternative knowledge emerging from the interface of ethics, politics, and knowledge. One question remains unanswered, however. What is theological in this proposal?

The last quarter of the twentieth century witnessed the emergence of a host of social action groups in India inspired by Christian faith. The tragic realization that the postcolonial state is an extension of the imperial logic of governance in indigenous attire, the violence that diverse social conflicts perpetuate on the powerless, and the disillusionment with the Church for its failure to be "the sign and sacrament" of the Reign of God, were the major causes for young people to experiment with new patterns of witnessing to the God of life. Some of these groups became part of different peoples' movements while others initiated new movements. In short, peoples' movements have been a theological category in India for the last three decades.

M. M. Thomas, a source of inspiration for the emergence of the fellowships of social action groups in India, provides us with a theological perspective to approach the social movements. For Thomas, social movements are the agency of the people for selfhood through self-awakening. Self-awakening is a materialist awakening. The struggle against poverty, therefore, becomes an expression of peoples' self-awakening. "Our humanity is destroyed by poverty and therefore it is for the sake of justice to our humanity that we want bread… Bread is an expression of selfhood."[62]

The struggle for self-awakening and enabling moral agency are deeply interrelated. Self-awakening is the affirmation of peoples' sovereignty over their lives. This is nothing but the reclamation of their moral agency. In the contemporary world, the spiritual quest for selfhood and moral agency is situated in the materiality of subaltern struggles for survival and self-representation. Social movements as sites of reclaiming moral agency and challenging claims of lordship over the selfhood of the people are engaged in a spiritual praxis.

Enrique Dussel, in his analysis of the Chiapas movement and the 1994 Maya rebellion, enables us to ethically reflect upon social movements.[63] For Dussel the Chiapas movement insisted on "the dignity of the negated historical subject." The native has been known as a functional part of the system, reduced to the status of a thing. It is the social movement that proclaimed the native as a person oppressed within the system. This ethical affirmation of the Other's personhood is also an affirmation that the Other is different from the system.

Thomas places the theological significance of the self-awakening of the people, mediated by the agency of the social movements, in his vision of salvation. To paraphrase him, it is the corporate expression of sin that colonizes and dehumanizes the lifeworld. It becomes imperative for us then to bring these principalities and power under the judgment of God within an eschatological framework that recognizes the reality of new "falls." In spite of the fragmentary realizations of the self-awakening, these movements point to eschatological humanization as their judgment and fulfillment.[64] Here, Thomas not only recognizes the inherent possibility for human initiatives in history to "fall," but also affirms that in spite of the fragmentary nature of the struggles and their achievements, social movements for self-awakening are engaged in the politics of the reign of God.

This politics of the reign of God, according to Thomas, involves "the denial of a certain god for the sake of a new God or for a God beyond God." Here, Thomas makes a distinction between spirituality and institutionalized religion. Recalling the story of Job, Thomas proposes that protest atheism is essential for authentic God experience. "It was a protest against God in the name of divine justice; a protest atheism in search of a God who is for us, for humanity, for social justice. Anti-religion, protest atheism, are all in terms of a positive fulfillment of the new spiritual awakening to justice."[65] Social movements are not products created out of theological blueprints; they are also not projects of any institutionalized religions. Rather, they confront the Divine in their struggle for self-awakening. The non-religious faith and spirituality of the social movements is succinctly articulated by M. J. Joseph:

> We are not religious people and no way interested in the revival of these religions or the gods they uphold. But what we have in common are: faith in the purposiveness of history where people can transcend bondage and death and are prepared to offer one's own life for it. This faith affirms that no one's death is meaningless if his/her life has been charged

with significance. However, the discovery of this faith is not through the systematic study of any dogmas but by trying to respond to the situation of oppression, injustice, depravity and death, people discover the living faith dimensions. When the poor and the marginalized join together in their search for fulfillment and purpose they discover a faith in that process.[66]

The spirituality of the social movements emerged out of their struggles of resistance and re-creating alternatives that transcend religious categories. It is this faith and spirituality of combat that sustain them in their struggles.

Conclusion

Theology, as collective autobiographical testimonials of communities at the grassroots, is not the story of heroes and heroines. Rather, it is the communal testimonials of dangerous memories of erasure. These dangerous memories are invoked in the new text to contest the dominant episteme and the regime of truth. Contemporary social movements are hence theological texts that can inform us in our search for a world devoid of the axis of domination and alienation.

This constructive proposal to develop a grassroots earth ethics is a journey of discipleship because it arises out of the conviction that as knowledge, politics, and ethics are integrally related in the political praxis of the subordinated others, their vantage point of the reality and visions of alternatives can provide us a better perspective which has the potential to interpret and to transform radically the desacralized earth and sinful social relations. To paraphrase Chandra Mohanty theologically, the mediation of the collective testimonials of the social movements are crucial not because they present an unmediated version of the "truth" but because they have the potential to destabilize the regimes of truth and pave the way for alternative praxis that is life affirming.[67] This book proposes new ways of doing theology and ethics that enable the faith communities to witness to the God of life relevantly and meaningfully by participating actively in the subaltern political praxis to resist all manifestations of the idols of death, and to affirm and celebrate life. Social movements of our times, as authentic texts with authority, can inform us in this journey.

4 Mapping Grassroots Earth Ethics: Methodological Musings

Introduction

The colonization of the lifeworld, mediated by the regime of truth, continues to be the everyday experience of the subordinated others all over the world. This hegemonic bandwagon not only unleashes a hurricane of death and destruction on living beings, but it also paralyzes their ability to envision a world devoid of the axis of domination by erasing their moral agency. It is on this horizon of shattered dreams and scattered lives that the collective, resilient consciousness of the subalterns becomes flesh in the form of social movements reclaiming their moral agency, engaging in praxis toward alternatives, and witnessing to the dawn of a different world. As sites of this alternative politics, subaltern social movements are alternative texts.

The realization that social movements embody, as texts of alternative political praxis, sites of radical social transformation should compel those who do Christian ethical reflections to be in solidarity and conversation with these movements. Being in organic solidarity with such movements' political praxis can lead to the construction of a grassroots subaltern earth ethics informed by these very texts called social movements. This chapter constructs a grassroots earth ethics – a prolegomenon of grassroots earth ethics – informed by the Narmada Bachao Andolan.

Methodological Standpoints

Before we begin this constructive journey, it is essential to spell out the methodological standpoints of this project. The grassroots earth ethics being constructed here emerges at the interface of ethics, politics, and knowledge. To do so requires reflection on this interface, mediated through the testimonies of the Narmada Bachao

Andolan. As prior chapters explained, knowledge that emerges from the crucible of the collectivity of the subalterns informed by their body-mediated experiences is oppositional as it challenges the regime of truth. The politics of such oppositional knowledge creates new and particular discourses, and these discourses inform their political praxis to decolonize their lifeworld through resistance and re-creation. This process begins with an *a priori* ethical standpoint that affirms the moral agency of the community to create a different world, one less contaminated by the instrumental rationality of the colonizing forces.

How can this methodological standpoint be explained in the language of Christian ethics and theology? Christian ethics, as this project perceives it, is a theological and ethical praxis in the crucible of subaltern politics to reclaim the moral agency of the people in order to realize their visions of liberation. The reclamation of moral agency is a theological and ethical imperative because it empowers the people in their struggles for selfhood. The purpose of Christian ethics is not to derive Christian behavior or attitude from the "given" sources of Scripture and tradition. Rather, as Enrique Dussel rightly puts it, ethics denotes "the future order of liberation, the demands of justice with respect to the poor, the oppressed, and their project of salvation."[1] The struggle against the colonization of the lifeworld as proleptic signs of the eschatological vision of the redeemed earth is hence the discursive arena mediating the construction of authentic Christian ethics.

The rejection of the "given" sources in this project raises questions about the very purpose of theology. Theology happens in a community's quest for selfhood, in the context of the recolonization of their lifeworld. It is a praxis informed by the "resources" of the community which include scriptures and religious traditions. This quest is neither a metaphysical speculation on metacosmic doctrines, nor a translation or application of "given" sources to contemporary situations. Rather, theology is a thoroughly this-worldly affair, problematizing, in the light of the vision of the redeemed earth, the threat to the movement of life caused by the "powers and principalities" which continue to commodify all life forms including human beings. It is not that we apply "given" doctrines to this existential reality or invoke God to intervene in concrete situations. Rather, we meet the Divine in a special way in the sufferings and the resistance of the victims. Dalit theologian Arvind Nirmal articulates this position in a compelling way: "The 'original' and the 'given' in this context is our own situation, our own history, our own struggles, our own aspirations, our own fears and our own hopes. God is dynamically present in these. He [sic] is savingly active in these. This is where we have to discern the Gospel happening and becoming."[2]

Social movements, as agents of counter-hegemonic praxis, are partakers in the salvific project of decolonization where the Gospel is happening. So the challenge that the social movements pose is a radical shift in our theological method. It invites us to rethink the "given" sources for doing theology. It transforms theology into a transformative political praxis initiated by "the wretched of the earth" to enable the blossoming of the redeemed earth in our own particular local contexts. It does not begin with God, nor end in God. Rather, in its commitment to witness to the emergence of the Reign of God, theological praxis, as Sebastian Kappen puts it, becomes *theandric* practice.[3] Wherever the victims develop an oppositional consciousness and collectively struggle to reclaim their selfhood and decolonize their lifeworld, the Spirit which hovered over the waters becomes ontologically present, transforming their fragmentary victories from the "bondage to decay," into foretastes of the eschatological "freedom of the glory of the children of God."

At the same time, the theological affirmation of social movements as agents of the *theandric* practice of the Reign of God underscores the situatedness of theological praxis in their particular experiences. Differently said, the ethical and theological reflections coming out of the discursive practices of the social movements are inherently antithetical to totalizing theological and ethical claims. Nor do they claim eternal validity and universality. The ethical reflections mediated by social movements affirm the provisional nature of all ethical theories. Larry Rasmussen's reflections on the environmental justice movement are instructive here: "They work from concrete injuries of injustice and seek incremental remedies, relishing victories savory enough for another day's sweat."[4] It is the incremental, fragmentary, and provisional victories of the people – the fragmentary victories to survive and self-represent – that make the eschatological utterly this-worldly.

The ethical standpoint narrated above is profoundly Christian. It keeps alive the creative tension between the "already" and the "not yet" by trusting in the promise of the ultimate reconciliation of all things on earth and in heaven in Christ Jesus. In a persuasive way M. M. Thomas articulates it: "The meaning of every historical action directed to love and justice in history and every fragmentary realization of truth, goodness and beauty in life, is protected, redeemed and fulfilled in the End. How, we do not know. But our guarantee is the Risen Jesus Christ."[5]

The rationale for the focus on earth ethics instead of environmental ethics is explained in the Introduction, along with the meaning in which we use the term "subaltern" in this book. The grassroots is the standpoint from which we look at the reality and attempt to construct this earth ethics. Hence, the focus of this project is a constructive one – to construct a grassroots earth ethics from the interface of subaltern politics, ethics, and knowledge mediated through social movements – rather than to establish polemically the rationale for a grassroots earth ethics by critically reviewing the literature in the field of Christian environmental ethics.

To recapitulate the reasons for not working on yet another book on environmental ethics, the standpoint of the present work is that the distress of the earth and its inhabitants is more than an environmental problem. Rather the crisis we face today is the colonization of the lifeword that enslaves the whole creation into the "bondage to decay." Colonization is a project to annihilate the Divine breath and creativity that created and continues to sustain all living beings. In other words, it is the negation of the Divine. Doing grassroots earth ethics from the standpoint of the subalterns is therefore more than a "tech fix" or "greening of the minds." It begins with a critical look at prevailing social relations to understand the asymmetrical power relations and the imperialist hegemonic regime of truth which sanctions and perpetuates the colonization of the lifeworld. The grassroots standpoint, therefore, enables us to perceive the crisis from the interface of the "cry of the poor and the cry of the earth."

Cartography of a Grassroots Earth Ethics

Based on these methodological standpoints we now begin the search for a grassroots earth ethics. We begin by following the methodology of Latin American liberation theology, articulated by Clodovis

Boff and Leonardo Boff,[6] to systematically present this project. This choice has political and methodological reasons. Politically, I place this project in the tradition of the irruption of the subaltern theological praxis from the margins generically known as third world theologies of liberation. Methodologically, I consider the Latin American model as able to articulate clearly and present systematically the cartography of a grassroots earth ethics.

The methodology of liberation theology affirms commitment as the first act of doing theology. It is followed by three mediations, namely: social analytical mediation, hermeneutical mediation, and praxeological mediation. Leonardo Boff, in the light of his theological awareness of the ecological crisis, reformulated these categories as four moments of doing theology, namely: seeing, judging, acting, and celebrating.[7] In this chapter I will use the principles of the Latin American method to develop relevant categories that can systematically articulate grassroots earth ethics.[8]

Seeing: The Subaltern Oppositional Gaze

It is a common theme in third world liberation theologies that commitment and solidarity are the primary acts of doing theology. Translating this methodological affirmation to the context of the distress of the earth, it is our solidarity with the wounded earth, our commitment to heal its wounds, and to prevent further victimization that gives us credibility to engage in the construction of theology. This experience of seeing enables us to reject the lenses that we have been using as a technological civilization for which nature is nothing but "a supermarket or a self-service restaurant." Seeing further helps us to realize that the logic that continues to exploit the communities at the grassroots and subject them to the economic and political interests of the rich is the same logic that devastates and rapes the earth.

However, a grassroots earth ethics informed by peoples' movements interprets seeing differently. As Juan Luis Segundo observed correctly, the conversion of the professional class of theologians to focus on the issues of the poor led to the category of seeing in Latin American liberation theology. "Thus it was not the oppressed people, but the middle classes, beginning with students, who received the first features of this liberation theology as a joyful conversion and a new commitment."[9] With the moral authority bestowed on them by their conversion and commitment to the causes of the people, they constructed theologies that universalized particular experiences of oppression and alienation with the grand vision of liberation.[10]

For Segundo, however, liberation theology is more than the theological appropriation of peoples' experiences by a professional class of theologians. Rather the in-breaking of a new theological discourse happened in Latin America thanks to the engagement of the people at the basic Christian communities with the Bible, mediated by their lived experiences. Vítor Westhelle articulates succinctly this type of seeing mediated by the collectivity of the subalterns called the basic Christian communities.

> Instead of the Exodus motif stressed by theologians who would see themselves leading the people away from the land of slavery, or a John the Baptist calling for repentance and announcing the coming of a new person, now the images were reversed. Instead of Exodus, there was *eisodus*, the entry into the lives of the people, the incarnation, and *kenosis*.[11]

Put differently, the poor are not just a category that provides the professional theologians the missing data – their experience of impoverishment, oppression, and exploitation; rather, the poor in their collectivity is an epistemic community that creates oppositional knowledge. It is the seeing from the vantage point of the collectivity of the subalterns that has the potential to create oppositional knowledge. A grassroots earth ethics, therefore, emerges from seeing as oppositional gaze.

Deeper analysis of the description of the contemporary ecological crisis in most of the theological literature on eco-theology and environmental ethics reveals the common approach to the issue of a "view from nowhere." Such views, based on the image of the earth from space, identify the problem as dualism and anthropocentrism which can be rectified through interconnectedness, relationships, community, and the like. But Rasmussen reminds us that in the context of the environmental justice movement, "the history of coercion, brutality, cultural genocide, and worse is not part of the moral memory and narrative of most environmental organizations."[12] As a result, theological environmentalism has become a "feel-good" issue.[13]

Grassroots earth ethics, on the other hand, emerges out of the subaltern oppositional gaze. Being an oppositional gaze, it naturally challenges the imperial and development gaze, based on experience of the colonization of their lifeworld. It further questions the claim of the normativity of the dominant gaze and affirms the agency of their oppositional gaze to interpret their particular reality and to transform it radically.[14] The affirmation of seeing as subaltern oppositional gaze provides grassroots earth ethics a new perspective, one distinct from other ethical reflections on earth and environment. James Cone's penetrating question, "Whose earth is it, anyway?",[15] is a robust example of the distinct perspective that the subaltern oppositional gaze brings into ethical reflections.

Joerg Rieger articulates in a compelling way the theological and ethical significance of seeing as subaltern oppositional gaze. "Ecotheological concerns shift if we begin not with the contemporary picture of reality but on the streets, in tensions and conflicts, in situations of pressure where there is suffering and oppression – in places that for Christians bear some resemblance to places where the disciples saw Jesus at work."[16] For Rieger, the mediation of the subaltern oppositional gaze is theologically imperative because it shares the same standpoint of the Jesus movement which perceived particular experiences of brokenness, sickness, alienation, suffering, and oppression as structural manifestations of sin. Reflecting on the reality of environmental racism, Larry Rasmussen makes the following observation: "To discuss human alienation from nature and the land without the history of white supremacy is not only an intellectual crime, it is a theological and moral one."[17] In short, Christian ethics begins from a subaltern oppositional gaze where particular experiences of the reign of death are problematized in relation to the "powers and principalities."

Let us now turn to the subaltern oppositional gaze of the NBA, to see how the movement perceives the colonization of their lifeworld. As Medha Patkar rightly puts it, "Who uses the resources? To what end? At what cost? Seeking answers to these questions is environmentalism for us."[18] The subaltern oppositional gaze does not begin with grand ecological and cosmological visions and narratives; rather, it begins with issues of survival and livelihood. Addressing the issue of the displacement of adivasis by the dam, Sanjay Sangvai articulates how the NBA's perception is different from the dominant environmentalisms which tend to romanticize and museumize the indigenous communities: "The issue at stake is to achieve the right to life, livelihood, autonomy, dignity, and justice within a heterogeneous complex political system like India and not some insulated island of apolitical anthropology."[19] In short, the subaltern oppositional gaze of the NBA perceives the crisis as a political issue of neo-colonial pillage, one that disempowers the community by taking away their moral agency. Stated differently, the subaltern oppositional gaze poses the question, "Whose earth is it, anyway?"

Social Analytical Mediation: The Subaltern Mediation of Social Theories

The social analytical mediation informed by the subaltern oppositional gaze enables earth ethics to move beyond a romantic fascination for pristine nature and conservationism into a radical critique of the prevailing social relations, and the instrumental rationality of our civilization. The subaltern oppositional gaze requires other mediations, such as social analytical, to grow into a subaltern oppositional knowledge. This underscores the methodological significance of social theories for theological and ethical reflections. Before we begin to examine a variety of social theories that have been used by subaltern social movements, it is important to recognize the standpoint from which social movements approach social theories. The social movements in general and the NBA in particular are not creations of social theories. It is not the awareness received from the social theories that led to the emergence of the social movements. Rather, social theories help social movements to mediate the transition from oppositional gaze to oppositional consciousness and politics. Again, such a transition does not happen as a disembodied engagement with theories per se, but it is in the coming together of diverse identities and movements that these social theories become mediatory and prompt oppositional knowledge and praxis.

The Narmada Bachao Andolan has always recognized the significance of the mediation of social theories in their struggle to decolonize their lifeworld. The complex and multiple identities of the communities in the valley compelled the NBA to reject all totalizing theories and to embrace social theories that are politically committed to radical changes in social relations while recognizing differences. In other words, the social theories enable the NBA to combine struggles for redistribution, recognition, and alternatives. These theories can be broadly categorized as social ecology perspectives, Gandhian perspectives, eco-feminist perspectives, adivasi and dalit perspectives, and eco-socialist perspectives.

Social ecology perspectives

The emergence of social ecology as a social theory to mediate the crisis of earth and its inhabitants needs to be understood in relation to dominant environmental theories such as deep ecology,[20] which legitimize and perpetuate the enclosure of the land, water, and forests in the name of conservation. They diagnose the problem as anthropocentrism with its claim of human uniqueness with intrinsic worth to dominate other species, and propose biocentrism or biocentric egalitarianism as the alternative to save the planet. The subaltern oppositional gaze rejects such theories because they are misanthropic, racist, and social Darwinistic.[21]

This is the context in which subaltern movements opt for the social analytical mediation of social ecology. For Murray Bookchin, the founder of social ecology, "the idea of dominating nature stems from human domination, initially in hierarchical forms as feminists so clearly understand, and later in class and statist forms."[22] This position underscores the importance of perceiving the ecological crisis as a crisis of prevailing social relations. In other words, the colonization of the lifeworld, which reduces nature to a passive object for exploitation and alienates human beings from their livelihoods, is the crisis that we face today.

The commitment of social ecology to denounce all forms of domination and hierarchy further exposes the interrelationship between ecocide and impoverishment. Reharmonization between humans and humans is essential for the reharmonization between humans and nature. This points to the significance of combining struggles for redistribution, recognition, and ecological justice. Stated differently, for subaltern communities ecological consciousness is a radical discernment of their exclusion and marginalization, and how they contribute to the distress of earth and its children. That means ecological action is a radical political action to transform the way our society is organized. This awareness will motivate the community to denounce the capitalist growth model, which reduces them to commodities and alienates them from their livelihoods.

Gandhian perspectives

Mahatma Gandhi has been a source of inspiration for many in the NBA including Baba Amte and Medha Patkar in their struggles to de-colonize the lifeworld. Gandhian groups and movements are active in the National Alliance of Peoples' Movements (NAPM). As William F. Fisher rightly articulates, Gandhi has been used as an icon by both the pro-dam lobby and the NBA to gain legitimization for their re-spective causes.[23] While the proponents of the dam claim that the dam would integrate Nehru's modernist vision with the Gandhian preferential option for the poor in rural India, the Andolan would invoke the Gandhian legacy of self-sufficiency and resistance against imperialism, and place it on the continuum of subaltern politics against colonization by affirming self-determination. Hence, it is im-portant to see how the NBA appropriates the Gandhian legacy as a means for social analytical mediation.

For Gandhi, the political struggle for *swaraj* (self-rule) was part of his spiritual quest for truth through non-violent means. Stated dif-ferently, the Gandhian models of political resistance against forces of colonization – civil disobedience, *satyagraha* (fast unto death), boycotting foreign goods, etc. – have a profound theological signifi-cance as acts of *tapas* (self-purification). As Gandhi observed, "The fact is that all spiritual fasts always influence those who come within the zone of their influence. That is why spiritual fasting is described as *tapas*. And all *tapas* invariably exert purifying influence on those on whose behalf it is undertaken."[24] Here Gandhi discerns the domi-nant imperialistic social relations as manifestations of sin, and resis-tance to systemic sin is, therefore, a spiritual quest; the only way to witness to the truth. He further argues that since resistance against sinful structures is *tapas*, it enables those who participate in the resis-tance to purify themselves so that they can embody the change that they dream about.

Gandhi's ecological philosophy was based on the "economy of permanence" as narrated in his oft-quoted statement, "the earth provides enough to satisfy everyman's need, but not everyman's greed."[25] Here Gandhi identifies human greed to accumulate more as the basis for all manifestations of imperialism and conquest. Conservationism and wilderness therefore do not find space in the Gandhian ecological philosophy, or a shift from anthropocentrism to biocentrism. Rather, consistent resistance against the capitalist mode of production, with a genuine commitment to revitalize village-centered economies based on the vision of *swaraj*, is the soul of Gandhi's ecological philosophy.[26]

The Gandhian vision of *swaraj* has the potential to inspire postcolonial communities in their struggles against neo-liberal imperialism which devours their livelihoods and landscapes. For Gandhi, self-rule, self-sufficiency, and self-determination are foundational to his village-centered economics. The colonization of the lifeworld can be resisted only when communities have self-rule, economic self-sufficiency, and the freedom to make decisions on their lives. The spinning wheel and the *khadi* cloth symbolize the determination of the communities to be the subjects of their destiny. "Real *swaraj* will come not by acquisition of authority by a few but by the acquisition of the capacity by all to resist authority when it is abused."[27]

Eco-feminist perspectives

The strong presence of women in leadership is unique in contemporary peoples' movements in India. They are at the forefront of organizing road blocks, sit-ins on fasts unto death, going to jail, facing rising waters, negotiating with the government, and creating alternatives. Women's leadership in movements like the NBA brings a new dimension to the struggle. Even though eco-feminism as an interdisciplinary initiative attempts to expose the connection between violence against women and the destruction of nature valorizing the essential traits of women in protecting nature, we approach it differently from the perspective of Indian feminist scholars who associate with movements such as the NBA.[28]

Unlike the dominant strands in eco-feminism which build the theory based on "biological" and "essential" connections between women and nature, feminists from the South approach the issue from the vantage point of women's right to have control over resources and their struggle against patriarchal, caste, and economic violence. They begin with a plea to reject the dominant feminist attempt to present women as a unitary category, and to recognize the reality of multiple forms of domination such as caste, class, and race. As Aruna Gnanadason rightly observes, this will lead to the discernment that, "ecofeminist analysis must acknowledge the internal contradictions among women and cannot ignore that there are systems and structures in place that distribute power over the use of the resources of the earth unjustly and unequally, even among women."[29] Such discernment enables us to go beyond totalizing eco-feminist theories and to learn how women integrate their particular experiences of domination with the distress of earth and participate actively in the struggles for survival.[30]

The concept of "production of life" developed by feminist theologian and social activist Gabrielle Dietrich is important here. According to Dietrich, the sexual division of labor is, along with capitalist and market exploitation, one of the root causes of the contemporary ecological crisis. The production and sustenance of life is considered a private affair of women devoid of any monetary value, but glorified as an ecological virtue. Dietrich proposes to address the sexual division of labor not by drawing "women into the market economy, brutalizing their ecological perceptions, but it has to happen in such a way that it draws men into the field of production and sustenance of life and humanizes their perceptions."[31] Dietrich in her eco-feminist perspective goes beyond the essentialist attempt to valorize women as natural environmentalists and instead proposes a radical critique of the sexual division of labor and asserts production of life as the foundational criterion to determine our production and consumption patterns, to create sustainable communities.

Bina Agarwal's concept of "feminist environmentalism" further strengthens this position. According to her, because women are the primary victims of environmental destruction due to their location in the sexual division of labor, their experience would provide a "gendered impulse" to their response and resistance to the distress of earth. Women being the repositories of knowledge about nature, their resistance is mediated by the spirit of production and sustenance of life. Here Agarwal does not argue for an essentialist view of women as natural environmentalists; rather, she locates the adivasi and dalit women's responses and perspectives in their material reality of dependence on nature for survival with actual physical engagement with nature, and the knowledge generated in that process. Like Dietrich, she too calls for universalizing the ethos of production of life "by declassing and degendering the ways in which productive and reproductive activities are organized (within and outside the home) and how property, resources, knowledge and power are distributed."[32] Agarwal summarizes the alternative proposal of feminist environmentalism as follows:

An alternative approach ... needs to be *transformational* rather than welfarist – where development, redistribution and ecology link in mutually regenerative ways. This would necessitate complex and interrelated changes such as in the *composition* of what is produced, the *technologies* used to produce it, the processes by which decisions on products and technologies are arrived at, the *knowledge systems* on which such choices are based, and the class and gender *distribution* of products and tasks.[33]

Adivasi and dalit perspectives[34]

The primary victims of the earth's distress in India are the adivasis and the dalits. Industrialization, big dams, expressways, mining, agrobusiness, the green revolution, biological parks – all these add new layers of oppression to the subaltern groups. Survival is the greatest ecological crisis that the adivasis and the dalits face today. The colonization of the lifeworld through development and globalization alienates them from their common property resources such as land, forest, and water, and thereby makes them environmental refugees. Adivasi and dalit perspectives therefore bring new questions such as who has control over common property resources, who determines national interest when the subaltern landscapes and livelihoods are snatched away from them in the name of progress and national interest, and who decides what is progress and development.

It is in this context that the concept of "ecological ethnicity," developed by Pramod Parajuli, becomes significant. It represents communities such as adivasis and dalits who "maintain the rhythm of circularity and regenerative cycles of nature's economy by cultivating appropriate cosmovisions, observing related rituals, and practicing prudence in the ways they care about nature, harvest from nature, nurture nature, and in turn are nurtured."[35] Nature for ecological ethnicities is integral to their livelihoods and survival. Their engagement with nature is primarily mediated through their struggle for survival.[36] Such an engagement brings radically different perspective to their understanding of nature.

The dominant discourse of our times oscillates between nature as a resource pile waiting to be plundered and engineered, and nature as wilderness to be fenced off from human – ecological ethnicities – use. It is in this context that the observation by C. K. Janu, the adivasi leader of Kerala, of the semiotic metamorphosis of "jungle" into "forest" becomes poignant.[37] Jungle, the organic abode of the ecological ethnicities, became forest – a stockpile of resources under state control – thanks to the intervention of the state and market forces through various forest acts and development projects. In India, right from the colonial period, in the name of conservation, deforestation, social forestry, biological reserves, and national parks, the state enacted various forest acts which resulted in the exclusion of ecological ethnicities from their traditional habitats. The postcolonial state in its commitment to "progress" and "development" unleashed a regime of ethnocide displacing millions from their homelands. "Eighty percent of the nation's mineral wealth and seventy two percent of the forests, water, and other natural resources are found in tribal lands. Thus, mines, industrial estates, hydroelectric projects, urban centers, and planned population transfer signaled the internal colonization of tribal homelands."[38]

The adivasi and dalit perspective is based on a symbiotic relationship between ecological ethnicities and their homelands mediated through their struggle for survival. The crisis of earth for them, therefore, is a crisis of survival. So an adivasi and dalit perspective affirms the issue of livelihood as foundational to any discourse on earth ethics. Further, for them, land is not *terra nullius* – wilderness or resource without meaning and ownership – rather it is a cultural landscape where the landscape is constructed, formed, and evolved through the symbiotic relationship between ecological ethnicities and nature. The landscape is also the site of the affirmation of their identity and historic resistance against all manifestations of colonial invasions. The *terra nullius* of development intervention is a sacred space permeated with the spirits of the ancestors, the gods, the goddesses, and the demons. It is the diverse meanings that the above mentioned symbiosis brings to nature that makes self-rule or autonomy the political focus for adivasi perspectives on nature.[39]

An earth ethics from the standpoint of the ecological ethnicities is a critical praxis "of asserting the importance of place, of seeking greater control over one's life and life sphere, of redefining what independence and freedom mean, of strengthening self-governance, of reclaiming the sovereignty that has been systematically taken away, …[and] of seeking to democratize the state and other economic and cultural processes."[40] In an anthology of the adivasi resilience for autonomy in Kerala, the etymological meaning of the Malayalam word for courage (*thantedam*) has been interpreted as the striving for one's own space (*thante idam*).[41] The adivasi and dalit perspectives in other words clamor for the unalienable right of the community to have self-determination over their lives and their livelihoods. In the ultimate analysis, reclaiming one's own space is the reclamation of the symbiotic relationship that has been erased by development interventions. This is the unique perspective that mediation of the theories of ecological ethnicities brings to our discourse.

Eco-socialist perspectives

Medha Patkar of the NBA in an interview back in 1992 categorically said that "the combination of green and red values and ideas has constituted our ideological position."[42] "Green and red" has been part of the environmental rhetoric for a long time, though for many the term "eco-socialism" is an oxymoron. It is in this context that we try to understand eco-socialist perspectives to lift up the significance of eco-socialism for grassroots earth ethics. Eco-socialism emerges out of the belief that ecology and socialism share in common a rejection of the thingification of life forms under the dictatorship of money. It is a perspective that identifies the insatiable quest for accumulation and profit of the capitalist project that leads to catastrophic disaster for earth and its inhabitants. The contemporary eco-socialist reflections have initiated a new, but deep and critical, engagement with Marxism to understand critically the causes of, and the solutions for, the ecological crisis.[43]

An eco-socialist analysis would inform us that the ecological crisis is inherently connected with the capitalist mode of production and consumption based on the logic of unlimited accumulation. It further exposes how the ecological crisis threatens the very survival of the subalterns through a variety of consequences such as impoverishment, alienation, and displacement from their livelihoods. From an eco-socialist point of view, the challenge is to "re-embed" the economy in the social and natural environment, where choices and priorities of production and consumption are no longer determined by the "invisible hand." For Joel Kovel, it requires the emergence of an alternative ecological mode of production which re-centers production toward the creation of the flourishing and integrity of the community of creation.[44] In this sense, as Michael Lowy observes, "breaking with the productivist ideology of progress – in its capitalist and/or bureaucratic form – and opposed to the infinite expansion of a mode of production and consumption that destroys nature, it [ecosocialism] represents the original attempt to connect the fundamental ideas of Marxian socialism to the gains of critical ecology."[45]

For Kovel, eco-socialism is "both destination and the road to be built as we travel."[46] As a destination beyond capital, it is utopian but ever remains an open project. For both Lowy and Kovel, the *telos* of eco-socialism is the realization of a "moral economy." This moral economy perceives human beings as active and transformative agents in the process of reintegrating the economic into the ecological, the social, and the political. According to Lowy, the transition to the eco-socialist society would lead "not only to a new mode of production and an egalitarian and democratic society, but also to an alternative mode of life, a new ecosocialist civilization, beyond the reign of money, beyond consumption habits... and beyond the unlimited production of commodities... that are harmful to the environment."[47] Kovel, in his vision of this moral economy of eco-socialism, goes further and states that "in the changed need structure that emerges, mutual obligation, respect for limits, and feelings of solidarity and spiritual wholeness arise; and these can overcome the hunger of possession and domination that propels the capitalist economy."[48] In short, the combination of green and red in the eco-socialist project is not just the stirring of different social theories. Rather, it is the historical alliance of working-class movements and ecological movements along with other grassroots movements at the periphery striving to de-colonize the lifeworld.

As we have seen in this section, the mediation of social theories occurs in the social movements through a coalition of diverse movements and identities. The coming together of diverse social theories in the context of historic struggles against the colonization of the lifeworld refines social movements' political commitment by transforming them from totalizing grand narratives to mediators of oppositional consciousness and alternative politics.

Hermeneutical Mediation: Subaltern Engagement with Religious Resources

Hermeneutical mediation, as the title itself suggests, is an attempt to draw insights from the religious traditions of communities to understand the crisis of the earth, and to become envisioned for creating a redeemed earth. Explaining the significance of hermeneutical mediation, Leonardo Boff asserts that liberation theology was born out of a twofold experience: political and theological. While the political perspective affirmed the poor as a social and epistemological locus and developed not only a social critique but also a social praxis that would make the dreams of the victims a historical reality, theology, the second experience, occurred to deepen the first. The base Christian communities realized that "the best way to interpret the pages of scripture was to compare with the pages of life."[49] Such hermeneutical engagement revealed to them that God is the giver of life and the one who inspires the victims to organize and struggle against the idols of death. This understanding of theology as the second experience is relevant for developing a grassroots earth ethics from the epistemological locus of wounded earth and wounded humanity. Engagement with the religious resources of communities from these bleeding points of our times will enable us to see the Divine who motivates us to strive for a redeemed earth and humanity.

As we discussed briefly in the third chapter, the mediation of religious resources in the political praxis of secular social movements in a religiously pluralistic society is risky business. In the Indian context, with the growth of religious fanaticism and the communalization of the social fabric of the nation, engagement with religious resources and ascribing them universal authority and preeminence is nothing but dangerous. Further, with the patriarchal and casteist nature of the "given" religious sources and traditions, hermeneutical mediation can continue to valorize and perpetuate social relations of exclusion and domination.[50]

This is the context in which we lift up the hermeneutical mediation as practiced by the NBA. As we have seen earlier, River Narmada is Narmada *Mata* for the inhabitants in the valley. Both the Hindu and the indigenous traditions share a pantheistic worldview which inspires them to respect and protect the landscape. The NBA invokes such myths and symbols extensively in its campaign.[51] For example, the age-old practice of *Parikarma* (circumambulating the banks of the river) has been used as a campaign to create awareness in the valley and to organize the community around their sacred river and landscape. The temples in the valleys are used intentionally for the meetings of the movement because using such locations defy the religious ideologies of exclusion which prevent dalits and other socially ostracized people from entering the sacred space. The religious festivals of various communities and festive observations such as Ambedkar Jayanti (the birthday of Ambedkar) are celebrated by the NBA as part of their resistance and re-creation. The NBA's assertion of the valley as the cultural landscape of the communities has been a foundational argument against the project of "accumulation by displacement." During the monsoon season, when the communities face submergence, they incorporate adivasi rituals into their rites of facing waters. In 1989 in Hapeshwar the hill adivasis by the thousands gathered in a ritual of holding their bows and arrows up in the air, with the Narmada water in their palms, renewing their determination to resist the dam until their last breath. What is the significance of such hermeneutical mediations? How is it different from the appropriation of religious myths and symbols by the religious right? William Fisher's observations in the valley are helpful here in our search to find answers to these questions:

> Here, the environment is not merely a stockroom of resources, but a living landscape where the natural and the supernatural are intricately intertwined. Spiritual power which resides within trees, rocks, or hills is perceived as intervening actively in people's lives. Virtually all of them emphasized their ties to ancestral land, to the river, to the goddess Narmada, and to the local spiritual world: "our gods cannot move from this place," one said to me; "how can we move without them?"[52]

A re-reading of, and a re-engagement with, the religious resources in light of the political gives profound spiritual meaning to the struggle against the colonization of the lifeworld. The slogans, the songs, the poetics, and the alternative re-creations that have emerged in the struggle are manifestations of this spirituality. Unlike the saffronized green movements, hermeneutical mediation in the case of the NBA functions to support political praxis. For example, evocation of the metaphor of mother Narmada has strengthened the agency and leadership of women in the valley and in the movement than the revival of cultural nationalism. This is evident in the fact that the NBA provided an alternative political gamut by uniting people from diverse religious and ethnic backgrounds.

Before concluding this section, I will provide an in-depth analysis of one religious metaphor that has been used frequently by both the dam lobby and the Andolan to understand the politics of hermeneutical mediation. Sacrifice is a metaphor that has been used widely by the state to legitimize its colonization of the lifeworld. Drawing from the religious and nationalist traditions, the state gave a clarion call to the inhabitants in the valley to sacrifice for the "common good" and "national interest." Way back in 1948, addressing the displaced of the Hirakud dam, Prime Minister Nehru exhorted: "If you are to suffer, you should suffer in the interest of the country."[53] The story of the sixty years of independence and development, for the majority of the Indian population, has been nothing but a tryst with this exhortation, to suffer for the common good.

Sacrifice as a religious metaphor is of profound significance to the communities in the Narmada valley as the River Narmada is considered the supreme symbol of sacrifice, and the NBA too invokes this character of Narmada. However, hermeneutical mediation of the NBA has never condoned the exhortation to suffer. Rather, they challenged the legitimacy of such religiously motivated exhortations by affirming the moral agency of the community to make decisions for their livelihood, landscape, and community resources. At the same time, the NBA appropriates the metaphor of suffering and sacrifice in an oppositional way. Political campaigns of resistance, such as fasting unto death and *Jal Samadhi* (facing waters), are perfect examples of the highest commitment to offer one's life in the struggle to decolonize their lives and their lifeworlds.

To conclude, the NBA recognizes the religious traditions of the communities as important resources in their struggle to decolonize their lifeworld. Here they appropriate the religious traditions as resources that can inspire the communities to resist the process of desacralization of the river, the valley, and the communities. The attempt here is not to romanticize either the movement or the religious traditions. Rather, as Gabriele Dietrich rightly observes, "while the people unite in the struggle with the slogan: '*Amu Akha Ek Che!*' (we are all one) transgressing the boundaries set by the state [and religions], they also quietly subvert the divisiveness of their own culture, overcome exploitation and finally transcend their limitations forging unity without giving up on their identity."[54] This is the politics and spirituality of hermeneutical mediation.

Praxeological Mediation: Subaltern Alternative Politics

The oppositional consciousness of the subalterns, as we have learned from the Narmada Saga, is transformational as it emerges out of threats to the very survival of the subalterns. Praxeological mediation represents the transformative action, where the oppositional consciousness becomes flesh through concrete political actions. In the case of social movements such as the NBA, praxeological mediation involves both resistance and re-creation: resistance against all manifestations of the colonization of the lifeworld, and re-creating alternatives. It is not a macro project per se of bringing about holistic change based on grand narratives or theories. Rather, it is an engagement with concrete instances of colonization and alienation at the micro level. However, mediated by critical social theories, such micro engagements discern the rootedness of the particular crisis in the prevailing pattern of social relations. In other words, the transformative politics of the subaltern praxeological mediation is located at particular instances of colonization and alienation, but committed to the wider politics of creating a different world.

The story of the Narmada Bachao Andolan is the story of a valley's resilient determination to resist mega dams. In the course of this historic struggle against the development interventions of the state and the capitalist project of "accumulation by displacement," the praxeological mediation of the NBA has gone beyond the issue of mega dams, while keeping the resistance against the dams alive. Some of the slogans to have emerged in the social movements in India underscore this oppositional consciousness of linking local struggles to wider struggles for justice, recognition, and life. The NBA's slogan *Narmada Bachao, Manav Bachao* (Save Narmada, Save Humanity), and the National Fishworkers' Federation's slogan "Protect Waters, Protect Life" are robust examples of this alternative politics. For them, the local struggles to protect their land, water, and forest from capitalist plunder and development interventions are integral to the wider commitment to "have life and to have it abundantly." The title of a nationwide campaign organized by the National Alliance of Peoples' Movements was *Desh Bachao, Desh Banao Andolan* (Save the Nation, Re-create the Nation Movement). Here, praxelogical mediation combines both resistance and re-creation. In the light of these two characteristics of grassroots subaltern alternative politics – an oppositional consciousness of the embeddedness of local instances of colonization in the prevailing social relations, and the combination of resistance and re-creation – let us examine the praxeological mediation of social movements.

Alternative politics and neo-colonialism

Social movements in India, like the NBA, in their politics to reclaim moral agency confront particular instances of colonization and alienation. In the context of neo-colonial onslaught, such localized struggles for *roji, roti, kapda aur makan* (employment, bread, clothing, and shelter) have profound political significance. For example the movement against the Coca Cola plant in Plachimada, Kerala is fighting against the environmental problems caused by the plant, such as the plundering of water resources and pollution through waste disposal. However, the movement has become a symbol of peoples' resilience against neo-colonial invasion through asserting peoples' right over their common property resources. Reclaiming peoples' right to life and livelihood is an absolute rejection of the privatization and commodification of natural resources, and hence antithetical to the logic of neo-liberalism. Re-creating peoples' alternatives in the fields of water harvesting, power generation and the like dismantle the neo-liberal myth that there are no viable alternatives to the logic of market. In short, the subaltern praxeological mediation is essentially an alternative politics against neo-colonialism.

Alternative politics and the internal colonization of the lifeworld

The appropriation of the Habermasian concept of lifeworld in the Indian context cannot ignore the pervasiveness of the internal colonization of the lifeworld by patriarchy, caste system, cultural nationalism, homophobia, and communalism. As we have seen earlier, external colonization directly and indirectly strengthens the forces of internal colonization. As Gabriele Dietrich rightly observes, "without the interaction of progressive social movements, the lifeworld will either easily disintegrate … or it will fossilize into rigid patriarchal and chauvinistic forms which project religious, ethnic or caste-based community identity at the cost of women, children, and all democratically-minded sections."[55] Arif Dirlik further elaborates this issue by integrating the struggles against both internal and external colonization: "The local is valuable as a site for resistance to the global, but only to the extent that it also serves as the site of negotiation for abolishing inequality and oppression inherited from the past."[56] Realization of the need to combine the struggles against external forms of colonization with the struggles against internal colonization is a unique characteristic of the praxeological mediation of social movements in India. In other words, subaltern praxeological mediation involves an unwavering commitment to the struggles for redistribution and recognition.

Alternative politics and the state and governance

Unlike the "old social movements," in theory and in practice the new social movements are not interested in capturing state power by violent means. Rather, the alternative transformative politics of the new social movements are committed to bringing in alternative forms of participatory and socialist democracy. Resistance against the "oppressive, omnipotent and omnipresent" state does not mean that the social movements are against the institution of the state. The NBA has been criticizing all institutions of parliamentary democracy in India including the Judiciary for not exercising their authority to protect the fundamental and constitutional rights of communities. The slogan *Hamare gaon mein hamare raj* (Our rule in our villages) was not a rejection of the state, but rather "an assertion of the rights and decentralized decision-making by the people on the issues affecting their life."[57] As the NAPM categorically explains its dialectical approach towards the State, the social movements affirm the role of the State "to fulfill its historic role of protector of social justice and social welfare and not be the *chowkidar* (watchman) of corporate interests, as is being done today, in the age of Globalization."[58]

The re-assertion of the institution of state needs to be understood in the context of the alternative discourse on governance. The Earth Charter realized its importance and determines to "Strengthen democratic institutions at all levels, and provide transparency and accountability in governance, inclusive participation in decision-making, and access to justice."[59] The Provisions of Panchayats (Extension to the Scheduled Areas) Act, 1996, is just such an example from India which envisions an alternative vision of governance and democracy. This Act recognizes the local community in the adivasi villages as the highest authority to determine decisions and policies for their life and livelihood. Social movements like the NBA are, in their praxeological mediation, taking seriously local forms of democratic institutions to translate their vision of governance, and participatory and socialist democracy.

Alternative politics and the economy of permanence

Grassroots subaltern alternative politics, in its commitment to experiment with alternatives to the dominant models, is developing an economy of permanence. This model derives from the realization that the capitalist pattern of production and consumption, based on the logic of accumulation and profit, can be challenged only by developing viable alternative patterns of production and consumption that are labor intensive, ecologically sensitive, democratic, participatory, and just. The shift from the capitalist economy of accumulation to a socialist economy of permanence is not just an "improved form of capitalism." For capitalism, religion, spirituality, rice, beans, and even our bodies are nothing but commodities. The alternative vision is not the globalization of market and profit mechanisms, but the affirmation and celebration of alternative values such as solidarity, equality, and respect for diversity. This vision of an economy of permanence calls for a new economic order, a new concept of ownership, and different social and ecological relations. For K. C. Abraham, the new values that emerge out of alternative politics such as "conservation, not consumerism; need, not greed; enabling power, not dominating power, [and] integrity of creation, not exploitation of creation" provide a new direction to ethics.[60]

How do we achieve it? According to Bastiaan Wielenga, "whatever can be done to upgrade eroded soils, introduce sensible water-harvesting methods, save a wide variety of seeds, block crazy mega projects, genetically manipulated crops and so on, is a contribution to the future in which a different type of society will hopefully evolve after long struggles."[61] It is a negation of the instrumental reason and an affirmation that to know is to enter into communion with the other. It is a search for a redeemed science and technology that collaborates with an economy of permanence in affirming and celebrating life and freedom, beginning with those whose lives and freedom are threatened.

An economy of permanence also leads to the emergence of alternative lifestyles. The discourse on lifestyle in the crucible of the political praxis of social movements is entirely different from the dominant environmentalist discourses on lifestyle. The attempt here is not to exhort the wretched of the earth to control and limit their consumption to save the planet. Instead, the lifestyle debate in the social movements aims to improve quality of life. The alternative politics of the social movements perceives "good life" differently from the dominant worldview. For Maria Mies and Vandana Shiva, the debate on lifestyle is a debate over values:

> Self-sufficiency, co-operation instead of competitiveness with others and with nature, respect for all creatures on the earth and their diversity, belief in the subjectivity of not only human beings but also non-human beings, communality instead of aggressive self-interest, creativity instead of the 'catching-up-with-the-Joneses' factor that is responsible for much superfluous consumption in our societies and to find satisfaction and joy in one's work and life.[62]

Sanjay Sangvai of the NBA observes that the fetish of consumerism fails to recognize the human flourishing and enrichment that the "non-commodity aspects of life" offer to personal and community life. "An alternative lifestyle is conducive to an enriched individual and social life as it provides spaces for plurality, more diverse and authentic expressions of aesthetic and cultural values of individuals and communities. It brings forward the productive capacities and creativity in all individuals and groups, besides providing a dignified livelihood."[63] In short, grassroots subaltern alternative politics is an outright rejection of the fetishism and absolutization of the economy of accumulation, and it is done by re-creating alternative economies of permanence.

Alternative politics and a new internationalism

Social movements, in spite of their local embeddedness in resisting particular instances of colonization, are not isolated inward-looking islands. Rather, they are part of an alternative politics at the global level: the politics of a new internationalism. This new internationalism is a rainbow coalition of a host of social movements which not only strengthen one another through solidarity, but also enable one another to be cautious of the internal colonization of the lifeworld.

It is important here to recognize that the alternative politics of new internationalism is suspicious of the homogenizing and totalizing tendencies inherent in "global" projects such as global ethics and "globalization from below." Barbara Rossing's compelling analysis of the concept of *oikoumene* is instructive here. Exegeting the biblical meaning of *oikoumene*, and its use in the historical tradition, Rossing states that "the ecumenical history of the Roman Empire reminds us that those at the center will tend to construct a single unified household in which those at the margins are silenced for the sake of unity and universality."[64] This has been the experience of minorities in postcolonial societies under nationalist movements. The particular struggles of the minorities were forcefully subsumed within the dominant agenda of the nationalist movements.[65] Grassroots earth ethics in its alternative praxeological mediation strives to be vigilant about this inherent danger of domination of overarching agendas. The alternative politics of new internationalism always keeps alive the tension between conflict and consensus. Unlike the monocolor of the flag of *oikoumene,* the flags of the new internationalism form a rainbow, affirming the commitment to protect life while recognizing pluriformity.

Celebration: Subaltern Spirituality of Life in Community

Celebration, for grassroots earth ethics, is the stage at which we realize that our transformative action is the anticipatory sign of the reign of God. It is "the advent of divine redemption mediated through historical-social liberations, the moment when the utopia of integral liberation is anticipated under fragile signs, symbols and rites."[66] It is an option for life; a confrontation with the logic of death and the celebration of life.

At the office of the NBA in Barwani, Madhya Pradesh, there is an inscription on the wall of the main hall where the community gathers frequently to share, reflect, plan, and strategize together: *Sangharsh hi Jiwan he* (Struggle is Life). This slogan provides profound meaning to the movement. In one sense it is autobiographical; their life is an unending narrative of struggle. Their very survival is a struggle. But it is also a statement of their collective faith. It is in their struggle to resist and re-create that they find meaning of life and celebrate it. Celebration of life in grassroots earth ethics does not translate to festivities for political victories. Rather, it is the affirmation of the community's resolve to be alternative: to become a sustainable community of moral agents. When a community becomes an intentional community, reclaiming its moral agency, and experimenting with the re-creation of viable alternatives to the logic and manifestations of internal and external colonization, life blossoms.

Towards a Grassroots Earth Ethics: A Foretaste

The cartography of grassroots earth ethics drawn above articulates the alternative constructive method that this book proposes. But there remains a question still unanswered: What is theological in this proposal? The attempt in this final section is not to "Christianize" grassroots earth ethics, but to understand grassroots earth ethics as theological and ethical praxis.

Grassroots earth ethics as theological praxis uses hermeneutical mediation to visualize its project of the realization of a different world. However, unlike the dominant ethical models in Christian ethics, grassroots earth ethics does not consider the "given" sources such as scripture and tradition as the authoritative sources. Rather, scripture and traditions are useful resources as long as they inform and enrich their projects of liberation. It is not a rejection of the place of the Bible in Christian ethics, but a rejection of the claim of inherent authority of the text apart from the community that reads it. In and of itself the Bible has no authority; it becomes revelatory when it enables the community to experience the epiphany in the altered earth and among wounded humanity. When inspired by the presence of the Divine in their experience of otherness, and the stories of the biblical communities living out their faith in the Divine by challenging the claims of the absolute sovereignty of the empires and the powers and principalities, the authority is being shifted from the Bible to the intentional communities of our times who continue this tradition of bearing witness to the movement of life. So the Bible becomes the Word of God when it unveils this experience of epiphany, and empowers the victims of our times to believe in the possibility of a "beyond of totality" inspired by the epiphany of the absolute Other.

Movements of Testimony

Drawing inspiration from Rebecca Chopp's concept of "poetics of testimony," I would like to call social movements, "movements of testimony." For Chopp, "poetics" stands for unconventional expressions that fashion and reshape the prevailing discourse by questioning its very logic and validity. Poetics is not controlled by theory, but it engages theory "to rename and refigure the real against the representations of dominant discourses."[67] Testimony is bearing witness, and it is sealed by the willingness to die. "The telling of these stories is for life, for the mending of life, the healing of life, the ability of life to live and survive and thus conquer this extremity."[68]

Social movements, from a theological and ethical point of view, are movements of testimony. They are a counter-hegemonic presence that consistently reject the prevailing sinful social relations, and tirelessly strive to create alternative social relations that are life affirming. Social movements as collectivities of the victims of capitalist and development gaze are testimonies of peoples' determination to survive. When "one is not authorized to live, then surviving is both resistance and hope,"[69] and hence their testimonies are profoundly Christian as they keep the flame of hope alive, proclaiming to the darkness, "we beg to differ."

Experiencing God: The Face of the Other as the Site of Epiphany

The testimonies of the social movements, as self expressions of collective resistance and hope, invoke an ethical response. This ethical response is called for from an experience of epiphany in the naked face of the Other. Jeffrey Stolle's interpretation of the Levinasian reading of the *Akedah* clarifies this point.[70] The Moriyya experience enabled Abraham to hear a new voice; God's voice in the face of the other. That experience of epiphany led to the metamorphosis of Isaac from a mute sacrificial victim to a speaking and knowing agent. And finally Abraham's response to the ethical summons of the naked face of the Other led to stopping murder. In other words, an ethical relation to the Other leads to an experience of epiphany and the reclaiming of the agency and the selfhood of the Other. For grassroots earth ethics, it is a new revelation of God: the revelation of the being and the politics of God.

The experience of epiphany in the face of the Other, says Enrique Dussel, is the basis for an ethics of liberation. The "de-base of the system" and striving for alternatives are the ethical praxis that is incumbent upon us in the era of neo-liberal colonization. For Dussel, the dismantling of the system is a deep act of faith: "The 'sin of the flesh' or the 'sin of Adam' is, precisely, idolatry, fetishism; it is treating the 'totality' as the ultimate, absolute totality and by so doing denying the existence of the other (Abel) and so of God (the absolute

Other)."[71] The testimonies of alternative political praxis to reject the totality of the system are hence profound spiritual acts of confessing the Divine as the absolute Other.

The ethics of liberation further affirms that it is the face-to-face political communion with the Other that summons ethical action. "The metaphysical (and eschatological) exteriority of the poor…situates them as the key (historical) reality and (epistemological) category of the whole ethics of liberation."[72] It is their being as exterior to the logic of the system that makes them the locus of Divine epiphany, and it is their real presence that empowers us to envision alternatives that transcend the totality of the system. This understanding of epiphany is the foundation for the ethics of liberation to confess God as the absolute Other; the One whose very presence is the negation of the totalizing claims of all manifestations of the system. When the system strips the community of its moral agency by taking away its right to remain exterior to the logic of system, we confront sin in its most hegemonic form, as it removes the community's ability to dream alternative visions. The Narmada as Other – a valley that refuses to die and a community that exposes the deception of the claims of totality of the system – summons us to alternative ethical praxis based on the conviction that the experience of the epiphany provides us: the dominant is not absolute and ultimate. In other words, the ethical praxis that strives to dismantle the totality of the system is grounded in faith in God – the Absolute Other.

Being Human: A New Humanity in the Community of Creation

The second half of the twentieth century witnessed a genuine attempt to analyze and address the ecological crisis from various perspectives in order to redeem nature from the "bondage to decay." All this analysis cites anthropocentrism as the root cause for the ecocide that we face as an earth community, exposing how the dominant theological anthropology and philosophical understanding of what it means to be human have intensified the degradation of nature and non-human beings. However, as we saw earlier, the dominant critique of anthropocentrism unfortunately led to misanthropy and reduced theological reflections on ecology and environment to conservationism and greening of mind. That makes it imperative for a grassroots earth ethics to initiate a subaltern discourse on theological anthropology to construct a non-anthropocentric anthropology that affirms the being and becoming of a new humanity in the community of creation.

The Yahwist narrative of the biblical creation story is instructive here. According to the J narrative, human beings are not created in the image of God, but out of *adama,* the arable soil. For Theodore Hiebert, this common origin of humanity from the arable soil affirms the relationality of human beings with the community of creation. Even the breath of life is shared by all creatures and hence human beings cannot claim any superiority in terms of having a soul or spiritual nature different from non-human beings. So *adam* is linked to *adama* in two ways: "*adama* is the stuff out of which *adam* is made and is also the primary object of his labor."[73]

The human vocation, according to the Yahwist, is to till and to cultivate the arable soil. The word that is used here for cultivation is different from *kabas* (subdue) which is used by the Priestly writers. It is *abad* which means to serve. It underscores human dependence on earth and not their domination over it. So the vision of human beings that emerged from a farming community – a community of ecological and social relations of solidarity and communion which is antithetical to the logic of the system – is that of dependent and responsible members of the ecosystem with the vocation to be farmers. A vision from the margins of imperial power rejects the spirit/matter dichotomy and thereby critiques all manifestations of domination, alienation, exclusion, and commodification. It proclaims the subaltern wisdom that, as dependent creatures, the welfare of the earth and each member of the ecosystem are integral to the flourishing of all. The concept of human vocation as serving the soil is an outright rejection of the colonial invading spirit that is inherent in contemporary systemic projects.

In her "Brief Credo," Sallie McFague affirms a brief but profound non-anthropocentric faith affirmation. The affirmation of God as embodied and incarnate is the foundation of this affirmation. The notion of God as "radical relationality, in intimate relationship with everything as the source, sustainer, and goal of every scrap, every quark, of creation"[74] provides a new sense of being a human in the world. She then presents the concept of world as God's body. Through this panentheistic position, she articulates God as both radically transcendent and radically immanent. For her, "Christian anthropology occurs within theology" because our understanding of who we are, and what we are, stem from who God is, and what God has done and is doing.

Based on the affirmation of God as embodied radical relationality and world as God's body, McFague develops her anthropology. "The view of the self or subject that emerges…is not the individual who is 'saved' for life in another world, but a thoroughly embodied, relational subject who understands herself or himself as interdependent with everyone and everything else."[75] The notion of world as God's body proclaims all creation as God "spread out" and God incarnate. Our task is to live in intimate relationship with God which means to live in intimate relationship with all manifestations of divine embodiment. McFague relates this to evil and soteriology. Sin and evil, according to her, are the belief that we can live outside this relationality. It is the unwillingness to reflect the image of God in us through our interrelatedness. The life and story of Jesus tells human beings how to do that. It is an experience of incarnation; a new creation.

> Deification, becoming like God or following Christ, means, then, becoming involved in such matters as ecological economics, the just distribution of resources on a sustainable basis. Deification, becoming like the incarnate God, means making the body of God healthier and more fulfilled. Salvation is worldly work. Human existence 'in the Spirit' means working 'in the body' so that it may flourish.[76]

McFague's constructive theology draws much from the eastern Orthodox tradition. In Orthodox theology human beings are understood as a microcosm which rejects all dichotomies and integrates human beings with the rest of the nature. The liturgy of the feast of the Baptism of our Lord proclaims creation as participating in Christ's saving work. Through the immersion of the incarnate Son of God, water becomes a vehicle for the salvific mission. The rationale for the Orthodox theological affirmation of human beings as the priests of creation is well articulated by Paulos Mar Gregorios:

> Replacing the concept of domination with the concept of stewardship will not lead us very far, for even in the latter there lies the hidden possibility of the objectification and alienation which are the root causes of the sickness of our civilization. Nature would remain some kind of property, owned not by us, of course, but by God, given into our hands for efficient and productive use.[77]

Humanity, as priests, has the vocation to mediate the creative and redemptive project of God with the whole creation while being thoroughly embedded in the community of creation.

The third world theologies of liberation nuance further this understanding of new humanity. For Leonardo Boff, anthropocentrism is not human beings per se; rather, it is "the imperial and anti-ecological anthropology at work in the contemporary dreams, projects, ideals, institutions and values."[78] In other words, anthropocentrism is being and becoming human according to the worldview of the totality. Sallie McFague rightly calls the anthropocentric anthropology's vision of human beings as "the hegemonic human being." "He is the figure in Leonardo da Vinci's drawing of a human being with arms and legs outstretched to the four corners of the cosmos; he is the 'man' of the American Declaration of Independence who is given life, liberty, and the pursuit of happiness; he is also the human being who is the object of consumer advertising."[79] This anthropology of anthropocentrism is sinful as it leads to both ecocide and fratricide.

For Boff, the construction of a non-anthropocentric anthropology is based on his affirmation of human beings as moral agents. Human beings are distinguished from the rest of creation not by biological superiority but by the character of human beings as moral entities. They are the only creatures in creation conceived and conceiving of themselves as ethical beings.

> Only human beings can, like the Samaritan in the Bible, stoop to aid the weaker party, protecting, supporting, renouncing, and compensating the other. But human beings can also break, destroy, and endanger the whole planetary system. Human beings become an ethical subject in that they can become a subject of history, fulfilling or failing it, for only humankind can produce tragic or fortunate results. The destiny of the whole earth system can depend on the ethical choices made by humanity.[80]

So while Boff denounces anthropocentrism, which is the product of imperialism and neo-liberalism, he affirms the agency of human beings as ethical beings in bringing about healing to wounded humanity and the wounded earth. "As sons and daughters of God, and not as despots, we prolong the creative activity of God, cultivating nature, improving it, and multiplying it, responsibly. In this way, not only God is creator, but so also, by divine plan, are we."[81]

How do we become co-creators in the Divine plan? As we have seen earlier, the confession of God the creator is the affirmation of the exteriority of the system and its logic as the site of Divine epiphany. The moral agency to become the co-creators, hence, belongs "to those who hunger, to the sick, to those tied down by a thousand chains. This imagination has its own historical agents, the sum total of those who make up the universe of the two-thirds of humanity who are marginalized and socially deprived."[82] In other words, the subalterns are the co-creators of the Divine plan.[83]

The theological anthropology of grassroots earth ethics is the affirmation of both the vocation of human beings to be the servants of the *adama*, and the responsibility of the human beings as ethical beings whose choices determine life and death. This anthropology rejects anthropocentrism as it is imperial and legitimizes atoning sacrifices for progress. It celebrates relationality, harmony, and the integrity of all creation, while respecting the right of each one to be different. A non-anthropocentric anthropology is therefore a faith in the possibility of a new humanity which mediates the praxis of a redeemed earth, beyond totality.

Creation and New Creation: The Subaltern Vision of a Redeemed Earth

The biblical visions of creation and new creation are foundational to the construction of a grassroots earth ethics. These visions of creation and new creation are the poetics of the testimonies of the Other. While the first creation story of the Priestly narrative reflects the pathos of exile, the vision of the new heaven and new earth narrated in the Book of Revelation is soaked with the blood and sweat of communities in the colonies of the Roman empire who are "stripped of their exteriority, of their dignity, of their rights, of their freedom, and transformed into instruments for the ends of the dominator, the Lord, the Idol, the Fetish."[84] In other words, the biblical visions of creation and new creation are the theological articulations of the ethics of liberation of the Other.

We live in a world where the dominant discourse always begins and ends with the affirmation of the absoluteness of the totality. The exteriority of the totality, we are told, has no ethical or epistemological significance. This was the context in which the subjugated knowledge of the dispossessed, the displaced, the enslaved, and the exiled got insurrected envisioning the visions of creation and new creation outside the logic of the system. The confessional affirmation of the exiled community, that God, the absolute Other is the Creator of the universe, is an affirmation of the sovereignty of the Divine over against the claims of the system. "If 'in the beginning God created' (Gen. 1: 1), it is because the Other is prior to the very principle of the cosmos, the system, the 'flesh'."[85]

As God's creation, all created beings share the trans-systemic being of the absolute Other. The theological anthropology of the first creation story where human beings are created in the image of God needs to be understood from this perspective. For the exiled community, the confession of God the creator and the affirmation of human beings as created in the image of God is more than a creation story. It is the subaltern theological foundation for resisting the colonization of their lifeworld.[86]

The Book of Revelation, on the other hand, emerged in the context of the imperial totalizing claims of the Roman Empire. The apocalyptic vision of the new heaven and the new earth is therefore the longings of a community and their landscape thingified by the imperial desire for accumulation, affirming the possibility of a "redeemed earth" beyond the totality. A closer analysis reveals that the apocalypse is a poetics of testimony, a vision that is born out of the determination of a community that refused to attribute the worth to receive "power and wealth and wisdom and might and honor and glory and blessing" to the imperial system. Rather, the dispossessed and the enslaved proclaim that "worthy is the Lamb that was slain." In other words, in the absurd poetics of dreaming visions that are illogical to the colonized imaginations, the Other becomes the site for a new discourse and praxis that envision a redeemed earth beyond the logic of the system.

Revelations' musings on the metaphor of water is foundational here. According to the seer, "the sea was no more" on the redeemed earth. As Catherine Keller states, it is a vision of hope as "the new creation entails the evaporation of the salt waters of tears and of seas."[87] But a deeper engagement with the text and the context is essential to make sense of the vision of the absence of sea. For Barbara Rossing, the Book of Revelation is a critique of the "realized eschatology" of Rome.[88] Because of its political and economic might as an imperial state, Rome considered itself eternal and sovereign. The sea was the primary agency for exercising this might and power – to invade, plunder, destroy, and enslave communities and nature in the colonies. To put it differently, the sea was the "route" to the state of "realized eschatology."

The city of Babylon reached this state of "realized eschatology" thanks to its imperial political economy. The list of cargos mentioned in Revelation 18 reveals how the landscape and the communities at the peripheries were commodified to this end.[89] The very presence of slaves among the cargo list underscores the pervasiveness of the colonization of the lifeworld. The realized eschatology of the system is always built on the colonized bodies of the other – the communities and nature. They are the ones destined to sacrifice at the altar of the Empire. The "realized eschatology" of the imperial political economy is hence inherently violent and destructive.

The vision of the new creation emerging from this dangerous experience of living under the sway of the idols of death is inherently a trans-systemic praxis that believes "beyond totality." Hence "and the sea was no more" is a profound ethical imperative that can emerge only from the site of alternative political praxis – the Other and the subalterns. The New Jerusalem is antithetical to the political economy of greed and accumulation. The alternative vision of the Other reclaims the metaphor of water as the agent of healing and redemption. The water, which was stripped of its exteriority in the city of Babylon and reduced to being the route to its realized eschatology, is metamorphosed into a free gift available for all. The river of the water of life which nourishes and nurtures the city of Jerusalem is surrounded by the trees whose leaves bring healing to the nations.

Conclusion

From a subaltern earth ethics point of view, this vision of the "beyond of totality" is paradigmatic. It exposes the apparatus of the imperial political economy which not only plunders and rapes communities and nature, but also strips them of their moral agency by co-opting them into the "realized eschatology" of the system. It categorically rejects the option of transforming the totality and instead unleashes an alternative politics of the Other inspired by the Lamb who was slain – the Absolute Other and the Absolute Subaltern. Further, it widens our understanding of the salvific process in history by affirming the agency of nature in creating a redeemed earth.

The struggle in the Narmada valley is a struggle to reclaim the waters. The communities and their land, water, and forests are not "created" as a "route" to reach the "realized eschatology" of development and progress in the globalized world. The very assertion that they are created by a Being who is beyond totality makes it imperative to reclaim them from the altar of Mammon where their exteriority is stripped to service the system. The "accumulation by dispossession" reduced the river into a reservoir for capitalist interests, and the communities into refugees in one's own country. It is from this experience of subalternity and otherness that the vision of a new earth emerges.

> It is not either anthropocentric or bio-centric or eco-centric, but the challenge we are facing is to learn to be deeply concerned about human life – both individually and collectively – *and* about all other forms of life *and* about the planet earth, about society *and* nature, about human history *and* the cosmos, about the struggle for justice *and* water harvesting, about red *and* green.[90]

Conclusion

The journey in search of a grassroots earth ethics is guided by the grammar of an ethics of liberation. It begins with the realization that the present is a totality, and absolutization of the totality is an ethical problem. This realization challenges us to stop our search for goodness within the Empire and the prevailing order because ethics is more than reforming the system. The journey also involves the vision of a "beyond of totality"; a vision mediated by the subalterns whose very presence negates this logic, and the claims of the infinity of the present. It is in this journey from totality to the utopia of the subalterns that a grassroots earth ethics emerges.

The affirmation that grassroots earth ethics evolves in the political praxis of subaltern social movements marks a radical discontinuity with the prevailing hegemonic God-talk. The God-talk of totality stems from the knowledge that it is the veil of divinity that provides the system its legitimacy and support. On the other hand, the God-talk of grassroots earth ethics does not originate from a hegemonic agenda. Rather, it emerges from the politics of the Divine. As revealed in the life of Jesus, the only possible locus of epiphany in the context of a colonized lifeworld is the Other. Such a radical realization of the centrality of the subaltern social movements for God-talk hence belongs to the spirit of the Divine project in history. It is a discernment of the perennial possibility of the Other in history, to acknowledge them as the vehicle of salvation, and to identify with them in search of a redeemed earth.

The age-old imperial project of stripping the moral agency of the subordinated others continues to be a contemporary reality. The subaltern is being alienated by way of taking away its exteriority and being grafted into the system to find meaning in life by becoming subservient to capital. The imperial project, through colonial discourses, has constructed the Other as a category of degenerate communities incapable of leading a "successful" life in the system. When this colonial discourse of inherent degeneracy of the Other became the "truth," new messiahs emerged on the horizon, accompanied by apparatuses of social engineering christened as "progress," "growth," "development," and "globalization" to intervene and practice the "politics of rescue." The success of this "politics of rescue" lies in its hegemonic character, masquerading as an apolitical machine which denudes the communities of their moral agency. This is the tragic narrative of our times.

It is in this context that grassroots earth ethics emphasizes reclaiming the moral agency of the subalterns. Moral agency is that which empowers a community to dream and to design their destiny. When confronted by the powers of domination, supremacy, and exclusion, moral agency enables the community to become a subversive presence that challenges the very codes of the prevailing order. This subversive presence unfolds as a redeeming grace for both the subaltern communities and the proponents of the totality who are busy creating the Other all along its course. The self-proclaimed messiahs of the world and their "politics of rescue" face existential crisis when the community reclaims its moral agency. Moral agency, in short, subverts the imperial project of the colonization of the lifeworld. Reclaiming moral agency is profoundly theological as it enriches the community in their search for selfhood, "to have life and to have it abundantly." The nurturing of the movement of life is integrally related to this journey towards selfhood. Subaltern social movements, as sites of enabling moral agency, are hence *ekklesia* happening in our times where the Divine is deeply present as they strive to translate their love for the movement of life into a contemporary reality.

The new ethics that emerges in the historic projects of the subalterns is in eternal conflict with the prevailing moral order of the system. Transgression of the moral codes of the status quo is essential and foundational to the subaltern search for being ethical. Their struggles for survival and reclaiming commons are illogical and immoral to the worldview of the system. Faith in the possibility of a reality beyond totality is heresy. The grand inquisitors of all times are on the lookout for the transgressors and the heretics. The search for a grassroots earth ethics thus becomes a discipleship journey following the One who became immoral to the morality of the system in order to incarnate the possibility of the "beyond of totality" as the Absolute Subaltern.

An ethics that is antithetical to the morality of the system is founded on the principles of solidarity and responsibility. Solidarity, when integrated with responsibility, transcends our ritualistic rhetoric of the preferential option for the poor. Solidarity for grassroots earth ethics is to affirm the subalterns as comrades in the historic projects of liberation. The affirmation of the Other as comrade involves a radical commitment, as it makes us vulnerable to the oppositional gaze of the Other. Solidarity in this sense is an invitation to be accountable and answerable to the Other. Comradeship of the Other leads us to a "groundless solidarity" which recognizes and celebrates differences among the subalterns and always remains alert not to fall into the pitfall of creating new totalities. It is a *communio* of "reconciled diversities," always resisting the inherent danger of internal colonization, while remaining watchful against the colonial strategy of "divide and rule."

Responsibility for grassroots earth ethics is our response-ability to the ethical challenge that the face of the subaltern poses before us. As sites of epiphany, the subaltern face invites us to a radical conversion. It is an invitation to "infinite responsibilities." Such response-ability demands us to resist and to re-create.

Grassroots earth ethics is about alternatives: *alternatives unincorporated*. The very rationale of grassroots earth ethics stems from the conviction that the Divine is "savingly present" outside the domain of totality. It further rejects all theological and ethical discourses mediated from detached and disembodied view from nowhere, and instead proposes alternative narratives informed by the oppositional gaze of the subalterns. Grassroots earth ethics is alternative as it subverts prevailing social and ecological relations. It does not stop there. By demystifying the doctrine of the totality – "there is no alternative" – grassroots earth ethics strives to create alternatives to celebrate the foretaste of a different world to demonstrate that there are alternatives.

Living in the era of globalization, the greatest challenge for grassroots earth ethics is to keep the hope alive. This demands a deeper commitment to believe in alternatives and to gain the political will to resist all temptations to become incorporated. Our hope lies in the Absolute Subaltern who lived out an alternative politics and spirituality yet remained eternally unincorporated. We meet her in today's Narmadas.

Notes

Introduction

1. I am indebted to Felix Wilfred for this insight, which he developed in "The Language of Human Rights," in *Frontiers in Asian Christian Theology*, ed. R. S. Sugirtharajah (Maryknoll, NY: Orbis Books, 1994), 206–20.

2. Nancy Fraser, *Unruly Practices: Power, Discourse and Gender in Contemporary Social Theory* (Minneapolis: University of Minnesota Press, 1992), 2.

3. See Bert Klandermans and Suzanne Staggenborg, eds., *Methods of Social Movement Research* (Minneapolis: University of Minnesota Press, 2002).

4. Some of the major works are Jürgen Moltmann, *God in Creation: A New Theology of Creation and the Spirit of God* (San Francisco: Harper and Row, 1985); Rosemary Radford Ruether, *Gaia and God: An Ecofeminist Theology of Earth Healing* (San Francisco: HarperSanFrancisco, 1992); Sallie McFague, *Life Abundant: Rethinking Theology and Economy for a Planet in Peril* (Minneapolis: Fortress Press, 2001); Leonardo Boff, *Cry of the Earth, Cry of the Poor* (Maryknoll, NY: Orbis Books, 1997); Ivone Gebara, *Longing for Running Waters: Ecofeminism and Liberation* (Minneapolis: Fortress Press, 1999); Larry L. Rasmussen, *Earth Community, Earth Ethics* (Maryknoll, NY: Orbis Books, 1996); Michael S. Northcott, *The Environment and Christian Ethics* (Cambridge: Cambridge University Press, 1996); and Poulose Mar Gregorios, *The Human Presence: An Orthodox View of Nature* (Geneva: WCC Publications, 1978). The Earth Bible project initiated by Norman Habel is a great resource which compiles biblical interpretations on eco-justice from different social locations. Among the Indian theological reflections on ecology, Sebastian Kappen, *Divine Challenge and Human Response* (Thiruvalla: CSS Books, 2001); K. C. Abraham, *Eco-Justice: A New Agenda for Church's Mission* (Bombay: BUILD Publications, 1992); Bastiaan Wielenga, *Towards an Eco-just Society* (Bangalore: Center for Social Action, 1999); Gabriele Dietrich, *A New Thing on Earth* (Delhi: ISPCK, 2001); and George Mathew Nalunnakkal, *Green Liberation* (Delhi: ISPCK, 1999) are important.

5. See Boff, *Cry of the Earth*; McFague, *Life Abundant*; Rasmussen, *Earth Community, Earth Ethics*; Wielenga, *Towards an Eco-just Society*; and James H. Cone, "Whose Earth is it Anyway?" in *Earth Habitat: Eco-injustice and the Church's Response*, eds. Dieter Hessel and Larry Rasmussen (Minneapolis: Fortress Press, 2001), 23–32.

6. The only works that place social movements as the primary source for environmental ethics to my knowledge are J. Ronald Engel, *Sacred Sands: The Struggles for Community in the Indiana Dunes* (Middletown, CT: Wesleyan University Press, 1983), and the article by Larry Rasmussen, "Environmental Racism and Environmental Justice: Moral Theory in the Making?," *Journal of the Society of Christian Ethics* 24, no. 1 (2004): 3–28. Joerg Rieger also proposes a new approach to eco-theology from the margins examining critically the eco-theologies of Sallie McFague and Leonardo Boff. While the earth ethics from the grassroots which we discuss in this book shares his critique of the eco-theologies, and opts for a view from the margins, Rieger does not go further in affirming the agency of the collectivity of the subalterns at the margins. Joerg Rieger, "Re-envisioning Ecotheology and the Divine from the Margins," *Ecotheology* 9, no. 1 (2004): 65–85.

7. Antonio Gramsci, *Selections from Cultural Writings*, trans. and eds. David Forgacs and Geoffrey Nowell Smith (London: Lawrence & Wishart, 1985), 206–8.

8. Ranajit Guha, "Preface," in *Subaltern Studies I: Writings on South Asian History and Society*, ed. Ranajit Guha (New Delhi: Oxford University Press, 1985), vii.

9. Mark Lewis Taylor, "Subalternity and Advocacy as Kairos for Theology," in *Opting for the Margins: Postmodernity and Liberation in Christian Theology*, ed. Joerg Rieger (Oxford: Oxford University Press, 2003), 29.

10. Ibid.

11. John Beverley, *Subalternity and Representation: Arguments in Cultural Theory* (Durham, NC and London: Duke University Press, 1999), 28.

12. Gayatri Chakravorty Spivak, "Can the Subaltern Speak?" In *Marxism and Interpretation of Culture*, eds. Carey Nelson and Lawrence Grossberg (Chicago: University of Chicago Press, 1988), 271–313.

13. Ilan Kapoor, "Hyper-self-reflexive Development? Spivak on Representing the Third World 'Other'," *Third World Quarterly* 25, no. 4 (2004): 632.

14. Arundhati Roy, "The Road to Hansud: The Death of a Town," available at http://www.zcommunications.org.

15. Kapoor, "Hyper-self-reflexive Development?" 630.

16. Ibid., 628.

17. Beverley, *Subalternity and Representation*, 71.

18. Kapoor, "Hyper-self-reflexive Development?" 635–6.

19. Gayatri Spivak, *In Other Worlds: Essays in Cultural Politics* (New York: Routledge, 1988), 201.

20. Kapoor, "Hyper-self-reflexive Development?" 644; original emphasis.

21. Jack A. Hill, "Teaching for Transformation: Insights from Fiji, India, South Africa, and Jamaica," *Teaching Theology and Religion* 8, no. 4 (2005): 223. Hill here uses the term *communitas* as defined by Victor Turner in his later works where he goes beyond his earlier definition *communitas*

as spontaneous communion of equal individuals belonging to indigenous communities to societies of greater complexity where they break down prevailing tribal boundaries to give rise to new relationships in the future.

22. Larry Rasmussen, "Epiphany," *The Lutheran* 19, no. 1 (January 2006): 23.

Chapter 1

1. Jürgen Habermas, *The Theory of Communicative Action Vol II: Life World and System* (Boston, MA: Beacon Press, 1987), 137. Also see Gary M. Simpson, *Critical Social Theory: Prophetic Reason, Civil Society, and Christian Imagination* (Minneapolis: Fortress Press, 2002), 108.

2. In this work, we use the concept of the colonization of the lifeworld in a limited and generic sense. The Habermasian project of system vs. lifeworld is not without problems. The goal of Habermas is to reconstruct the Enlightenment project in the context of the pathologies of modern society which, he explains, is due to the distortion of the communicative rationality of the lifeworld by the instrumental rationality of external forces such as market and state. In advanced capitalist societies this division of system and lifeworld may not exist because of the penetrating potential of the market ethos. The notion of lifeworld as a pristine state of primordial bliss and harmonious living is nothing more than a fairy tale. Moreover, the lifeworld has been colonized from within by ideologies and social practices such as patriarchy, caste system, racism, feudalism, and cultural nationalism. The resistance against the colonization of the lifeworld by market forces and state hence recognizes the internal colonization and strives to confront them as well.

3. See Paul Lakeland, *Theology and Critical Theory: The Discourse of the Church* (Nashville, TN: Abingdon Press, 1990); Terrence W. Tilley, *Postmodern Theologies: The Challenge of Religious Diversity* (Maryknoll, NY: Orbis Books, 1995); Simpson, *Critical Social Theory*; Don S. Browning and Francis Schüssler Fiorenza, eds., *Habermas, Modernity, and Public Theology* (New York: Crossroad, 1992); Elizabeth M. Bounds, *Coming Together/ Coming Apart: Religion, Community, and Modernity* (New York: Routledge, 1997).

4. David Tracy, "Theology, Critical Social Theory, and the Public Realm," in *Habermas, Modernity, and Public Theology*, eds. Browning and Schüssler Fiorenza, 27.

5. Quoted in Enrique Dussel, *Beyond Philosophy: Ethics, History, Marxism and Liberation Theology*, ed. Eduardo Mendieta (Lanham, MD: Rowman and Littlefield, 2003), 173.

6. Lawrence Summers, "Let Them Eat Pollution" (Excerpt of Lawrence Summers' internal memo to the World Bank), *Economist* (February 8, 1992): 66. Also see Suzanne Bergeron, *Fragments of Development: Nation, Gender, and the Space of Modernity* (Ann Arbor, MI: University of Michigan Press, 2004), 91.

7. Luis Alfredo Arango, "Papel y Tusa," Guatemala, 1967, quoted in Mark Lewis Taylor, "Transnational Corporation and Institutionalized Violence: A Challenge to Christian Movements in the US," in *New Vision for the Americas: Religious Engagement and Social Transformation*, ed. David Batstone (Minneapolis: Fortress Press, 1993), 101.

8. Enrique Dussel, *The Invention of the Americas: Eclipse of the "Other" and the Myth of Modernity* (New York: Continuum Press, 1995), 35.

9. Quoted by Dussel, *The Invention of the Americas*, 51.

10. Larry Rasmussen, *"Give us Word of the Humankind We Left to Thee": Globalization and its Wake* (Cambridge, MA: Episcopal Divinity School, 1999), 4.

11. Quoted by Gilbert Rist, *The History of Development: From Western Origins to Global Faith* (London and New York: Zed Books, 1997), 55. We see the same argument in the contemporary world when the Empire considers it as a moral duty to export freedom and democracy worldwide by any means including pre-emptive war. "Every nation in every region now has a decision to make. Either you are with us or you are with the terrorists." Speech of President George W. Bush to a joint session of the US Congress on September 20, 2001, quoted in Ninan Koshy, *The War on Terror: Reordering the World* (Delhi: Left World Books, 2003), 2.

12. Dussel, *The Invention of the Americas*, 50.

13. Ibid.

14. Larry Rasmussen, *Moral Fragments and Moral Community: A Proposal for Church in Society* (Minneapolis: Fortress Press, 1995), 21.

15. Bounds, *Coming Together/Coming Apart*, 36.

16. Dussel, *The Invention of the Americas*, 48, 117.

17. Mark Lewis Taylor, "Spirit and Liberation: Achieving Postcolonial Theology in the United States," in *Postcolonial Theologies: Divinity and Empire*, eds. Catherine Keller, Michael Nausner and Mayra Rivera (St. Louis, CO: Chalice Press, 2004), 42.

18. Robert J. C. Young, *Postcolonialism: An Historical Introduction* (Oxford: Blackwell, 2001), 27.

19. Vandana Shiva, *Biopiracy: The Plunder of Nature and Knowledge* (Boston, MA: South End Press, 1997), 101–5. We find a similar analysis in James Mittelman. "Viewed historically, globalization may be best understood in terms of its continuities and discontinuities with the past... [T]he period before the sixteenth century may be construed as a time of *incipient globalization*. A second period, from the inception of capitalism in the West until the early 1970s, was an era of *bridging globalization*. Third, the

period since the early 1970s comprises *accelerated globalization*" (James H. Mittelman, *The Globalization Syndrome: Transformation and Resistance* [Princeton, NJ: Princeton University Press, 2000], 19).

20. Wolfgang Sachs, "Introduction," in *Development Dictionary: A Guide to Knowledge as Power*, ed. Wolfgang Sachs (London: Zed Books, 1992), 1; original emphasis.

21. Sachs, "Introduction," 1.

22. Richard Peet, *Theories of Development* (New York and London: Guilford Press, 1999), 1.

23. Ivan Illich, "Needs," in *Development Dictionary: A Guide to Knowledge as Power*, ed. Wolfgang Sachs (London: Zed Books, 1992), 96.

24. Jan Nederveen Pieterse, *Development Theory: Deconstructions/Reconstructions* (London: Sage Publications, 2001), 18.

25. Walt W. Rostow, *The Stages of Economic Growth: A Non-Communist Manifesto* (Cambridge: Cambridge University Press, 1960).

26. Ibid., 164.

27. The aeronautical metaphor of "take-off" originally belongs to Rosenstein-Rodan's formulation which dates back to 1957: "Launching a country into self-sustaining growth is a little like getting an airplane off the ground. There is a critical ground speed which must be passed before the craft can become airborne." Quoted in Rist, *The History of Development*, 95.

28. Rostow, *The Stages of Economic Growth*, 6.

29. Ivan Illich, "Development as Planned Poverty," in *The Post-Development Reader*, eds. Majid Rahnema and Victoria Bawtree (London: Zed Books, 1997), 95.

30. The main proponents of the post-development school of development theory are Gustavo Esteva, Arturo Escobar, Majid Rahnema and Wolfgang Sachs. The writings of Gilbet Rist, Ashis Nandi, Claude Alvares, James Ferguson and Frederique Apffel Marglin are also important. For critical commentaries on post-development school see Ray Kiely, Jan Nederveen Pieterse and Meera Nanda.

31. Gustavo Esteva, "*Basta!* Mexican Indians say 'Enough!'" in *The Post-Development Reader*, eds. Majid Rahnema and Victoria Bawtree (London: Zed Books, 1997), 302.

32. Morgan Birgg, "Post-development, Foucault and the Colonization Metaphor," *Third World Quarterly* 23, no. 3 (2002): 421–2.

33. James Ferguson, *The Anti-Politics Machine: "Development," Depoliticization, and Bureaucratic Power in Lesotho* (Cambridge: Cambridge University Press, 1990), 256.

34. Arturo Escobar, *Encountering Development: The Making and Unmaking of the Third World* (Princeton, NJ: Princeton University Press, 1995), 6.

35. Edward Said, *Orientalism* (New York: Vintage Books, 1979), 3.

36. Homi Bhabha, *The Location of Culture* (London and New York: Routledge, 1994), 70.

37. Harry S. Truman (Inaugural Address, January 20, 1949), quoted in Gustavo Esteva, "Development," in *The Development Dictionary: A Guide to Knowledge as Power*, ed. Wolfgang Sachs (London: Zed Books, 1992), 6.

38. Esteva, *"Basta,"* 7.

39. Escobar, *Encountering Development*, 44.

40. Escobar, *Encountering Development*, 52–3.

41. Rist, *The History of Development*, 77.

42. Pieterse, *Development Theory*, 25.

43. Ibid., 26.

44. Jose Maria Sbert, "Progress," in *The Development Dictionary*, ed. Sachs, 197; original emphasis.

45. Heather Eaton and Lois Ann Lorentzen, "Introduction," in *Ecofeminism and Globalization: Exploring Culture, Context and Religion*, eds. Heather Eaton and Lois Ann Lorentzen (Lanham, MD: Rowman and Littlefield, 2003), 4; original emphasis.

46. Giles Mohan, "Contested Sovereignty and Democratic Contradictions: The Political Impacts of Adjustment," in *Structural Adjustment: Theory, Practice and Impacts*, eds. Giles Mohan et al. (London and New York: Routledge, 2000), 76.

47. Rebecca Todd Peters, *In Search of the Good Life: The Ethics of Globalization* (New York and London: Continuum Press, 2004), 78.

48. Cynthia D. Moe-Lobeda, *Healing a Broken World: Globalization and God* (Minneapolis: Fortress Press, 2002), 23.

49. Escobar, *Encountering Development*, 33.

50. Susan George, "A Short History of Neo-Globalism: Twenty Years of Elite Economics and Emerging Opportunities for Structural Change," in *Global Finance: New Thinking on Regulating Speculative Capital Markets*, eds. Walden Bello et al. (London: Zed Books, 2000), 27–35.

51. Bob Milward, "What is Structural Adjustment?" in *Structural Adjustment: Theory, Practice and Impacts*, eds. Giles Mohan et al. (London and New York: Routledge, 2000), 33.

52. Fidel Castro, "Complete text of President Castro's speech at the opening session of the South Summit, April 12, 2000." See http://www.puertorico.com/forums/open-board/13160-supporters-terrorism.html.

This grand narrative of the discourse of globalization can be summarized in the words of D. L. Sheth in the following way. "Conceived and led by the victors of the cold war, it claimed to establish a new global order which would put an end to the old one that had kept the world 'divided' – economically, culturally and politically. In its place it not just promised, but communicated a virtual experience (as if that world was upon us!) of the world becoming one economy, (possibly) one culture and (eventually) one polity! Such a world could do, globally, without the messy institutions of representational democracy, even as such institutions were to be made mandatory internally for every individual country. It assured that this new global order would be managed by a set of global institutions (served by experts and freed from the cumbersome procedures of representational accountability), which, being set up and controlled by the world's few 'self-responsible' and 'advanced' democracies, would guarantee peace and order to the whole world. Moreover, since the monopoly of violence (including its technology) will be withdrawn from a large number of individual and often 'irresponsible' nation states (whose natural location is in the south) and be placed collectively in the hands of a few nation states, which also are 'responsible' and 'civilized' democracies (whose natural location is of course in the north), it not only will eliminate international wars, but alleviate poverty wherever it exists." D. L. Seth, "Globalization and New Politics of Micro-Movements," *Economic and Political Weekly*, 39 no. 1 (2004).

53. Karl Polanyi, *The Great Transformation* (New York: Farrar & Rinehart, 1944), 73.

54. Susan George and Fabrizio Sabelli, *Faith and Credit: The World Bank's Secular Empire* (London: Penguin Books, 1994), 67. This quotation comes from a personal communication to Susan George from CamFed's Ann Cotton. Here the attempt is not to make any moralistic judgment on sexuality. The recent attempts of the sex workers to organize and unionize themselves and their demand for considering prostitution as work raise new questions on the moralistic intervention to "save women."

55. Vandana Shiva, "The Suicide Economy of Corporate Globalization" (2004), http://www.countercurrents.org/glo-shiva050404.htm

56. The suicide of Lee Kyung Hae is important here as he was able to make his death a political issue. He was the leader of the Korean Federation of Advanced Farmers' Association. He was a staunch anti-globalization activist who organized the farmers in his country and also participated in several demonstrations against the global financial institutions. While participating in the protest at the WTO meeting in Cancun, he took his life in public protesting the killing of farmers by the WTO. The following excerpts from the statement that he distributed just before his death articulates his call for resistance against the colonization of the lifeworld. "My warning goes out to all citizens that human beings are in an endangered situation. That uncontrolled multinational corporations and a small number of big WTO members are leading an undesirable globalization that is inhumane, environmentally degrading, farmer-killing, and undemocratic. It should be stopped immediately. Otherwise the false logic of neo-liberalism will wipe out the diversity of global agriculture and be disastrous to all human beings." Quoted in Laura Carlsen, "WTO Kills Farmers: In Memory of Lee Kyung Hae" (2005), http://www.cipamericas.org.

57. "Desh Bachao Kisan Mahaphanchayat," *Lokayan Bulletin* 13, no. 1 (July-August 1996): 67.

58. M. P. Joseph, "Present is not Eternal," *Agape Immaginaria* 2 (Italy) (December 2000): 13.

59. Upali Cooray, "The International Debt Crisis," in *Debt Crisis and People's Struggle* (Hong Kong: Documentation for Action Groups in Asia, 1987), 91.

60. Naomi Klein, "Free Trade is War," *The Nation* 277, no. 9 (2003).

61. David Baake, "The Sorrows of Globalization: Capitalism and Slavery" (2005), http://www.zcommunications.org.

62. Ibid.

63. See M. P. Joseph, "Religious Fundamentalism: A Political Strategy for Global Governance," *Voices from the Third World* XXV, no. 1 & 2 (December 2002) and P. Radhakrishnan, "Religion under Globalization," *Economic and Political Weekly* 39 no. 13 (2004).

64. Riaz Ahmad, "Gujarat Violence: Meaning and Implications," *Economic and Political Weekly* 37, no. 20 (2002): 1872.

65. Hindutva stands for the right-wing Hindu ideology based on cultural nationalism. The proponents of Hindutva consist of Bharatiya Janata Party, the Rashtriya Swayam Sevak Sangh, the Vishva Hindu Parisat, and the Bhajarang Dal.

66. Quoted in Naomi Klein, "Free Trade is War," *The Nation* (September 29, 2003), http://www.thenation.com/article/free-trade-war?page=full

67. Vandana Shiva, "Globalization and Talibanization," 2004, http://www.outlookindia.com. She further explains how globalization fuels fundamentalism. "1) Fundamentalism is a cultural backlash to globalization as alienated and angry young men of colonized societies and cultures react to the erosion of identity and security. 2) Dispossessed people robbed of economic security by globalization cling to politicized religious identities and narrow nationalisms for security. 3) Politicians robbed of economic decision making as national economic sovereignty is eroded by globalization, organize their vote banks along lines of religious and cultural difference on the basis of fear and hatred. 4) Imperialist forces, using the divide and rule strategy, also exploit religious conflicts to fragment the opposition to globalization."

68. Ibid.

69. Ibid.

70. J. Rifkin's following description of enclosure which radically changed social relations in Europe is important in this context: "Enclosure introduced a new concept of human relationship into European civilization that changed the basis of economic security and the perception of human life. Land was no longer something people belonged to, but rather a commodity people possessed. Land was reduced to a quantitative status and measured by its exchange value. So, too, with people. Relationships were reorganized. Neighbors became employees or contractors. Reciprocity was replaced with hourly wages. People sold their time and labor where they used to share

their toil. Human beings began to view each other and everything around them in financial terms. Virtually everyone and everything became negotiable and could be purchased at an appropriate price." J. Rifkin, *The Biotech Century* (New York: Putnam, 1998), 40–1.

71. Naomi Klein, "The Rise of Disaster Capitalism," *The Nation* 280, no. 17 (2005): 9. It is important to mention here the controversial statement made by the US State Secretary Condolezza Rice on January 2005 describing the tsunami as "a wonderful opportunity" that "has paid great dividends for us."

72. Dwight N. Hopkins, "The Religion of Globalization," in *Religions/Globalizations: Theories and Cases*, eds. Dwight N. Hopkins et al. (Durham, NC and London: Duke University Press, 2001), 9.

73. Sebastian Kappen, *Spirituality in the Age of Recolonization* (Bangalore: Visthar, 1995), 3.

74. Adam Smith, *Wealth of Nations* (New York: Prometheus Books, 1991), 13. Here we use self-interest and self-love to mean the capitalist interest to enhance wealth. There are emerging voices from the oft silenced communities affirming self-interest and self-love as positive.

75. Hopkins, "The Religion of Globalization," 13.

76. Joseph, "Present is not Eternal," 14.

77. M. P. Joseph, "Towards a Theological Critique of Globalization," in *Globalization and Human Solidarity*, ed. Tissa Balasuriya (Thiruvalla: CSS Books, 2000), 10.

78. M. P. Joseph, "Beyond Bandung: The Market, the Empire and an Enquiry of Religious Meaning," in *Building Spirituality and Culture of Peace*, ed. Josef P. Wdiyatmadja (Hong Kong: Christian Conference of Asia, 2004), 181.

79. Moe-Lobeda, *Healing a Broken World*, 36.

Chapter 2

1. Eric Delson, ed., *Ancestors: The Hard Evidence* (New York: A. R. Liss, 1985), 334–8.

2. The nomenclature adivasi is used to represent communities known as tribals or indigenous people.

3. Sanskritization is a concept popularized by M. N. Srinivas, a renowned Indian social scientist. It refers to the tendency of lower caste people to assimilate upper caste practices and customs to move upward in the social hierarchy of the caste society. See M. N. Srinivas, *Social Change in Modern India* (Berkeley, CA: University of California Press, 1966).

4. Amita Baviskar, *In the Belly of the River: Tribal Conflicts over Development in the Narmada Valley* (Delhi: Oxford University Press, 1995), 88.

5. For an English translation of the *gayana*, see Baviskar, *In the Belly of the River*, 262–72. *Pooja* means ritual.

6. Baviskar, *In the Belly of the River*, 162.

7. Ibid., 165.

8. S. Santhi, *Sardar Sarovar Project: The Issue of Developing River Narmada* (Thiruvananthapuram: INTACH, 1995), 37.

9. Ascribing the title of "natural environmentalists" to women and adivasis is a controversial issue in contemporary literature on environmentalism in general and ecofeminism in particular. Ramachandra Guha's and Madhav Gadgil's ecological classification of Indian population as omnivores, ecosystem people and ecological refugees, is based on the principle of binary opposites between the urban population and the rural poor. Guha and Gadgil, *Ecology and Equity: The Use and Abuse of Nature in Contemporary India* (London: Routledge, 1995); Vandana Shiva in her own work *Staying Alive: Women, Ecology and Survival in India* (New Delhi: Kali for Women, 1988) and her work with Maria Mies, *Ecofeminism* (New Delhi: Kali for Women, 1993) also operates within the category of binary opposites in an essentialist manner where she privileges women as "custodians of biodiversity" and natural environmentalists. Pramod Parajuli's concept of "ecological ethnicity" can also be accused of essentialism (Pramod Parajuli, "Learning from Ecological Ethnicities: Toward a Plural Political Ecology of Knowledge" in *Indigenous Traditions and Ecology: The Interbeing of Cosmology and Community*, ed. John A. Grim [Cambridge, MA: Harvard University Press, 559–90]). However, the mediation of social movements such as the Zapatista movement and the Narmada Bachao Andolan in the construction of this concept provides it a non essentialist political meaning. For critical analysis of essentialist categories in environmentalism and ecofeminism see Meera Nanda, *Prophets Facing Backward: Postmodern Critique of Science and Hindu Nationalism in India* (London: Rutgers University Press, 2003); and Lois Ann Lorentzen, "Indigenous Feet: Ecofeminism, Globalization, and the Case of Chiapas," in *Ecofeminism and Globalization: Exploring Culture, Context, and Religion*, eds. Heather Eaton and Lois Ann Lorentzen (Lanham, MD: Rowman and Littlefield, 2003). James C. Scott's "Forward" to *Agrarian Environments* which critically evaluates the standard narrative of second-generation environmentalists shares the concerns of several other scholars. "The colonizers, the market, and the state were the agents of ecological degradation while indigenous peoples, the more Neolithic the better, were nature's natural conservators. It is a narrative that has been exported or independently invented almost everywhere." Arun Agarwal and K. Sivaramakrishnan, eds., *Agrarian Environments: Resources, Representations and Rule in India* (Durham, NC: Duke University Press, 2000), vii.

10. Chris Deegan, "The Narmada: Circumambulation of a Sacred Landscape," in *Hinduism and Ecology: The Intersection of Earth, Sky and*

Water eds. Christopher Key Chapple and Mary Evelyn Tucker (Cambridge, MA: Harvard University Press, 2000), 390.

11. Ancient Hindu texts such as *Vayu purana*, *Skanda purana*, *Matsya purana* and *Narmada purana* contain descriptions of Narmada. Classical Sanskrit poets such as Kalidas and Bahabhatt also mentioned Narmada in their literary works.

12. Ayodhya Prasad Dwivedi, *Sanskruti Srotaswini Narmada* (Hindi) (Bhopal: Madhya Pradesh Hindi Grandh Academy, 1987), 5.

13. Royina Grewal, *Sacred Virgin: Travels along the Narmada* (New Delhi: Penguin Books, 1994), 21.

14. According to Narmada Purana, Narmada earned the *bardan* (gifts) through her *tapasya* (ascetic practice) of ten thousand years, which includes "to be *amara* (forever); to be holy; to have her *bhakti's* (devotee's) sins washed away by bathing in her waters; to be the Southern Ganga; to offer whatever rewards one gets from other rivers; to enable those who do *tapsya* on her banks to find a place with Sankara (Shiva); to be forever known as a sin cleanser; to have those who live and die on her north bank go to *Amarpuri* (where the gods are); to have those who live and die on her south bank to go to *Pitrloka* (where their ancestors are)." Cited in Deegan, "The Narmada: Circumambulation of a Sacred Landscape," 395.

15. Chris Deegan, "The Narmada in Myth and History," in *Toward Sustainable Development: Struggling over India's Narmada River*, ed. William F. Fisher (Armonk, NY: M. E. Sharp, 1995), 65.

16. Vijay Paranjype, "The Cultural Ethos," *Lokayan Bulletin* (May–August 1991), 22.

17. In a religiously pluralistic country like India, with the rise of cultural nationalism and religious fanaticism, the revival of religious symbols and legends can be dangerous as it has the potential to communalize the lifeworld. The saffronization of the lifeworld, including the peoples' movements, is a contemporary reality in India. In such a context, appropriation of the religio-cultural ethos of the communities needs to be done carefully in secular movements. This issue will be discussed in detail later.

18. For an extensive study in this line see Anjuman Ali-Bogaert, "Imagining Alternatives to Development: A Case Study of the Narmada Bachao Andolan in India," PhD dissertation, Kent University, 1997.

19. Partha Chatterjee, *Nationalist Thought in the Colonial World: A Derivative Discourse* (Delhi: Oxford University Press, 1986). For a Marxist critical reading of Chatterjee's analysis, see Sumit Sarkar, "Orientalism Revisited: Saidian Frameworks in the Writing of Modern Indian History," in *Mapping Subaltern Studies and the Postcolonial*, ed. Vinayak Chaturvedi (London: Verso, 2000), 239–55.

20. Chatterjee's classification of the Gandhian "moment of maneuver" as outside of post-Enlightenment rationality is a debatable issue.

21. Chatterjee, *Nationalist Thought*, 66.

22. Gabriele Dietrich and Bastiaan Wielenga, *Towards Understanding Indian Society* (Madurai: Centre for Social Analysis, 1998), 170.

23. Gyan Prakash, "Writing Post-Orientalist Histories of the Third World: Perspectives from Indian Historiography," in *Mapping Subaltern Studies*, ed. Chaturvedi, 171.

24. Dalits in India in general have a different perception of modernity. The liberal values of equality, freedom, rights and dignity inspired the dalit pursuit of modernity. Babasaheb Ambedkar was critical of Gandhi's romanticization of Indian villages. "This is the village republic of which the Hindus are so proud. What is the position of the untouchables in this Republic? They are not merely the last but are also the least...in this Republic there is no place for democracy. There is no room for equality. There is no room for liberty and there is no room for fraternity. The Indian village is a very negation of Republic. The republic is an Empire of the Hindus over the untouchables. It is a kind of colonialism of the Hindus designed to exploit the untouchables. The untouchables have no rights... They have no rights because they are outside the village republic and because they are outside the so-called village republic, they are outside the Hindu fold" (V. Moon, ed., *Dr. Babasaheb Ambedkar Writings and Speeches*, vol. 5 [Bombay: Government of Maharashtra, 1979], 25–6). Ambedkar welcomed modernization and industrialization as it enabled dalits to escape from the caste-ridden villages in pursuit of modernity to claim social and economic capital. The British army during the colonial period, and the industries that started as part of the modernization paradigm of the new government, provided the dalits opportunities to come out of their traditional occupations defined by the caste system. For a comparative study of the notion of village in Gandhi, Nehru and Ambedkar see Sureender S. Jodhka, "Nation and Village: Images of Rural India in Gandhi, Nehru and Ambedakr," *Economic and Political Weekly*, August 10, 2002. However, there are other voices among the dalit scholars who see the dalit pursuit of modernity differently. For example, in his critique of the bourgeois modernity Gopal Guru observes that "Modernity has not generated new spaces (territorial) which could give dalits a sense of dignity and equality. It has offered only a crippled and fragmentary sense of time and corresponding notion of freedom to dalits" (Gopal Guru, "Dalits in Pursuit of Modernity," in *India: Another Millennium?* ed. Romila Thapar [New Delhi: Penguin Books, 2000], 125).

25. Jawaharlal Nehru, *Jawaharlal Nehru's Speeches, vol. 3, March 1953–August 1957* (New Delhi: Publication Division, Ministry of Information and Broadcasting, 1958), 3.

26. Cited in R. Rangachari et al., *Large Dams: India's Experience WCD Case Study Final Report: November 2000* (Cape Town: World Commission on Dams, 2000), 2–3.

27. There was a radical shift in Nehru's position regarding big dams towards the end of his life. In his address to the annual meeting of the Central

Board of Irrigation and Power on November 17, 1958, Nehru articulated this position. "For some time past, however, I have been beginning to think that we are suffering form what we may call 'the disease of gigantism'. We want to show that we can build big dams and do big things. This is a dangerous outlook developing in India... [T]he idea of big – having big undertakings and doing big things for the sake of showing that we can do big things – is not a good outlook at all... It is...the small industries and the small plants for electric power, which will change the face of the country far more than half a dozen big projects in half a dozen places." C. V. J. Sharma, ed., *Modern Temples of India: Selected Speeches of Jawaharlal Nehru at Irrigation and Power Projects* (Delhi: Central Board of Irrigation and Power, 1989), 40–9.

28. Available at http://www.sardarsarovardam.org. Sardar Sarovar Project is the terminal dam in the Narmada Valley Development Project.

29. Available at http://www.nri-gujarat.com/sardar.htm (accessed 2005).

30. Patrick McCully, *Silenced Rivers: The Ecology and Politics of Large Dams* (Hyderabad: Orient Longman, 1998), 75.

31. An excerpt from an official letter from the government of Madhya Pradesh to the Narmada Control Authority (NCA) written in May 2001, "As such there is need for considering suitable amendments in Sub-Clause IV (7) of Clause XI of the NWDT (Award), and introducing a provision on the option of the oustee to accept *compensation in full in one settlement* to enable him to purchase land and settle down as his choice" [emphasis added]. Quoted in Dilip D'Souza, *The Narmada Dammed: An Enquiry into the Politics of Development* (New Delhi: Penguin Books, 2002), 49.

32. Ibid., 47.

33. Justice B.N. Kirpal, after retiring from the Supreme Court of India as the Chief Justice of India, currently heads the Indian Environmental Council of the Hindustan Coca-Cola Beverages Private Limited. Recently he publicly criticized the Kerala High Court order restraining Coke from mining ground water in Plachimada, Kerala.

34. L. C. Jain, *Dam vs Drinking Water: Exploring the Narmada Judgment* (Pune: Parisar, 2001), 19.

35. Bradford Morse and Thomas Berger, *Sardar Sarovar: The Report of the Independent Review* (Ottawa: Resource Futures International, 1992), 62.

36. B. G. Verghese, *Winning the Future: From Bhakra to Narmada, Tehri, Rajasthan Canal* (New Delhi: Konark, 1994), 167.

37. Jain, *Dam vs Drinking Water*, 13.

38. Morse and Berger, *Sardar Sarovar*, xxiv–xxv.

39. See *Words on Water* for a video clip of the speech of Advani on October 31, 2000.

40. William F. Fisher, "Sacred Rivers, Sacred Dams: Competing Visions of Social Justice and Sustainable Development along the Narmada," in *Hinduism and Ecology: The Intersection of Earth, Sky and Water*, eds.

Christopher Key Chapple and Mary Evelyn Tucker (Cambridge, MA: Harvard University Press, 2000), 401–21.

41. Ibid., 409–10.

42. Fisher, "Sacred Rivers, Sacred Dams," 410.

43. Ibid., 411.

44. Arundhati Roy, *The Greater Common Good* (Bombay: India Book Distributors, 1999), 28.

45. See Jürgen Habermas, "New Social Movements," *Telos* 49 (Fall 1981).

46. This does not mean that the NBA fits into the characteristics of the Habermasian New Social Movements. A detailed discussion about the theories of social movements is beyond the scope of this chapter. The third chapter will address this issue.

47. For a historical narrative and analysis of subaltern protest in the Narmada valley during the colonial period, see Baviskar, *In the Belly of the River*. It is important here to be aware of the distinctiveness of subaltern politics. Ranajit Guha in his critical analysis of the dominant historiography observes that, "parallel to the domain of elite politics there existed throughout the colonial period another domain of Indian politics in which the principal actors were not the dominant groups of the indigenous society or the colonial authorities but the subaltern classes and groups constituting the mass of the laboring population and the intermediate strata in town and country – that is, the people. This was an *autonomous* domain, for it neither originated from elite politics, nor did its existence depend on the latter" (Ranaji Guha, "On Some Aspects of the Historiography of Colonial India," in *Mapping Subaltern Studies and the Postcolonial*, ed. Vinayak Chaturvedi [London: Verso, 2000], 3).

48. See Sangvai, *The River and Life*, 37.

49. Ramachandra Guha, *Environmentalism: A Global History* (New Delhi: Oxford University Press, 2000), 99–108.

50. See Amita Baviskar, "Red in Tooth and Claw? Looking for Class in Struggles over Nature," in *Social Movements in India: Poverty, Power and Politics*, eds. Raka Ray and Mary Fainsod Katzenstein (Lanham, MD: Rowman & Littlefield, 2005), 161–72, and Gail Omvedt, "Dams and Bombs," *The Hindu* (August 5, 1999).

51. Arundhati Roy has popularized NBA nationally and internationally through her writings and campaigns both in the valley and other parts of the world. She was even sentenced to imprisonment by the Supreme Court for her alleged contempt of court by questioning the majority verdict in the SSP case. Her celebrity identity provided her more coverage in both the print and electronic media. Gail Omvedt, a feminist social scientist and Ramachandra Guha, an eminent environmental historian, published an open letter and an article respectively in the national newspapers questioning her role in the

movement. These articles created a long debate on the topic of representation, the role of "outsiders" and the like.

52. Subodh Wagle, "The Long March for Livelihoods: Struggle against the Narmada Dam in India," in *Environmental Justice: Discourses in International Political Economy*, vol. 8, eds. John Byrne et al. (New Brunswick: Transaction Publishers, 2002), 80–1.

53. Ibid., 81.

54. Ranjit Dwivedi, "Resisting Dams and 'Development': Contemporary Significance of the Campaign against the Narmada Projects in India," *European Journal of Development Research* 10, no. 2 (1998): 166.

55. Sripad Dharmadhikari, "Advocacy Skills and Systems," in *Experiences of Advocacy in Environment and Devleopment*, eds. Joshi et al. (Bangalore: Development Support Initiative, 1997), 16–36. Dharmadhikari narrates how NBA sought the assistance of Vijay Pareshpai, a Poona-based economist, to develop a cost–benefit analysis of the project. "We try to suggest to him, well before he had taken up the study that he should take up a cost benefit analysis of the project. For that he came to the valley and had long discussions and he met the affected people, so he was in a way a part of the process. He saw things for himself. In that sense setting the agenda, not making him sit there and telling him that he must write A B C D, but to let the priorities of the people set the terms of the research" (ibid., 31).

56. Baviskar, "Red in Tooth and Claw," 19.

57. Chittaroopa Palit, "Monsoon Risings: Mega-Dam Resistance in the Narmada Valley," *New Left Review* 21 (May–June 2003): 95–6. During my field research in the valley in July 2003, I was able to be part of a campaign in the Nimad region in Madhya Pradesh, which demonstrated the above mentioned organizational style of the Narmada Bachao Andolan (NBA). The movement wanted to cross check the official list of project affected people (PAPs), and whether they received compensation or not. The young volunteers who are from the community visited the affected villages as a team. During the day time, along with the village leaders the team visited each and every household in the village to check the accuracy of the official document. In the evening the community would gather together to discuss their concerns and they watched together the videos of the struggle. The NBA activists in Badwani office compiled the reports of the volunteers. A meeting of the representatives from all the villages in the region was convened, in which Medha Patkar and other activists and volunteers were also present. After detailed discussions, they made several decisions regarding the future course of action. The Badwani office then coordinated the implementation of the decisions.

58. The term *pari passu* is a Latin legal term which literally means without preference or priority, or in an equal or like way. This legal concept was used to rule out the demand to complete the resettlement and rehabilitation before the construction begins.

59. Claude Alvares, "Development: Much Ado about Nothing," *The Illustrated Weekly of India* (June 3, 1984): 15.

60. Quoted in Jain, *Dam vs Drinking Water*, 21.

61. Quoted in Roy, *Greater Common Good*, 6.

62. Jan Vikas Andolan, "A Draft Perspective and Some Questions," *Lokayan Bulletin* 8, no. 1 (January–February 1990): 69–73.

63. Dwivedi, "Resisting Dams," 159.

64. Vikas Andolan, "Draft Perspective," 70.

65. Gustavo Esteva and Madhu Suri Prakash, "Re-routing and Re-rooting Grassroots Initiatives: Escaping the Impasse of Sustainable Development for the Narmanda," *Lokayan Bulletin* 9 (1991): 115.

66. "Normative gaze" is a concept developed by Cornel West in his genealogy of race. See Cornel West, *Prophesy Deliverance!: An Afro-American Revolutionary Christianity* (Philadelphia: Westminster Press, 1982).

67. Smitu Kothari, "Damming the Narmada and the Politics of Development," in *Toward Sustainable Development: Struggling over India's Narmada River*, ed. William F. Fisher (Armonk, NY: M. E. Sharp, 1995), 426.

68. The monthly electricity charges are fixed in this order. Rs.10 for a tube light and Rs.30 for a television set.

69. Lyla Bavadam, "The Bilgaon Model," available at http://www.hinduonnet.com/fline/fl2021/stories/20031024001208700.htm

70. Ibid.

71. Ferguson, *The Anti-Politics Machine*.

Chapter 3

1. Simon de Beauvoir, *The Second Sex*, trans. H. M. Parshley (New York: Vintage, 1972), 161.

2. Aristotle, *Politics*, trans. Benjamin Jowett, in *The Basic Works of Aristotle*, ed. Richard McKeon (New York: Random House, 1941), 1260b.

3. This is a paraphrased version of the *Purusasukta* hymn in the *Rigveda*.

4. There are several works in Christian theology that address epistemological questions and challenge the regime of truth. See Mary McClintock Fulkerson, *Changing the Subject: Women's Discourse and Feminist Theology* (Eugene, OR: Wipf and Stock, 2001); Lucy Tatman, *Knowledge that Matters: A Feminist Theological Paradigm and Epistemology* (Cleveland, OH: Pilgrim Press, 2001); Mary M. Solberg, *Compelling Knowledge: A Feminist Proposal for an Epistemology of the Cross* (New York: State University Press of New York Press, 1997); Ada Maria Isasi-Diaz, *En La Lucha = In the Struggle: Elaborating a Mujerista Theology* (Minneapolis: Fortress Press, 2004); Vitor Westhelle, "Scientific Sights and Embodied Knowledges," *Modern Theology*

11, no. 3 (July 1995): 341–61, and Linda Thomas, "Womanist Theology, Epistemology, and a New Anthropological Paradigm," *Cross Currents: The Journal of the Association for the Religious and Intellectual Life* 8, no. 4 (Winter 1998–99): 488–99.

5. Lorraine Code, *What Can She Know: Feminist Theories and the Construction of Knowledge* (Ithaca, NY: Cornell University Press, 1991), 35.

6. Sandra Harding, *Whose Science? Whose Knowledge? Thinking from Women's Lives* (Ithaca, NY: Cornell University Press, 1991), 109–10.

7. Fulkerson, *Changing the Subject*, 5.

8. Quoted by Vítor Westhelle in his lectures at the Lutheran School of Theology at Chicago.

9. "My Name is Ubuntu," *New South Africa Outline* 6, no. 2-3 (2004): 10. Recently a church-wide event was christened Ubuntu, and they celebrated difference with Ubuntu sweat shirts and Ubuntu coffee mugs.

10. Available at http://www2.elca.org/assembly/05/VotingMatters/AfricanDescentMinistryStrategy.pdf

11. R. S. Sugirtharajah, *Postcolonial Reconfigurations: An Alternative Way of Reading the Bible and Doing Theology* (Danvers, MA: Chalice Press, 2003), 166–7.

12. Vítor Westhelle, "The Word and the Mask: Revisiting the Two-Kingdoms Doctrine," in *The Gift of Grace: The Future of Lutheran Theology*, eds. Neil Henrik Gregersen et al. (Minneapolis: Fortress Press, 2005), 178.

13. Gayatri Chakravorty Spivak, "Can the Subaltern Speak?" in *Marxism and Interpretation of Culture*, eds. Carey Nelson and Lawrence Grossberg (Chicago: University of Chicago Press, 1988), 271–313. For feminist reflections on Sati, see Lata Mani, *Contentious Traditions: The Debate on Sati in Colonial India* (Berkeley, CA: University of California, 1998); Rajeswari Sunder Rajan, *Real and Imagined Women: Gender, Culture and Postcolonialism* (London: Routledge, 1993); Romila Thapar, "Traditions versus Misconceptions," *Manushi* 42-43 (1987), and Ania Loomba, "Dead Women Tell no Tales: Issues of Female Subjectivity, Subaltern Agency and Tradition in Colonial and Postcolonial Writings on Widow Immolation in India," *History Workshop Journal* 36 (1993).

14. Patricia Hill Collins, *Fighting Words: Black Women and the Search for Justice* (Minneapolis: University of Minnesota Press, 1998), xii.

15. Fulkerson, *Changing the Subject*, 25; original emphasis.

16. Tatman, *Knowledge that Matters*, 103.

17. Donna Haraway, "Situated Knowledges: The Science Question in Feminism and the Privilege of Partial Perspective," *Feminist Studies* 14, no. 3 (1988): 587.

18. Nancy Hartsock, "The Feminist Standpoint: Developing the Ground for a Specifically Feminist Historical Materialism," in *Discovering Reality: Feminist Perspectives on Epistemology, Metaphysics and Philosophy of*

Science, eds. Sandra Harding and Merrill B. Hintikka (Dordrecht: D. Reidel, 1983), 285.

19. Haraway, "Situated Knowledges," 585.

20. Gopal Guru, "The Language of Dalit-Bahujan Political Discourse," in *Dalit Identity and Politics*, ed. Ghanshyam Shah (New Delhi: Sage Publications, 2001), 97.

21. Ibid., 102. See also Kancha Ilaiah, "Dalitism vs Brahmanism: The Epistemological Conflict in History," in *Dalit Identity and Politics*, ed. Ghanshyam Shah (New Delhi: Sage Publications, 2001), 108–28.

22. Sharmila Rege, "'Real Feminist' and Dalit Women," *Economic and Political Weekly* 35, no. 6 (2000): 495. Also see her "Dalit Women Talk Differently: A Critique of 'Difference' and Towards a Dalit Feminist Standpoint," *Economic and Political Weekly* 33, no. 44 (1998): 39–46.

23. Collins, *Fighting Words*, 200.

24. Haraway, "Situated Knowledges," 581.

25. Ibid., 592.

26. Ibid., 584.

27. Beverly Wildung Harrison, "The Power of Anger in the Work of Love," in *Making the Connections: Essays in Feminist Social Ethics*, ed. Carol S. Robb (Boston, MA: Beacon Press, 1985), 13. This essay is Harrison's inaugural lecture at the Union Theological Seminary, New York and is considered as a classic in the field of Christian social ethics.

28. Uma Narayan, "Essence of Culture and a Sense of History: A Feminist Critique of Cultural Essentialism," in *Decentering the Center: Philosophy for a Multicultural, Postcolonial, and Feminist World*, eds. Uma Narayanan and Sandra Harding (Bloomington and Indianapolis: Indiana University Press, 2000), 80.

29. Ada Maria Isasi-Diaz, "*Lo Cotidiano*: A Key Element of *Mujerista* Theology," *Journal of Hispanic/Latina Theology* 10, no. 1 (2002): 13. In Mujerista theology, "lived experience identifies those experiences in our lives about which we are intentional. It is the sum of our experience which we examine, reflect upon, deal with specifically. In doing so we make it a building block for our personal and communal struggle for liberation. Because intentionality is required in order to reflect actively on what we experience, Latina's lived experience is the ground for our moral development, for our consciousness raising and conscience formation" (Ada Maria Isasi-Diaz, *En la lucha = In the Struggle: A Hispanic Women's Liberation Theology* [Minneapolis: Fortress Press, 1993], 173).

30. Patricia Hill Collins, "Defining Black Feminist Thought," in *The Second Wave: A Reader in Feminist Theory*, ed. Linda Nicholson (New York: Routledge, 1997), 253.

31. Collins, *Fighting Words*, 224.

32. Ibid., 48.

33. bell hooks, "The Oppositional Gaze: Black Female Spectators," in *Feminist Postcolonial Theory: A Reader*, eds. Reina Lewis and Sara Mills (New York: Routledge, 2003), 218, emphasis added.

34. Chandra Talpade Mohanty, *Feminism without Borders: Decolonizing Theory, Practicing Solidarity* (Durham, NC and London: Duke University Press, 2003), 46. The Dalit feminist standpoint position is important here. "An internal critique does not call for non-dalit women to freeze into guilt or to celebrate an uncritical dalit womanism. Neither does it imply a submission to some 'imagined authenticity of homogenized dalit women's voice,' it means a recognition of connections of power that exist between women... It requires not a narrow identitarian politics, but is precisely to avoid such a narrow alley that a rewriting of our histories is called for." Rege, "Dalit Women Talk Differently," 41.

35. Haraway, "Situated Knowledges," 579.

36. Ibid., 583.

37. Donna Haraway, *Simians, Cyborgs, and Women: The Reinvention of Nature* (New York: Routledge, 1991), 198.

38. Shari Stone-Mediatore, "Chandra Mohanty and the Revaluing of 'Experience'," in *Decentering the Center: Philosophy for a Multicultural, Postcolonial, and Feminist World*, eds. Uma Narayan and Sandra Harding (Bloomington and Indianapolis: Indiana University Press, 2000), 119.

39. Collins, *Fighting Words*, 44–76.

40. Loomba, "Dead Women Tell No Tales," 221.

41. Polanyi, *The Great Transformation*, 73.

42. Ibid., 130.

43. The major Indian works on social movements are by T. K. Oommen, *Protest and Change: Studies in Social Movements* (New Delhi: Sage Publications, 1990); Gail Omvedt, *Reinventing Revolution: India's New Social Movements and the Socialist Tradition in India* (Armonk, NY: M. E. Sharpe, 1993); D. N. Dhangare, *Peasant Movements in India* (Delhi: Oxford University Press, 1983); Ghanashyam Shah, *Social Movements in India: A Review of Literature* (New Delhi: Sage Publications, 1990); and Rajendra Singh, *Social Movements, Old and New: A Post-modernist Critique* (New Delhi: Sage Publications, 2001).

44. Alberto Melucci, *Challenging Codes: Collective Action in the Information Age* (Cambridge: Cambridge University Press, 1996), 1.

45. Alain Touraine, *The Voice and the Eye: An Analysis of Social Movements* (Cambridge: Cambridge University Press, 1981); Jürgen Habermas, *The Theory of Communicative Action, Vol. II: Lifeworld and System* (Boston, MA: Beacon Press, 1987); *Legitimation Crisis* (Boston, MA: Beacon Press, 1975); *The Structural Transformation of the Public Sphere* (Cambridge, MA: MIT Press, 1989); Alberto Melucci, *Nomads of the Present: Social Movements and Individual Needs in Contemporary Society* (Philadelphia: Temple University

Press, 1989); and *Challenging Codes: Collective Action in the Information Age* (Cambridge: Cambridge University Press, 1996).

46. Nick Crossley, *Making Sense of Social Movements* (Buckingham: Open University Press, 2002), 151–2.

47. Habermas, *The Theory of Communicative Action*, vol. 2, 392.

48. Omvedt, *Reinventing Revolution*, xv. A similar attempt is seen in the response of D. N. Dhangare and J. John to the article "Nine Theses on Social Movements" by Andre Gunter Frank and Marta Fuentes. Responding to the observation of the "Nine Theses" that the new movements are "grass roots" and apolitical, Dhangare and John observed that it was a theoretical conspiracy "to take away political consciousness from the exploited classes and bestow upon them an apolitical force of morality and social power." D. N. Dhanagare and J. John, "Cyclical Movements Toward the 'Eternal'," *Economic and Political Weekly* (May 21, 1988). Also see Andre Gunter Frank and Marta Fuentes, "Nine Theses on Social Movements," *Economic and Political Weekly*, 22 no. 35 (August 29, 1987).

49. Sharmila Rege, "'Real Feminist' and Dalit Women," *Economic and Political Weekly* 25, no. 6 (2000): 494.

50. Alain Touraine's observation serves as an example. "The striking feature of developments since the early 1980s is that the movements that have had the greatest effect on public opinion because of their content, and not just their context, have usually been those formed to defend the cultural rights… It obviously does not mean that the problems of jobs and wages are no longer important, but it does mean that the formation of actors, and therefore the renewal of public life, usually takes the form of a demand for cultural rights and that is kind of struggle, rather than movements that directly oppose the logic of neoliberalism, that deserve to be called 'social movements' because it goes without saying that social movements cannot exist unless they both assert something and reject something." Alain Touraine, *Beyond Neoliberalism* (Cambridge: Polity, 2001), 48. As we have seen in the second chapter, the NSMs in India like the NBA are organized around the slogan *sangharsh aur nirman* (to resist and to recreate). They have already convincingly demonstrated how the struggles for self-determination and cultural rights are integrally related to the struggle against neo-liberalism.

51. Omvedt, *Reinventing Revolution*, 318.

52. Nancy Fraser, *Justice Interruptus: Critical Reflections on the "Postsocialist" Condition* (London: Routledge, 1997), 1–5.

53. The theory of Public Sphere is elaborated in Habermas, *Structural Transformation*. A critical look at this Habermasian concept can be found in Craig Calhoun, ed., *Habermas and the Public Sphere* (Cambridge, MA: MIT Press, 1992); and Fraser, *Justice Interruptus*. For a theological appraisal of the theory of public sphere, and Nancy Fraser's concept of subaltern counterpublics, see Benjamin Valentine, *Mapping Public Theology: Beyond*

Culture, Identity and Difference (Harrisburg, PA: Trinity Press International, 2002).

54. Valentine, *Mapping Public Theology*, 120.

55. Collins, *Fighting Words*, 22–32.

56. Ibid., 81.

57. Valentine, *Mapping Public Theology*, 124.

58. Singh, *Social Movements, Old and New*, 20; original emphasis.

59. Melucci, *Nomads of the Present*, 63.

60. Ibid., 74.

61. T. V. Reed, *Fifteen Jugglers, Five Believers: Literary Politics and the Poetics of American Social Movements* (Berkeley, CA: University of California Press, 1992), 18.

62. M. M. Thomas, "The Power that Sustains Us," in *The Church's Mission and Post-modern Humanism*, ed. M. M. Thomas (Thiruvalla: CSS Books, 1996), 71.

63. Enrique Dussel, "Ethical Sense of the 1994 Maya Rebellion in Chiapas," in *Beyond Philosophy: Ethics, History, Marxism and Liberation Theology*, ed. Eduardo Mendieta (New York: Rowman & Littlefield, 2003), 167–83.

64. M. M. Thomas, *Salvation and Humanization: Some Critical Issues in the Theology of Mission in Contemporary India* (Madras: Christian Institute for the Study of Religion and Society–Christian Literature Society, 1971), 1–19.

65. Thomas, *The Church's Mission*, 75.

66. M. J. Joseph, "Search for Community," in *Peoples' Struggles*, ed. Abraham Eapen (Thiruvalla: Program for Social Action, 1987), 9.

67. Mohanty, *Feminism without Borders*, 244.

Chapter 4

1. Enrique Dussel, *Ethics and Community* (Maryknoll, NY: Orbis Books, 1988), 28.

2. Quoted in Franklin J. Balasundaram, *Prophetic Voices of Asia – Part II* (Colombo: Logos, 1994), 81.

3. Sebastian Kappen, "Towards an Indian Theology of Liberation," in *Readings in Indian Christian Theology*, vol. 1, eds. R. S. Sugirtharajah and Cecil Hargreaves (London: SPCK, 1993), 25. According to Kappen, the Divine comes to us as gift and challenge. As a gift we experience the Divine in beauty, love, community and solidarity. As challenge the Divine confronts us to engage in transformative actions of recreating ourselves and the world. Kappen calls the human response to these theophanies *theandric* practice. For him it is the experience of the absoluteness of beauty, community, love

and solidarity that mediates the human revolt against structural manifestations of evil. At the same time the annunciation of the Divine in our midst can be experienced only in our political projects to create an alternative future. "In it [*theandric* practice] are blended contemplation and action, celebration and creation, safeguarding and subverting, memory and hope, self-transformation and world-transformation. It is in *theandric* practice and what it brings into being that the gift-call of the Divine becomes flesh. If so, Revelation is, in a sense, mankind's [sic] historical task. Humans have as much to create the truth about the Divine as they have to discover it" (ibid.). I am aware of the gender exclusive nature of the term *theandric*. Probably *theanthropic* could be a better term.

4. Rasmussen, "Environmental Racism," 4.

5. M. M. Thomas, *The Secular Ideologies of India and the Secular Meaning of Christ* (Madras: Christian Literature Society, 1976), 203.

6. See Clodovis Boff and Leonardo Boff, *Introducing Liberation Theology* (Maryknoll, NY: Orbis Books, 1987); Clodovis Boff, *Theology and Praxis: Epistemological Foundations* (Maryknoll, NY: Orbis Books, 1987); and Clodovis Boff, "Methodology of the Theology of Liberation," in *Systematic Theology: Perspectives from Liberation Theology*, eds. Jon Sobrino and Ignacio Ellacuria (Maryknoll, NY: Orbis Books, 1993), 1–21. This method has its roots in the Catholic Action which developed the formula "to see, to judge, and to act" during the first decade of the last century. For a historical account of this method see Vitor Westhelle, "Elements for a Typology of Latin American Theologies," in *Prejudice: Issues in Third World Theologies*, ed. Andreas Nehring (Madras: Gurukul Lutheran Theological College and Research Institute, 1996), 84–101.

7. Boff, *Cry of the Earth*, 109–10.

8. For a similar appropriation of the Latin American "hermeneutical circle" for Christian ethics, see Miguel A. De La Torre, *Doing Christian Ethics from the Margins* (Maryknoll, NY: Orbis Books, 2004), 58–69. Here the categories are rephrased as 1) Observing – An Analysis, 2) Reflecting – Social Analysis, 3) Praying – A Theological and Biblical Analysis, 4) Acting – Implementing Praxis, and 5) Reassessing – New Ethical Perspectives.

9. Juan Luis Segundo, *Signs of the Times: Theological Reflection*, trans. Robert R. Barr (Maryknoll, NY: Orbis Books, 1993), 71.

10. For a robust critic of liberation hermeneutics see R. S. Sugirtharajah, *The Bible and the Third World* (Cambridge: Cambridge University Press, 2001), 203–43. His critical engagement with the interpretation of Job by Gustavo Gutierrez and Paul by Elsa Tamez is important.

11. Westhelle, "Elements for a Typology," 91–2.

12. Rasmussen, "Environmental Racism," 10.

13. For a robust critique of mainstream theological environmentalism see Rieger, "Re-envisioning Ecotheology," 65–85.

14. See our earlier discussion on Cornel West's concept of "normative gaze." West, *Prophesy Deliverance!*, 47–65.

15. Cone, "Whose Earth is it, Anyway?"

16. Rieger, "Re-envisioning Ecotheology," 68.

17. Rasmussen, "Environmental Racism," 11.

18. Medha Patkar, "Following with Full Force," *First City* (June 1998).

19. Sanjay Sangvai, *The River and Life: People's Struggle in the Narmada Valley* (Mumbai: Earthcare Books, 2000), 154.

20. Deep ecology is an influential movement in the West popularized by Earth First!, a movement of the North American conservationists. The Norwegian philosopher Arne Naess is considered as the founder of deep ecology. His "eight points of deep ecology" is the charter of deep ecology. For a systematic understanding of deep ecology, see Arne Naess, *Ecology, Community and Lifestyle* (Cambridge: Cambridge University Press, 1989); George Sessions, ed., *Deep Ecology for the 21ˢᵗ Century: Readings on the Philosophy and Practice of the New Environmentalism* (Boston, MA and London: Shambhala, 1995); and Eric Katz et al., eds., *Beneath the Surface: Critical Essays in the Philosophy of Deep Ecology* (Cambridge, MA and London: MIT Press, 2000).

21. In the North American context, deep ecology has been used to blame the communities of color with their comparatively higher population rate for the environmental crisis. Based on this assumption there are environmental groups in the US which demand changes in the immigration policy of the government to save the planet. The theoretical mediation of deep ecology has been used in postcolonial nations such as India to create a reign of terror in the forest lands to forcefully oust adivasis and other subsistence communities who for generations have lived in communion with nature, to create new enclosures such as biological parks and wildlife sanctuaries to protect nature and to encourage ecotourism among the urban middle class. This has resulted in the emergence of a new category of refugees – the environmental refugees – constituted by adivasis in the millions who finally end up in the city slums as wage laborers for capitalist production. In India communities living in close proximity to wildlife sanctuaries are always under the threat of wild animals destroying their crops and attacking and killing them. According to the law, the compensation paid for a human being killed by a tiger is Rs 5,000 (US$110), whereas the fine for killing a tiger is Rs 50,000 (US$1100) plus 10 years' imprisonment! This law exposes the racist, misanthropic and social Darwinistic nature of our environmental theories and policies. See Wielenga, *Towards an Eco-just Society* for a detailed critique of conservationism in India.

22. Murray Bookchin, *The Modern Crisis* (Philadelphia: New Society Publishers, 1986), 71. Also see Bookchin, *The Ecology of Freedom: The Emergence and Dissolution of Hierarchy* (Montreal: Black Rose Books, 1991); *Toward an Ecological Society* (Montreal: Black Rose Books, 1980);

The Philosophy of Social Ecology: Essays on Dialectical Naturalism (Montreal: Black Rose Books, 1996); and Andrew Light, ed., *Social Ecology after Bookchin* (New York: Guilford Press, 1998).

23. Fisher, "Sacred Rivers, Sacred Dams," 406.

24. M. K. Gandhi, *My Religion*, ed. Bharatan Kumarappa (Ahmedabad: Navjivan Press, 1955), 67.

25. Quoted in Mark Shepherd, *Gandhi Today: The Story of Mahatma Gandhi's Successors* (John Cabin, MD: Seven Locks Press, 1987), 63.

26. We have already discussed the Dalit critique of Gandhi's emphasis on village. Village being the cradle of inhumane practices of caste system, the idealization of the village economy in the Gandhian project fails to address the issues of social division, and subsequent victimization of the powerless, caused by caste, class and patriarchy.

27. Quoted in Subrata Mukherjee, *Gandhian Thought: Marxist Interpretation* (New Delhi: Deep and Deep Publications, 1991), 33.

28. For further research on eco-feminism see Shiva, *Staying Alive*; Mies and Shiva, *Eco-Feminism*; Carolyn Merchant, *The Death of Nature: Women, Ecology and the Scientific Revolution* (San Francisco: Harper & Row, 1980); and Heather Eaton, *Introducing Eco-feminist Theologies* (London and New York: T & T Clark International, 2005).

29. Aruna Gnanadason, "Traditions of Prudence Lost: A Tragic World of Broken Relationships," in *Ecofeminism and Globalization: Exploring Culture, Context, and Religion*, eds. Heather Eaton and Lois Ann Lorentzen (Lanham, MD: Rowman & Littlefield, 2003), 79.

30. Bina Agarwal's critique of the Western ecofeminist discourses provides more insight for our discussion on eco-feminism. "First, it posits 'women' as unitary category and fails to differentiate among women by class, race, ethnicity, and so on. It thus ignores forms of domination other than gender which also impinge critically on women's position. Second, it locates the domination of women and of nature almost solely in ideology, neglecting the material sources of this dominance. Third, even in the realm of ideological constructs, it says little about the social, economic and political structures within which these constructs are produced and transformed... Fourth, the ecofeminist argument does not take into account women's lived material relationship with nature, as opposed to what others or they themselves might conceive that relationship to be. Fifth, those strands of ecofeminism that trace the connection between women and nature to biology may be seen as adhering to a form of essentialism (some notion of a female 'essence' which is unchangeable and irreducible)." Bina Agarwal, "The Gender and Environment Debate: Lessons from India," in *Gender and Politics in India*, ed. Nivedita Menon (New Delhi: Oxford University Press, 1999), 100.

31. Gabriele Dietrich, "Development, Ecology and Women's Struggles," In *Women's Movement in India: Conceptual and Religious Reflections*, ed. Gabriele Dietrich, 176 (Bangalore: Breakthrough Publications, 1988).

32. Agarwal, "The Gender and Environment Debate," 133.

33. Ibid., 134; original emphasis.

34. The attempt here is not to homogenize the adivasis and Dalits, nor to suggest that they approach environmental crisis from a single perspective. Drawing from the concept of "ecological ethnicities" (which I will explain further in this section), we are trying to lift up and understand the unique perspectives that the ecological ethnicities (in the Indian context mainly adivasis and Dalits) bring into the discourse on earth ethics.

35. Parajuli, "Learning from Ecological Ethnicities," 560.

36. As Parajuli rightly observes, "What is in nature is directly experienced and lived through plants, crops, and other sources of sustenance, an interaction mediated through rituals associated with production, collection, preparation, and distribution of food. In the most primal sense, it is through the search for food, nutrition, and medicine that ecological ethnicities communicate with nature." Ibid.

37. Bhaskaran, *Janu: C. K. Januvinte Jeevithakatha* (in Malayalam) (Kottayam: D. C. Books, 2003), 38.

38. Pradip Prabhu, "In the Eye of the Storm: Tribal Peoples of India," in *Indigenous Traditions and Ecology*, ed. Grim, 62. It is important to recognize here the Panchsheel Policy (Five Principles of Good Governance) of Prime Minister Nehru in which the nation affirmed the adivasi right to dignity and self-rule. The policy affirmed that "1) people should develop along the lines of their own genius and the state should avoid imposition, instead encouraging their own traditional arts and culture; 2) tribal rights in land and forests should be respected; 3) the state should train their own people to do the work of administration and development; 4) the state should not overadminister these areas or overwhelm them with a multiplicity of schemes, but work through and not in rivalry with their own social and cultural institutions; 5) the government should judge results not by statistics or the amount of money spent, but by the quality of human character involved." Ibid., 61. However this policy has never been implemented.

39. There are several international documents and declarations that articulate the indigenous perspective on nature. For example the Draft Declaration of Rights of Indigenous Peoples (DDRIP) prepared by the UN Working Group on Indigenous Population includes the following principles. "Right to self-determination, representation and full participation, Right to religious freedom and protection of sacred sites and objects, including ecosystems, plants, and animals, Right to own, develop, control, and use the lands and territories, including the total environment of the lands, air, waters, coastal seas, sea ice, flora and fauna, and other resources which they have traditionally owned or otherwise occupied or used, Right to special measures to control, develop, and protect their sciences, technologies, and cultural manifestations, including human and other genetic resources, seeds,

medicines, knowledge of the properties of fauna and flora, oral traditions, literatures, designs, and visual and performing arts."

40. Smitu Kothari, "Sovereignty and Swaraj: Adivasi Encounters with Modernity and Majority," in *Indigenous Traditions and Ecology*, ed. Grim, 457.

41. Dileep Raj, ed., *Thantedangal: Kerala Samooha Bhoopadam: Muthanga Samarathinusesham* (Kottayam: D. C. Books, 2003), 8.

42. Quoted in Pratyusha Basu and Jael Silliman, "Green and Red, not Saffron: Gender and the Politics of Resistance in the Narmada Valley," in *Hinduism and Ecology: The Intersection of Earth, Sky, and Water*, eds. Christopher Key Chapple and Mary Evelyn Tucker (Cambridge, MA: Harvard University Press, 2000), 423.

43. James O'Connor's concept of the second contradiction of capitalism is an example of this attempt. Here he proposes, along with Marx's first contradiction of capitalism – the contradiction between capital and labor (forces of production and relations of production) – a new category of contradiction which he calls the second contradiction of capitalism – between productive forces and the conditions of production. See James O'Connor, "Capitalism, Nature, Socialism: A Theoretical Introduction," *Capitalism Nature Socialism* 1 (Fall 1988). For a deeper engagement with eco-socialism, see John Bellamy Foster, Barry Commoner, Raymond Williams and Joel Kovel.

44. Joe Kovel, "The Ecofeminist Ground of Ecosocialism," *Capital Nature Socialism* 16, no. 2 (June 2005).

45. Michael Lowy, "What is Ecosocialism?" *Capitalism Nature Socialism* 16, no. 2 (June 2005): 18.

46. Kovel, "The Ecofeminist Ground of Ecosocialism," 3.

47. Lowy, "What is Ecosocialism?" 20.

48. Kovel, "The Ecofeminist Ground of Ecosocialism," 5.

49. Leonardo Boff, *Ecology and Liberation: A New Paradigm* (Maryknoll, NY: Orbis Books, 1996), 98.

50. For example, the analysis of the Hindu caste system as "a progenitor of the concept of sustainable development" has been used by several environmental activists and scholars. See O. P. Dwivedi, "Satyagraha for Conservation: Awakening the Spirit of Hinduism," in *Ethics of Environment and Development: Global Challenges, International Responses*, eds. J. Ronald Engel and Joan Gibb Engel (Tucson: University of Arizona Press, 1990), 208; Madhav Gadgil and Ramachandra Guha, *This Fissured Land: An Ecological History of India* (Delhi: Oxford University Press, 1992), 91–110; and Deane Curtin, *Chinnagounder's Challenge: The Question of Ecological Citizenship* (Bloomington and Indianapolis: Indiana University Press, 1999), 166. For a compelling critical analysis of the saffronization of the greens in India see Mukul Sharma, "Saffronising Green," *Seminar* 516 (August 2002): 26–30.

51. Commenting on the metaphor of Narmada *mata*, Medha Patkar stated that, "The concept of womanhood, of *mata*, has automatically got

connected with the whole movement, … the concept of Narmada as *mata* is very much part of the movement." Medha Patkar, "The Strength of a People's Movement," in *Indigenous Vision: Peoples of India, Attitudes to the Environment*, ed. Geeti Sen (Delhi: Sage Publications, 1992), 282.

52. Fisher, "Sacred Rivers, Sacred Dams," 413.

53. Sharma, ed., *Modern Temples of India*, 40–9. Also see Roy, *Greater Common Good*, 1.

54. Gabriele Dietrich, *A New Thing on Earth* (Delhi: ISPCK, 2001), 249.

55. Dietrich, *A New Thing on Earth*, 138.

56. Arif Dirlik, *After the Revolution: Waking to Global Capitalism* (Hanover and London: Wesleyan University Press, 1994), 108.

57. Sangvai, *The River and Life*, 202.

58. National Alliance of People's Movements, *Ayodhya Declaration: National People's Agenda* (Mumbai: National Alliance of Peoples' Movements, 2003), 4.

59. Available at http://www.earthcharter.org.

60. K. C. Abraham, "A Theological Response to the Ecological Crisis," in *Ecotheology: Voices from South and North*, ed. David G. Hallman (Geneva: WCC Publications, 1994), 70.

61. Wielenga, *Towards an Eco-Just Society*, 162.

62. Mies and Shiva, *Ecofeminism*, 254.

63. Sangvai, *The River and Life*, 201.

64. Barbara R. Rossing, "(Re)claiming *Oikoumene*?: Empire, Ecumenism, and the Discipleship of Equals," in *Walk in the Ways of Wisdom: Essays in Honor of Elisabeth Schüssler Fiorenza*, eds. Shelly Matthews, Cynthia Briggs Kittredge and Melanie Johnson-Debaufre (Harrisburg, PA: Trinity Press International, 2003), 84.

65. The nationalist movement in India under the banner of the Indian National Congress is the best example for this. When the Dalits under the leadership of Babasahab Ambedkar demanded separate electorates, Gandhi used his moral weapon of Satyagraha to persuade them to reconsider their struggle. Gandhi's moral coercion forced them to withdraw their demand. The particular struggle of the Dalits for freedom from internal colonization was thus suppressed by the nationalist movement for attaining political freedom from British colonial power.

66. Boff, *Cry of the Earth*, 110.

67. Rebecca S. Chopp, "Theology and the Poetics of Testimony," in *Converging on Culture: Theologians in Dialogue with Cultural Analysis and Criticism*, eds. Delwin Brown et al. (Oxford: Oxford University Press, 2001), 61.

68. Chopp, "Theology and Poetics of Testimony," 62.

69. Ibid., 62.

70. Jeffrey Stolle, "Levinas and *Akedah*," *Philosophy Today* (Summer 2001): 132.

71. Enrique Dussel, "An Ethics of Liberation," in *Beyond Philosophy: Ethics, History, Marxism, and Liberation Theology*, ed. Eduardo Mendieta (New York: Rowman & Littlefield, 2003), 139.

72. Dussel, "Ethics of Liberation," 140.

73. Theodore Hiebert, *The Yahwist Landscape: Nature and Religion in Early Israel* (New York: Oxford University Press, 1996), 35.

74. McFague, *Life Abundant*, 18.

75. Ibid., 31.

76. Ibid., 186.

77. Paulos Mar Gregorios, *The Human Presence: An Orthodox View of Nature* (Geneva: WCC Publications, 1978), 87.

78. Boff, *Cry of the Earth*, 70.

79. McFague, *Life Abundant*, 47.

80. Boff, *Cry of the Earth*, 31.

81. Ibid., 87.

82. Ibid., 104.

83. The concept of human beings as co-creators was popularized by Philip Hefner's concept of "created co-creator." Here we use this concept in a different meaning with the claim that the subalterns are the co-creators. See Philip Hefner, *The Human Factor: Evolution, Culture, and Religion* (Minneapolis: Fortress Press, 1993).

84. Dussel, "Ethics of Liberation," 140.

85. Ibid., 143.

86. For a postcolonial reading of the themes of "exile," see Daniel L. Smith-Christopher, *A Biblical Theology of Exile* (Minneapolis: Fortress Press, 2002). For a theological exposition of the creation of human beings according to the image and likeness of God, from a human rights perspective, see Roger Ruston, *Human Rights and the Image of God* (London: SCM Press, 2004).

87. Catherine Keller, "No More Sea: The Lost Chaos of the Eschaton," in *Christianity and Ecology: Seeking the Wellbeing of Earth and Humans*, eds. Dieter T. Hessel and Rosemary Radford Ruether (Cambridge, MA: Harvard University Press, 2000), 185.

88. Barbara Rossing, *The Choice between Two Cities: Whore, Bride, and Empire in the Apocalypse* (Harrisburg, PA: Trinity Press International, 1999).

89. "Cargo of gold, silver, jewels and pearls, fine linen, silk and scarlet, all kinds of scented wood, all articles of ivory, all articles of costly wood, bronze, iron, and myrrh, frankincense, wine, olive oil, choice flour and wheat, cattle and sheep, horses and chariots, slaves and human lives" (Rev. 18:11-13).

90. Wielenga, *Towards an Eco-just Society*, 137; original emphasis.

Bibliography

Abraham, K. C. *Eco-Justice: A New Agenda for Church's Mission*. Bombay: BUILD Publications, 1992.

—. "A Theological Response to the Ecological Crisis." In *Ecotheology: Voices from South and North*, ed. David G. Hallman, 65–88. Geneva: WCC Publications, 1994.

Agarwal, Arun, and K. Sivaramakrishnan, eds. *Agrarian Environments: Resources, Representations and Rule in India*. Durham, NC: Duke University Press, 2000.

Agarwal, Bina. "The Gender and Environment Debate: Lessons from India." In *Gender and Politics in India*, ed. Nivedita Menon, 96–142. New Delhi: Oxford University Press, 1999.

Ahmad, Riaz. "Gujarat Violence: Meaning and Implications." *Economic and Political Weekly* 37, no. 20 (2002): 1870–73.

Ali-Bogaert, Anjuman. "Imagining Alternatives to Development: A Case Study of the Narmada Bachao Andolan in India." PhD dissertation, Kent University, 1997.

Alvares, Claude. "Development: Much Ado about Nothing." *The Illustrated Weekly of India* (June 3, 1984).

—. *Science, Development and Violence: The Revolt against Modernity*. Delhi: Oxford University Press, 1994.

Arango, Luis Alfredo. "Papel y Tusa" (1967). Quoted in Mark Lewis Taylor, "Transnational Corporation and Institutionalized Violence: A Challenge to Christian Movements in the US." In *New Vision for the Americas: Religious Engagement and Social Transformation*, ed. David Batstone. Minneapolis: Fortress Press, 1993.

Aristotle. *Politics*. Trans. Benjamin Jowett. In *The Basic Works of Aristotle*, ed. Richard McKeon. New York: Random House, 1941.

Baake, David. "The Sorrows of Globalization: Capitalism and Slavery". 2005. Available at http://www.zcommunications.org

Balasundaram, Franklin J. *Prophetic Voices of Asia – Part II*. Colombo: Logos, 1994.

Basu, Pratyusha, and Jael Silliman. "Green and Red, not Saffron: Gender and Politics of Resistance in the Narmada Valley." In *Hinduism and Ecology: The Intersection of Earth, Sky, and Water*, eds. Christopher Key Chapple and Mary Evelyn Tucker, 423–52. Cambridge, MA: Harvard University Press, 2000.

Bavadam, Lyla. "The Bilgaon Model." 2003. Available at http://www.hinduonnet.com/fline/fl2021/stories/20031024001208700.htm.

Baviskar, Amita. *In the Belly of the River: Tribal Conflicts over Development in the Narmada Valley.* Delhi: Oxford University Press, 1995.
—. "Red in Tooth and Claw? Looking for Class in Struggles over Nature." In *Social Movements in India: Poverty, Power and Politics*, eds. Raka Ray and Mary Fainsod Katzenstein, 161–72. Lanham, MD: Rowman & Littlefield, 2005.
Bergeron, Suzanne. *Fragments of Development: Nation, Gender, and the Space of Modernity.* Ann Arbor, MI: University of Michigan Press, 2004.
Beverley, John. *Subalternity and Representation: Arguments in Cultural Theory.* Durham, NC and London: Duke University Press, 1999.
Bhabha, Homi. *The Location of Culture.* London and New York: Routledge, 1994.
Bhaskaran. *Janu: C. K. Januvinte Jeevithakatha* (in Malayalam). Kottayam: D. C. Books, 2003.
Birgg, Morgan. "Post-development, Foucault and the Colonization Metaphor." *Third World Quarterly* 23, no. 3 (2002): 421–36.
Boff, Clodovis. *Theology and Praxis: Epistemological Foundations.* Maryknoll, NY: Orbis Books, 1987.
—. "Methodology of the Theology of Liberation." In *Systematic Theology: Perspectives from Liberation Theology*, eds. Jon Sorbino and Ignacio Ellacuria, 1–21. Maryknoll, NY: Orbis Books, 1993.
Boff, Clodovis, and Leonardo Boff. *Introducing Liberation Theology.* Maryknoll, NY: Orbis Books, 1987.
Boff, Leonardo. *Ecology and Liberation: A New Paradigm.* Maryknoll, NY: Orbis Books, 1996.
—. *Cry of the Earth, Cry of the Poor.* Maryknoll, NY: Orbis Books, 1997.
Bookchin, Murray. *Toward an Ecological Society.* Montreal: Black Rose Books, 1980.
—. *The Modern Crisis.* Philadelphia: New Society Publishers, 1986.
—. *The Ecology of Freedom: The Emergence and Dissolution of Hierarchy.* Montreal: Black Rose Books, 1991.
—. *The Philosophy of Social Ecology: Essays on Dialectical Naturalism.* Montreal: Black Rose Books, 1996.
Bounds, Elizabeth M. *Coming Together/Coming Apart: Religion, Community, and Modernity.* New York: Routledge, 1997.
Browning, Don S., and Francis Schüssler Fiorenza, eds. *Habermas, Modernity, and Public Theology.* New York: Crossroad, 1992.
Calhoun, Craig, ed. *Habermas and the Public Sphere.* Cambridge, MA: MIT Press, 1992.
Carlsen, Laura. "WTO Kills Farmers: In Memory of Lee Kyung Hae." 2005. Available at http://www.cipamericas.org
Castro, Fidel. "Complete text of President Castro's speech at the opening session of the South Summit, April 12, 2000." http://www.puertorico.com/forums/open-board/13160-supporters-terrorism.html

Chatterjee, Partha. *Nationalist Thought in the Colonial World: A Derivative Discourse*. Delhi: Oxford University Press, 1986.

Chopp, Rebecca S. "Theology and the Poetics of Testimony." In *Converging on Culture: Theologians in Dialogue with Cultural Analysis and Criticism*, eds. Delwin Brown et al. 56–70. Oxford: Oxford University Press, 2001.

Clarke, Sathianathan. *Dalits and Christianity: Subaltern Religion and Liberation Theology in India*. New Delhi: Oxford University Press, 1998.

Code, Lorraine. *What Can She Know: Feminist Theories and the Construction of Knowledge*. Ithaca, NY: Cornell University Press, 1991.

Collins, Patricia Hill. "Defining Black Feminist Thought." In *The Second Wave: A Reader in Feminist Theory*, ed. Linda Nicholson, 241–59. New York: Routledge, 1997.

—. *Fighting Words: Black Women and the Search for Justice*. Minneapolis: University of Minnesota Press, 1998.

Cone, James H. "Whose Earth is it, Anyway?" In *Earth Habitat: Eco-injustice and the Church's Response*, eds. Dieter Hessel and Larry Rasmussen, 23–32. Minneapolis: Fortress Press, 2001.

Cooray, Upal. "The International Debt Crisis." In *Debt Crisis and People's Struggle*. Hong Kong: Documentation for Action Groups in Asia, 1987.

Crossley, Nick. *Making Sense of Social Movements*. Buckingham: Open University Press, 2002.

Curtin, Deane. *Chinnagouder's Challenge: The Question of Ecological Citizenship*. Bloomington and Indianapolis: Indiana University Press, 1999.

De Beauvoir, Simon. *The Second Sex*. Trans. H. M. Parshley. New York: Vintage, 1972.

De La Torre, Miguel. *Doing Christian Ethics from the Margins*. Maryknoll, NY: Orbis Books, 2004.

Deegan, Chris. "The Narmada in Myth and History." In *Toward Sustainable Development: Struggling over India's Narmada River*, ed. William F. Fisher, 47–70. Armonk, NY: M. E. Sharp, 1995.

—. "The Narmada: Circumambulation of a Sacred Landscape." In *Hinduism and Ecology: The Intersection of Earth, Sky and Water*, eds. Christopher Key Chapple and Mary Evelyn Tucker, 389–400. Cambridge, MA: Harvard University Press, 2000.

Delson, Eric, ed. *Ancestors: The Hard Evidence*. New York: A. R. Liss, 1985.

Dhanagare, D. N. *Peasant Movements in India*. Delhi: Oxford University Press, 1983.

Dhanagare, D. N., and J. John. "Cyclical Movements Toward the 'Eternal'." *Economic and Political Weekly* 23, no. 21 (1988): 1089–92.

Dharmadhikari, Sripad. "Advocacy Skills and Systems." In *Experiences of Advocacy in Environment and Development*, eds. S. Joshi et al., 16–36. Bangalore: Development Support Initiative, 1997.

—. *Water: Private, Limited: Fundamental Issues in Privatization and Corporatisation of Water in India*. Badwani, India: Manthan Adhyanayn Kendra, 2002.

Dietrich, Gabriele. "Development, Ecology and Women's Struggles." In *Women's Movement in India: Conceptual and Religious Reflections*, ed. Gabriele Dietrich, 174–86. Bangalore: Breakthrough Publications, 1988.

—. *A New Thing on Earth*. Delhi: ISPCK, 2001.

Dietrich, Gabriele, and Bastiaan Wielenga. *Towards Understanding Indian Society*. Madurai: Centre for Social Analysis, 1998.

Dirlik, Arif. *After the Revolution: Waking to Global Capitalism*. Hanover and London: Wesleyan University Press, 1994.

D'Souza, Dilip. *The Narmada Dammed: An Inquiry into the Politics of Development*. New Delhi: Penguin Books, 2002.

Duchrow, Ulrich. *Alternatives to Global Capitalism: Drawn from Biblical History, Designed for Political Action*. Utrecht: International Books, 1995.

Duchrow, Ulrich, et al. *Property for People, Not for Profit: Alternatives to the Global Tyranny of Capital*. Geneva: WCC Publications, 2004.

Dussel, Enrique. *Ethics and Community*. Maryknoll, NY: Orbis Books, 1988.

—. *The Invention of the Americas: Eclipse of the "Other" and the Myth of Modernity*. New York: Continuum Press, 1995.

—. "Ethical Sense of the 1994 Maya Rebellion in Chiapas." In *Beyond Philosophy: Ethics, History, Marxism, and Liberation Theology*, ed. Eduardo Mendieta, 167–83. Lanham, MD: Rowman & Littlefield, 2003.

—. "An Ethics of Liberation." In *Beyond Philosophy: Ethics, History, Marxism, and Liberation Theology*, ed. Eduardo Mendieta, 135–48. New York: Rowman & Littlefield, 2003.

Dwivedi, Ayodhya Prasad. *Sanskruti Srotaswini Narmada* (Hindi). Bhopal: Madhya Pradesh Hindi Grandh Academy, 1987.

Dwivedi, O. P. "Satyagraha for Conservation: Awakening the Spirit of Hinduism." In *Ethics of Environment and Development: Global Challenges, International Responses*, eds. J. Ronald Engel and Joan Gibb Engel. Tucson: University of Arizona Press, 1990.

Dwivedi, Ranjit. "Resisting Dams and 'Development': Contemporary Significance of the Campaign against the Narmada Projects in India." *European Journal of Development Research* 10, no. 2 (1998): 135–83.

Eaton, Heather. *Introducing Eco-Feminist Theologies*. London and New York: T & T Clark International, 2005.

Eaton, Heather, and Lois Ann Lorentzen, eds. *Ecofeminism and Globalization: Exploring Culture, Context, and Religion*. Lanham, MD: Rowman & Littlefield, 2003.

Engel, J. Ronald. *Sacred Sands: The Struggles for Community in the Indiana Dunes*. Middletown, CT: Wesleyan University Press, 1983.

Escobar, Arturo. *Encountering Development: The Making and Unmaking of the Third World*. Princeton, NJ: Princeton University Press, 1995.

Esteva, Gustavo. "Development." In *The Development Dictionary: A Guide to Knowledge as Power*, ed. Wolfgang Sachs, 6–25. London: Zed Books, 1992.

—. "*Basta!* Mexican Indians say 'Enough!'" In *The Post-Development Reader*, eds. Majid Rahnema and Victoria Bawtree. London: Zed Books, 1997.

Esteva, Gustavo and Madhu Suri Prakash, "Re-routing and Re-rooting Grassroots Initiatives: Escaping the Impasse of Sustainable Development for the Narmanda." *Lokayan Bulletin* 9 (1991).

Ferguson, James. *The Anti-Politics Machine: "Development," Depoliticization, and Bureaucratic Power in Lesotho*. Cambridge: Cambridge University Press, 1990.

Fisher, William F. "Sacred Rivers, Sacred Dams: Competing Visions of Social Justice and Sustainable Development along the Narmada." In *Hinduism and Ecology: The Intersection of Earth, Sky and Water*, eds. Christopher Key Chapple and Mary Evelyn Tucker, 401–22. Cambridge, MA: Harvard University Press, 2000.

Frank, Andre Gunter, and Marta Fuentes. "Nine Theses on Social Movements." *Economic and Political Weekly* 22, no. 35 (1987): 1503–10.

Fraser, Nancy. *Unruly Practices: Power, Discourse and Gender in Contemporary Social Theory*. Minneapolis: University of Minnesota Press, 1992.

—. *Justice Interruptus: Critical Reflections on the "Postsocialist" Condition.* New York: Routledge, 1997.

Fulkerson, Mary McClintock. *Changing the Subject: Women's Discourse and Feminist Theology*. Eugene, OR: Wipf and Stock, 2001.

Gadgil, Madhav, and Ramachandra Guha. *This Fissured Land: An Ecological History of India*. Delhi: Oxford University Press, 1992.

Gandhi, M. K. *My Religion*. Ed. Bharatan Kumarappa. Ahmedabad: Navjivan Press, 1955.

Gebara, Ivone. *Longing for Running Waters: Ecofeminism and Liberation*. Minneapolis: Fortress Press, 1999.

George, Susan. "A Short History of Neo-Globalism: Twenty Years of Elite Economics and Emerging Opportunities for Structural Change." In *Global Finance: New Thinking on Regulating Speculative Capital*, eds. Walden Bello et al., 27–35. London: Zed Books, 2000.

George, Susan, and Fabrizio Sabelli. *Faith and Credit: The World Bank's Secular Empire*. London: Penguin Books, 1994.

Gnanadason, Aruna. "Traditions of Prudence Lost: A Tragic World of Broken Relationships." In *Ecofeminism and Globalization: Exploring Culture, Context, and Religion*, eds. Heather Eaton and Lois Ann Lorentzen. Lanham, MD: Rowman & Littlefield, 2003.

Gramsci, Antonio. *Selections from Cultural Writings*, trans. and ed. David Forgacs and Geoffrey Nowell Smith. London: Lawrence & Wishart, 1985.

Gregorios, Paulos Mar. *The Human Presence: An Orthodox View of Nature*. Geneva: WCC Publications, 1978.

Grewal, Royina. *Sacred Virgin: Travels along the Narmada*. New Delhi: Penguin Books, 1994.

Guha, Ramachandra. *Environmentalism: A Global History*. New Delhi: Oxford University Press, 2000.

Guha, Ramachandra, and Madhav Gadgil. *Ecology and Equity: The Use and Abuse of Nature in Contemporary India*. London: Routledge, 1995.

Guha, Ranajit. *Subaltern Studies I: Writings on South Asian History and Society*. New Delhi: Oxford University Press, 1985.

—. "On Some Aspects of the Historiography of Colonial India." In *Mapping Subaltern Studies and the Postcolonial*, ed. Vinayak Chaturvedi, 1–7. London: Verso, 2000.

Guru, Gopal. "Dalits in Pursuit of Modernity." In *India: Another Millennium?*, ed. Romila Thapar, 123–36. New Delhi: Penguin Books, 2000.

—. "The Language of Dalit-Bahujan Political Discourse." In *Dalit Identity and Politics*, ed. Ghanshyam Shah, 97–107. New Delhi: Sage Publications, 2001.

Habermas, Jürgen. *Knowledge and Human Interest*. Boston, MA: Beacon Press, 1971.

—. *Legitimation Crisis*. Boston, MA: Beacon Press, 1975.

—. "New Social Movements." *Telos* 49 (Fall 1981): 33–37.

—. *The Theory of Communicative Action Vol. II: Life World and System*. Boston, MA: Beacon Press, 1987.

—. *The Structural Transformation of the Public Sphere: An Inquiry into a Category of Bourgeois Society*. Cambridge, MA: MIT Press, 1989.

Haraway, Donna. "Situated Knowledges: The Science Question in Feminism and the Privilege of Partial Perspective." *Feminist Studies* 14, no. 3 (1988): 575–99.

—. *Simians, Cyborgs, and Women: The Reinvention of Nature*. New York: Routledge, 1991.

Harding, Sandra. *The Science Question in Feminism*. Ithaca, NY: Cornell University Press, 1986.

—. *Whose Science? Whose Knowledge? Thinking from Women's Lives*. Ithaca, NY and London: Cornell University Press, 1991.

Harrison, Beverly Wildung. "The Power of Anger in the Work of Love." In *Making the Connections: Essays in Feminist Social Ethics*, ed. Carol S. Robb, 3–21. Boston, MA: Beacon Press, 1985.

Hartsock, Nancy. "The Feminist Standpoint: Developing the Ground for a Specifically Feminist Historical Materialism." In *Discovering Reality: Feminist Perspectives on Epistemology, Metaphysics and Philosophy of Science*, eds. Sandra Harding and Merrill B. Hintikka, 283–310. Dordrecht: D. Reidel, 1983.

—. *The Feminist Standpoint Revisited and Other Essays*. Boulder, CO: Westview Press, 1998.

Hefner, Philip. *The Human Factor: Evolution, Culture, and Religion*. Minneapolis: Fortress Press, 1993.

Hiebert, Theodore. *The Yahwist Landscape: Nature and Religion in Early Israel*. New York: Oxford University Press, 1996.

—. "The Human Vocation: Origins and Transformations in Christian Traditions." In *Christianity and Ecology: Seeking the Wellbeing of Earth and Humans*, eds. Dieter T. Hessel and Rosemary Radford Ruether, 135–53. Cambridge, MA: Harvard University Press, 2000.

Hill, Jack A. "Teaching for Transformation: Insights from Fiji, India, South Africa, and Jamaica." *Teaching Theology and Religion* 8, no. 4 (2005): 218–31.

hooks, bell. "The Oppositional Gaze: Black Female Spectators." In *Feminist Postcolonial Theory: A Reader*, eds. Reina Lewis and Sara Mills, 207–21. New York: Routledge, 2003.

Hopkins, Dwight N. "The Religion of Globalization." In *Religions/ Globalizations: Theories and Cases*, eds. Dwight N. Hopkins et al., 7–32. Durham, NC and London: Duke University Pres, 2001.

Ilaiah, Kancha. "Dalitism vs. Brahmanism: The Epistemological Conflict in History." In *Dalit Identity and Politics*, ed. Ghanshaym Shah, 108–28. New Delhi: Sage Publications, 2001.

Illich, Ivan. "Development as Planned Poverty." In *The Post-Development Reader*, eds. Majid Rahnema and Victoria Bawtree. London: Zed Books, 1997.

Isasi-Diaz, Ada Maria. *En la lucha = In the Struggle: A Hispanic Women's Liberation Theology*. Minneapolis: Fortress Press, 1993.

—. "*Lo Cotidiano*: A Key Element of *Mujerista* Theology." *Journal of Hispanic/ Latina Theology* 10, no. 1 (2002).

—. *En La Lucha = In the Struggle: Elaborating a Mujerista Theology*. Minneapolis: Fortress Press, 2004.

Jain, L. C. *Dam vs Drinking Water: Exploring the Narmada Judgment*. Pune: Parisar, 2001.

Jan Vikas Andolan. "A Draft Perspective and Some Questions." *Lokayan Bulletin* 8, no. 1 (January–February 1990): 69–73.

Jodhka, Sureender S. "Nation and Village: Images of Rural India in Gandhi, Nehru and Ambedkar." *Economic and Political Weekly* (August 10, 2002): 3343–54.

Joseph, M. J. "Search for Community." In *Peoples' Struggles*, ed. Abraham Eapen. Thiruvalla: Program for Social Action, 1987.

Joseph, M. P. "Present is not Eternal." *Agape Immaginaria* 2 (December 2000): 12–16.

—. "Towards a Theological Critique of Globalization." In *Globalization and Human Solidarity*, ed. Tissa Balasuriya, 7–16. Thiruvalla: CSS Books, 2000.

—. "Religious Fundamentalism: A Political Strategy for Global Governance." *Voices from the Third World* XXV no. 1 & 2 (December 2002): 151–62.

—. "Beyond Bandung: The Market, the Empire and an Enquiry of Religious Meaning." In *Building Spirituality and Culture of Peace*, ed. Josef P. Widyatadja, 175–87. Hong Kong: Christian Conference of Asia, 2004.

Kapoor, Ilan. "Hyper-self-reflexive Development? Spivak on Representing the Third World 'Other'." *Third World Quarterly* 25, no. 4 (2004): 627–47.

Kappen, Sebastian. "Towards an Indian Theology of Liberation." In *Readings in Indian Christian Theology*, eds. R.S. Sugirtharajah and Cecil Hargreaves, 24–36. London: SPCK, 1993.

—. *Spirituality in the Age of Recolonization*. Bangalore: Visthar, 1995.

—. *Divine Challenge and Human Response*. Thiruvalla: CSS Books, 2001.

Katz, Eric et al., eds. *Beneath the Surface: Critical Essays in the Philosophy of Deep Ecology*. Cambridge, MA and London: MIT Press, 2000.

Keller, Catherine. "No More Sea: The Lost Chaos of the Eschaton." In *Christianity and Ecology: Seeking the Wellbeing of Earth and Humans*, eds. Dieter T. Hessel and Rosemary Radford Ruether, 183–98. Cambridge, MA: Harvard University Press, 2000.

Klandermans, Bert, and Suzanne Staggenborg, eds. *Methods of Social Movement Research*. Minneapolis: University of Minnesota Press, 2002.

Klein, Naomi. "Free Trade is War." *The Nation* 277, no. 9 (2003): 10. http://www.naomiklein.org/articles/2003/09/free-trade-war

—. "The Rise of Disaster Capitalism." *The Nation* 280, no. 17 (2005): 9–11.

Koshy, Ninan. *The War on Terror: Reordering the World*. Delhi: Left World Books, 2003.

Kothari, Rajni. *Rethinking Development: In Search of Humane Alternatives*. Delhi: Ajantha Publications, 1988.

Kothari, Smitu. "Damming the Narmada and the Politics of Development." In *Toward Sustainable Development: Struggling over India's Narmada River*, ed. William F. Fisher, 421–44. Armonk: M.E. Sharpe, 1995.

—. "Sovereignty and Swaraj: Adivasi Encounters with Modernity and Majority." In *Indigenous Traditions and Ecology: The Interbeing of Cosmology and Community*, ed. John A. Grim, 453–64. Cambridge, MA: Harvard University Press, 2001.

Kovel, Joe. "The Ecofeminist Ground of Ecosocialism." *Capitalism Nature Socialism* 16, no. 2 (June 2005): 1–8.

Lakeland, Paul. *Theology and Critical Theory: The Discourse of the Church*. Nashville, TN: Abingdon Press, 1990.

Light, Andrew, ed. *Social Ecology after Bookchin*. New York: Guilford Press, 1998.

Loomba, Ania. "Dead Women Tell No Tales: Issues of Female Subjectivity, Subaltern Agency and Tradition in Colonial and Postcolonial Writings on Widow Immolation in India." *History Workshop Journal* 36 (1993): 209–27.

Lowy, Michael. "What is Ecosocialism?" *Capitalism Nature Socialism* 16, no. 2 (June 2005): 15–24.

Mani, Lata. *Contentious Traditions: The Debate on Sati in Colonial India*. Berkeley, CA: University of California, 1998.

McCully, Patrick. *Silenced Rivers: The Ecology and Politics of Large Dams*. Hyderabad: Orient Longman, 1998.

McFague, Sallie. *Life Abundant: Rethinking Theology and Economy for a Planet in Peril*. Minneapolis: Fortress Press, 2001.

Melucci, Alberto. *Challenging Codes: Collective Action in the Information Age*. Cambridge: Cambridge University Press, 1996.

—. *Nomads of the Present: Social Movements and Individual Needs in Contemporary Society*. Philadelphia: Temple University Press, 1989.

Merchant, Carolyn. *The Death of Nature: Women, Ecology and the Scientific Revolution*. San Francisco: Harper & Row, 1980.

Mies, Maria, and Vandana Shiva. *Ecofeminism*. New Delhi: Kali for Women, 1993.

Milward, Bob. "What is Structural Adjustment?" In *Structural Adjustment: Theory, Practice and Impacts*, eds. Giles Mohan et al., 41–58. London and New York: Routledge, 2000.

Mittelman, James H. *The Globalization Syndrome: Transformation and Resistance*. Princeton, NJ: Princeton University Press, 2000.

Moe-Lobeda, Cynthia D. *Healing a Broken World: Globalization and God*. Minneapolis: Fortress Press, 2002.

Mohan, Giles. "Contested Sovereignty and Democratic Contradictions: The Political Impacts of Adjustment." In *Structural Adjustment: Theory, Practice and Impacts*, eds. Giles Mohan et al., 75–94. London and New York: Routledge, 2000.

Mohanty, Chandra Talpade. *Feminism without Borders: Decolonizing Theory, Practicing Solidarity*. Durham, NC and London: Duke University Press, 2003.

Moltmann, Jürgen. *God in Creation: A New Theology of Creation and the Spirit of God*. San Francisco: Harper and Row, 1985.

Moon, V., ed. *Dr. Babasaheb Ambedkar Writings and Speeches*, vol. 5. Bombay: Government of Maharashtra, 1979.

Morse, Bradford, and Thomas Berger. *Sardar Sarovar: The Report of the Independent Review*. Ottawa: Resource Futures International, 1992.

Mukherjee, Subrata. *Gandhian Thought: Marxist Interpretation*. New Delhi: Deep and Deep Publications, 1991.

Naess, Arne. *Ecology, Community and Lifestyle*. Cambridge: Cambridge University Press, 1989.

Nalunnakkal, George Mathew. *Green Liberation*. Delhi: ISPCK, 1999.

Nanda, Meera. *Prophets Facing Backward: Postmodern Critique of Science and Hindu Nationalism in India*. London: Rutgers University Press, 2003.

Naryanan, Uma. "Essence of Cultural and a Sense of History: A Feminist Critique of Cultural Essentialism." In *Decentering the Center: Philosophy for a Multicultural, Postcolonial, and Feminist World*, eds. Uma Narayanan and Sandra Harding, 80–100. Bloomington and Indianapolis: Indiana University Press, 2000.

National Alliance of People's Movements. *Ayodhya Declaration: National People's Agenda*. Mumbai: National Alliance of Peoples' Movements, 2003.

Nehru, Jawaharlal. *Jawaharlal Nehru's Speeches vol. 3, March 1953–August 1957*. New Delhi: Publication Division, Ministry of Information and Broadcasting, 1958.

Northcott, Michael S. *The Environment and Christian Ethics*. Cambridge: Cambridge University Press, 1996.

O'Connor, James. "Capitalism, Nature, Socialism: A Theoretical Introduction." *Capitalism Nature Socialism* 1 (Fall 1988): 11–38.

Omvedt, Gail. *Reinventing Revolution: New Social Movements and the Socialist Tradition in India*. Armonk: M. E. Sharpe, 1993.

—. "Dams and Bombs." *The Hindu* (August 5, 1999): 10.

Oommen, T. K. *Protest and Change: Studies in Social Movements*. New Delhi: Sage Publications, 1990.

Palit, Chittaraoopa. "Monsoon Risings: Mega-Dam Resistance in the Narmada Valley." *New Left Review* 21 (May–June 2003): 81–100.

Parajuli, Pramod. "Learning from Ecological Ethnicities: Toward a Plural Political Ecology of Knowledge." In *Indigenous Traditions and Ecology: The Interbeing of Cosmology and Community*, ed. John A. Grim, 559–90. Cambridge, MA: Harvard University Press, 2001.

—. "Revisiting Gandhi and Zapata: Motion of Global Capital, Geographies of Difference and the Formation of Ecological Ethnicities." In *In the Way of Development: Indigenous Peoples, Life Projects and Globalization*, eds. Mario Blaser et al., 235–56. London and New York: Zed Books, 2004.

Paranjype, Vijay. "The Cultural Ethos." *Lokayan Bulletin* (May–August 1991): 21–31.

Patkar, Medha. "The Strength of a People's Movement." In *Indigenous Vision: Peoples of India, Attitudes to the Environment*, ed. Geeti Sen, 273–99. New Delhi: Sage Publications, 1992.

—. "Following with Full Force." *First City* (June 1998).

Peters, Rebecca Todd. *In Search of the Good Life: The Ethics of Globalization*. New York and London: Continuum Press, 2004.

Pieterse, Jan Nederveen. *Development Theory: Deconstructions/ Reconstructions*. London: Sage Publications, 2001.

Polanyi, Karl. *The Great Transformation*. New York: Farrar & Rinehart, 1944.

Prabhu, Pradip. "In the Eye of the Storm: Tribal Peoples of India." In *Indigenous Traditions and Ecology: The Interbeing of Cosmology and Community*, ed. John A. Grim, 47–70. Cambridge, MA: Harvard University Press, 2001.

Prakash, Gyan. "Writing Post-Orientalist Histories of the Third World: Perspectives from Indian Historiography." In *Mapping Subaltern Studies and the Postcolonial*, ed. Vinayak Chaturvedi, 163–90. London: Verso, 2000.

Radhakrishnan, P. "Religion under Globalization," *Economic and Political Weekly* 39, no. 13 (2004): 1403–1412.

Rahnema, Majid, and Victoria Bawtree, eds. *The Post-Development Reader*. London: Zed Books, 1997.

Raj, Dileep, ed. *Thantedangal: Kerala Samooha Bhoopadam: Muthanga Samrathinusesham* (in Malayalam). Kottayam: D. C. Books, 2003.

Rajan, Rajeswari Sunder. *Real and Imagined Women: Gender, Culture and Postcolonialism*. London: Routledge, 1993.

Rajendra, Cecil. *Dove on Fire: Poems on Peace, Justice and Ecology*. Geneva: WCC Publications, 1987.

Rangachari, R., et al. *Large Dams: India's Experience WCD Case Study Final Report: November 2000*. Cape Town: World Commission on Dams, 2000.

Rasmussen, Larry L. *Moral Fragments and Moral Community: A Proposal for Church in Society*. Minneapolis: Fortress Press, 1995.

—. *Earth Community, Earth Ethics*. Maryknoll, NY: Orbis Books, 1996.

—. *"Give us Word of the Humankind We Left to Thee": Globalization and its Wake*. Cambridge, MA: Episcopal Divinity School, 1999.

—. "Environmental Racism and Environmental Justice: Moral Theory in the Making?" *Journal of the Society of Christian Ethics* 24, no. 1 (2004): 3–28.

—. "Epiphany." *The Lutheran* 19, no. 1 (January 2006). http://www.thelutheran.org/article/article.cfm?article_id=5655.

Reed, T. V. *Fifteen Jugglers, Five Believers: Literary Politics and the Poetics of American Social Movements*. Berkeley, CA: University of California Press, 1992.

Rege, Sharmila. "Dalit Women Talk Differently: A Critique of 'Difference' and Towards a Dalit Feminist Standpoint." *Economic and Political Weekly* (October 31, 1998): 39–46.

—. "'Real Feminist' and Dalit Women." *Economic and Political Weekly* 25, no. 6 (2000): 492–95.

Rieger, Joerg. "Re-envisioning Ecotheology and the Divine from the Margins." *Ecotheology* 9, no. 1 (2004): 65–85.

Rifkin, J. *The Biotech Century*. New York: Putnam, 1998.

Rist, Gilbert. *The History of Development: From Western Origins to Global Faith*. London and New York: Zed Books, 1997.

Rossing, Barbara. *The Choice between Two Cities: Whore, Bride, and Empire in the Apocalyptic*. Harrisburg, PA: Trinity Press International, 1999.

—. "(Re)claiming *Oikoumene*?: Empire, Ecumenism, and the Discipleship of Equals." In *Walk in the Ways of Wisdom: Essays in Honor of Elisabeth Schüssler Fiorenza*, eds. Shelly Matthews, Cynthia Briggs Kittredge and Melanie Johnson-Debaufre, 74–87. Harrisburg, PA: Trinity Press International, 2003.

Rostow, Walt W. *The Stages of Economic Growth: A Non-Communist Manifesto*. Cambridge: Cambridge University Press, 1960.

Roy, Arundhati. *The Greater Common Good*. Bombay: India Book Distributors, 1999.

—. "The Road to Hansud: The Death of a Town." 2005. Available at http://www.zcommunications.org

Ruether, Rosemary Radford. *Gaia and God: An Ecofeminist Theology of Earth Healing*. San Francisco: HarperSanFrancisco, 1992.

Ruston, Roger. *Human Rights and the Image of God*. London: SCM Press, 2004.

Sachs, Wolfgang, ed. *Development Dictionary: A Guide to Knowledge as Power*. London: Zed Books, 1992.

Said, Edward. *Orientalism*. New York: Vintage Books, 1979.

Sangvai, Sanjay. *The River and Life: People's Struggle in the Narmada Valley*. Mumbai: Earthcare Books, 2000.

Santhi, S. *Sardar Sarovar Project: The Issue of Developing River Narmada*. Thiruvananthapuram: INTACH, 1995.

Sarkar, Sumit. "Orientalism Revisited: Saidian Frameworks in the Writing of Modern Indian History." In *Mapping Subaltern Studies and the Postcolonial*, ed. Vinayak Chaturvedi, 239–55. London: Verso, 2000.

Sbert, Jose Maria. "Progress." In *The Development Dictionary: A Guide to Knowledge as Power*, ed. Wolfgang Sachs, 192–205. London: Zed Books, 1992.

Segundo, Juan Luis. *Signs of the Times: Theological Reflection*, trans. Robert R. Barr. Maryknoll, NY: Orbis Books, 1993.

Sessions, George., ed. *Deep Ecology for the 21st Century: Readings on the Philosophy and Practice of the New Environmentalism*. Boston, MA and London: Shambhala, 1995.

Seth, D. L. "Globalization and New Politics of Micro-Movements." *Economic and Political Weekly* 39, no. 1 (2004): 45–58.

Shah, Ghanashyam. *Social Movements in India: A Review of Literature*. New Delhi: Sage Publications, 1990.

Sharma, C. V. J., ed. *Modern Temples of India: Selected Speeches of Jawaharlal Nehru at Irrigation and Power Projects*. Delhi: Central Board of Irrigation and Power, 1989.

Sharma, Mukul. "Saffronising Green." *Seminar* 516 (August 2002): 26–30.

Shepherd, Mark. *Gandhi Today: The Story of Mahatma Gandhi's Successors*. John Cabin, MD: Seven Locks Press, 1987.

Shiva, Vandana. *Staying Alive: Women, Ecology and Survival in India*. New Delhi: Kali for Women, 1988.

—. *Biopiracy: The Plunder of Nature and Knowledge*. Boston, MA: South End Press, 1997.

—. "Globalization and Talibanization." 2004. Available at http://www.outlookindia.com.

—. "The Suicide Economy of Corporate Globalisation." 2004. Available at http://www.countercurrents.org/glo-shiva050404.htm

Simpson, Gary M. *Critical Social Theory: Prophetic Reason, Civil Society, and Christian Imagination*. Minneapolis: Fortress Press, 2002.

Singh, Rajendra. *Social Movements, Old and New: A Post-modernist Critique*. New Delhi: Sage Publications, 2001.

Smith, Adam. *Wealth of Nations*. New York: Prometheus Books, 1991.

Smith-Christopher, Daniel L. *A Biblical Theology of Exile*. Minneapolis: Fortress Press, 2002.

Solberg, Mary M. *Compelling Knowledge: A Feminist Proposal for an Epistemology of the Cross*. New York: State University of New York Press, 1997.

Spivak, Gayatri Chakravorty. "Can the Subaltern Speak?" In *Marxism and Interpretation of Culture*, eds. Carey Nelson and Lawrence Grossberg, 271–313. Urbana/Chicago: University of Illinois Press, 1988.

—. *In Other Worlds: Essays in Cultural Politics*. New York: Routledge, 1988.

Srinivas, M. N. *Social Change in Modern India*. Berkeley, CA: University of California Press, 1966.

Stolle, Jeffrey. "Levinas and *Akedah*." *Philosophy Today* (Summer 2001).

Stone-Mediatore, Shari. "Chandra Mohanty and the Revaluing of 'Experience'." In *Decentering the Center: Philosophy for a Multicultural, Postcolonial, and Feminist World*, eds. Uma Narayanan and Sandra Harding, 110–27. Bloomington and Indianapolis: Indiana University Press, 2000.

Sugirtharajah, R. S. *The Bible and the Third World*. Cambridge: Cambridge University Press, 2001.

—. *Postcolonial Reconfigurations: An Alternative Way of Reading the Bible and Doing Theology*. Danvers, MA: Chalice Press, 2003.

Summers, Lawrence. "Let Them Eat Pollution" (Excerpt of Lawrence Summers' internal memo to the World Bank), *Economist* (February 8, 1992): 66.

Tatman, Lucy. *Knowledge that Matters: A Feminist Theological Paradigm and Epistemology*. Cleveland, OH: Pilgrim Press, 2001.

Taylor, Mark Lewis. "Subalternity and Advocacy as Kairos for Theology." In *Opting for the Margins: Postmodernity and Liberation in Christian Theology*, ed. Joerg Rieger, 23–44. Oxford: Oxford University Press, 2003.

—. "Spirit and Liberation: Achieving Postcolonial Theology in the United States." In *Postcolonial Theologies: Divinity and Empire*, eds. Catherine Keller, Michael Nausner and Mayra Rivera, 39–55. St. Louis, CO: Chalice Press, 2004.

Thapar, Romila. "Traditions versus Misconceptions." *Manushi* 42-43 (1987): 2–14.

Thomas, Linda. "Womanist Theology, Epistemology, and a New Anthropological Paradigm." *Cross Currents: The Journal of the Association for the Religious and Intellectual Life* 8, no. 4 (Winter 1998–99): 488–99.

Thomas, M. M. *Salvation and Humanization: Some Critical Issues in the Theology of Mission in Contemporary India*. Madras: Christian Institute for the Study of Religion–Christian Literature Society, 1971.

—. *The Secular Ideologies of India and the Secular Meaning of Christ*. Madras: Christian Literature Society, 1976.

—. "The Power that Sustains Us." In *The Church's Mission and Post-modern Humanism*, ed. M. M. Thomas, 70–77. Thiruvalla: CSS Books, 1996.

—. "Search for a New Ideology for Social Justice with Eco-Justice." In *The Church's Mission and Post-modern Humanism*, ed. M. M. Thomas, 78–85. Thiruvalla: CSS Books, 1996.

Tilley, Terrence W. *Postmodern Theologies: The Challenge of Religious Diversity*. Maryknoll, NY: Orbis Books, 1995.

Touraine, Alain. *Beyond Neoliberalism*. Cambridge: Polity, 2001.

Tracy, David. "Theology, Critical Social Theory, and the Public Realm." In *Habermas, Modernity, and Public Theology*, eds. Don S. Browning and Francis Schüssler Fiorenza, 19–42. New York: Crossroad, 1992.

Valentine, Benjamin. *Mapping Public Theology: Beyond Culture, Identity and Difference*. Harrisburg, PA: Trinity Press International, 2002.

Verghese, B. G. *Winning the Future: From Bhakra to Narmada, Tehri, Rajasthan Canal*. New Delhi: Konark, 1994.

Wagle, Subodh. "The Long March for Livelihoods: Struggle against the Narmada Dam in India." In *Environmental Justice: Discourses in International Political Economy*, vol. 8, eds. John Byrne et al., 71–96. New Brunswick, NJ: Transaction Publishers, 2002.

West, Cornel. *Prophesy Deliverance!: An Afro-American Revolutionary Christianity*. Philadelphia: Westminster Press, 1982.

Westhelle, Vítor. "Scientific Sights and Embodied Knowledges." *Modern Theology* 11, no. 3 (July 1995): 341–61.

—. "Elements for a Typology of Latin American Theologies." In *Prejudice: Issues in Third World Theologies*, ed. Andreas Nehring, 84–101. Madras: Gurukul Lutheran Theological College and Research Institute, 1996.

—. "The Word and the Mask: Revisiting the Two-Kingdoms Doctrine." In *The Gift of Grace: The Future of Lutheran Theology*, eds. Neil Henrick Gregersen et al., 167–78. Minneapolis: Fortress Press, 2005.

Wielenga, Bastian. *Towards an Eco-just Society*. Bangalore: Center for Social Action, 1999.

Wilfred, Felix. "The Language of Human Rights." In *Frontiers in Asian Christian Theology*, ed. R. S. Sugirtharajah, 206–20. Maryknoll, NY: Orbis Books, 1994.

Young, Robert, J. C. *Postcolonialism: An Historical Introduction*. Oxford: Blackwell, 2001.

Index